García de Cisneros

A Book of Spiritual Exercises and a Directory for the Canonical Hours

García de Cisneros

A Book of Spiritual Exercises and a Directory for the Canonical Hours

ISBN/EAN: 9783337851248

Printed in Europe, USA, Canada, Australia, Japan

Cover: Foto ©Lupo / pixelio.de

More available books at **www.hansebooks.com**

PAX.
MONASTIC GLEANINGS, No. II.

A

BOOK OF SPIRITUAL EXERCISES,

AND A

Directory for the Canonical Hours,

WRITTEN BY

GARCIAS CISNEROS,
OF THE ORDER OF ST. BENEDICT, ABBOT OF MONSERRAT.

TRANSLATED BY

A MONK OF ST. AUGUSTINE'S MONASTERY,
RAMSGATE.

LONDON: BURNS AND OATES,
Portman Street and Paternoster Row.
1876.

LONDON:
ROBSON AND SONS, PRINTERS, PANCRAS ROAD, N.W.

THE TRANSLATOR'S PREFACE.

THE end we have had in view in choosing for our second volume of *Monastic Gleanings*, the *Spiritual Exercises* of the Venerable Abbot Cisneros, has been to introduce to the knowledge of English Catholics a work in which the spirit of our holy father St. Benedict adapts itself alike to the wants of religious and of people living in the world. To the cheerful, large-minded asceticism of the Benedictine, Abbot Cisneros joins that keen discernment of spirits, which so well beseems a master in that school of ascetic writers, wonderfully suited to our times, whose works are known as books of Spiritual Exercises.

Garcias Cisneros was born at Toledo, of noble parents, in the year 1459. The influence of his uncle, the great Cardinal Ximenes, would have enabled him to pursue a brilliant career in the world; but the Spirit of God called him to the cloister, and he obeyed the call. At the age of twenty-one, he took his monastic vows in the celebrated Benedictine monastery of Valladolid. The great love he always had for our holy Rule, and the eagerness with which he sought after such practices of piety as are most in keeping with its spirit, were marked features in his religious life. His talents for governing were not left idle ; and, a few years after his profession, he was elected second Prior of his monastery, the head Superior of the house being Prior-General of the Congregation.

Ferdinand of Spain had taken warmly to heart the work of restoring the Benedictine Order in his kingdom, and Pope Alexander VI., at the king's request, issued a Bull, ordering the reformed discipline of Valladolid to be adopted by the abbey of Monserrat,* whose abbot, Peralta, had just been raised to the episcopate. The Bull was addressed to John of St. John, Prior-General of Valladolid. In the year 1493, the Prior-General, with several of his monks, among whom was Cisneros, went to Monserrat, to execute the Papal decree. Cisneros was chosen abbot, and confirmed for two years. Being reëlected each time that his term of government expired, he continued eighteen years abbot of Monserrat, till his death

---

* In this celebrated abbey St. Ignatius Loyola went through a course of Spiritual Exercises, under the direction of Father John Chanones, O.S.B.

in 1510. Though occasionally obliged to leave his monastery, as when he was sent by his sovereign ambassador to France, yet his whole heart and soul were in the work of monastic observance. It was his wish that his monks, as a rule, should be neither wholly active nor wholly contemplative, though he made special provision for such as obtained leave to lead the life of hermits or recluses, admitted by our holy patriarch. He often warned his monks against frequent intercourse with seculars, which, he was wont to say, cannot but extinguish devotion and monastic fervour. The education of youth was an object of his special care; and he wrote a rule in eighteen chapters for the use of the students educated in the abbey. As he writes in his *Exercises* that those only are fit for being Superiors who can suit themselves alike to the active and to the contemplative life, so he taught by example. He would often retire to a hermitage, to gain strength in prayer for his weighty charge. Like a true Benedictine, his government was mild and gentle, and it is said that none could speak with him without being cheered and consoled.

This wisdom and mildness of the Benedictine spirit he transferred into his book of *Spiritual Exercises*.

These Exercises form a sort of scientific manual, for leading the soul onward in the way of God, not at haphazard, but by those steps which, as He has taught His Saints and the Doctors of His Church, form the *usual* path to be trodden by His chosen ones in their journey towards the perfection attainable in this life. All that this manual contains is drawn from the writings of the Saints and Fathers of the Church; but the rays of their doctrine are here concentrated: like a faithful Beseleel, the writer carves, fits together, and adorns with the brightness of a simple and graceful eloquence the precious stones of God's temple.

Guided by those holy fathers whom he quotes in every page, Cisneros divides the career of holiness into three parts, which he calls the *Via Purgativa*, or Way of Purity; the *Via Illuminativa*, or Way of Enlightenment; and the *Via Unitiva*, or Way of Union—names that since his time have been made familiar to us by a host of ascetic writers. The first of these, as he tells us in his Prologue, answers to the virtue of faith; the second, to hope; the third, to charity. In the first, while bewailing our past sins, we see only the smoke of the coming fire; flame and smoke are mixed together in the second; while in the third, the fire of God's love burns bright and clear. In the first, the soul is cleansed from her foulness by the thought of past sins and of God's judgments; in the second, the Life and Passion of Christ shed a light on her path; in the third, she rests in the contemplation of His Godhead.

The first eleven chapters of the work form a prelude to the first week of meditations. Though not put into the form of meditations, they require to be read slowly and thought over well, especially chapter vi. From the eleventh to the nineteenth chapter follow the meditations of the first of the three *Viæ*. Although arranged for one week, it was not the intention of the author that beginners should, at the end of eight days' exercise, pass at once to a higher grade without being sure of their progress; and in the nineteenth chapter he tells us how long we should employ ourselves in this first stage, and by what signs we may tell that we have reaped the fruit of it.

Next follows the Way of Enlightenment. In this part we would advise our readers to insert a part of the fourth division of the book (on Contemplation, of which we shall speak presently), namely, from chapter xlix. to chapter lx. These chapters contain an exquisitely beautiful and devout course of meditations on the Life and Passion of Christ. The last chapter of the Way of Enlightenment, on the Lord's Prayer, is one of the most beautiful in the whole work.

To these three parts Cisneros adds a fourth, on Contemplation. The title looks as if the special object of this part were to deal only with those extraordinary workings of God's grace which form the subject of what is called Mystic Theology. It is, however, not so; and any child can read and understand it without difficulty, at least from chapter xlix. to lxix. Though Cisneros does here and there in the first few chapters mention these mystic gifts of God, yet, as he himself says, he writes this fourth part, as well as the rest, for the simple and unlettered. It is for the most part only a fuller explanation of things already said, and the greatest part of it belongs to the Way of Enlightenment. Instead of being, as might be imagined, a fourth stage, higher than that called the Way of Union, its distinctive character lies in having been written for such as have the will and convenience of wholly withdrawing themselves, at least for a time, from outward employments, to dwell on spiritual things alone.

From the last words of the sixty-ninth chapter we learn that the work was completed on the thirteenth of November, A.D. 1500. It was first written in Spanish, but was soon after translated into Latin. The editions we have used in our translation are those of Venice, printed in 1555, and of Cologne in 1644. In the first of these, the Directory for the Canonical Hours is put before the Book of Exercises; in the second, after it. In the Cologne edition is appended a treatise on Prayer, by Lodovico Barbo, founder of the Cassinese Congregation, which we hope to publish in a future volume. Among the editions of the work we have been able to see was a French translation by Dom Anselm Theuart, of the Congregation of St. Maur, Paris, 1655; and another in Italian by Giulio Zanchini, edited, with a dedication to the Benedictine nuns of S. Ambrogio in Rome, by D. Mauro da Genova, Cassinese abbot in St. Paul's in the year 1635.

S. Speco, Subiaco,
Feast of St. Benedict 1876.

CONTENTS.

	PAGE
TRANSLATOR'S PREFACE	iii
AUTHOR'S PREFACE	3
PROLOGUE	4

PART I. THE WAY OF PURITY.

CHAP.
I. That the devout man, who is bent on going onward in the spiritual life, will profit much by seeking the fellowship of good men and shunning that of the wicked 7
II. That spiritual exercises are much needed by a religious man for the cleansing of his soul . 9
III. Concerning the fruit to be gathered from fixed and settled exercises 10
IV. On the conditions with which a man should undertake these spiritual exercises . . 13
V. What kind of spiritual exercises we should choose, and by what rule they should be measured . 15
VI. On sundry good thoughts which should spur us on in our spiritual exercises 18
VII. That our vows and the holiness of the place we dwell in call upon us to be fervent in our good works 25
VIII. That our spiritual exercises should be duly fixed and settled, both in respect to the matter of the same and to the proper seasons and hours for fulfilling them 29
IX. Wherein is shown that for many reasons have holy men been led to lay down times and hours at which we may give ourselves to mental prayer 33

CONTENTS.

CHAP.		PAGE
X.	That beginners in the way of God must begin by fear, which is the beginning of divine wisdom; and concerning several kinds of fear	35
XI.	Concerning those things whereof we must always live in fear	39
XII.	Concerning the distribution of our meditations throughout the week, according to the way of purity.	42
XIII.	On the subjects for meditation on Tuesday morning.	57
XIV.	On the subjects for meditation on Wednesday morning.	61
XV.	In what pious thoughts the devout man should exercise himself on Thursday morning	64
XVI.	Subjects of meditation after the office of Matins on Friday	66
XVII.	On the subjects of meditation for Saturday morning.	70
XVIII.	On what subjects our meditation should be made after the Matins office on Sunday	73
XIX.	For how long a time a man should remain in the way of purity, and how he may know he has succeeded in purifying himself	76

PART II. THE WAY OF ENLIGHTENMENT.

XX.	That the man who wishes to begin the way of enlightenment must be first purged and cleansed from his sins in the way of purity, that he be not dazzled by the brightness of the divine light	78
XXI.	How the man who takes up these exercises should examine his conscience before beginning the way of enlightenment	80
XXII.	On the way of enlightenment according to blessed Dionysius	84
XXIII.	On the order in which the devout man, for the enlightening of his soul, should ponder the works of God's goodness according to the days of the week, and how he should give thanks for them	86
XXIV.	How the way of enlightenment receives the rays of its brightness from divers sources, but above all from the Lord's Prayer;	

CHAP.		PAGE
	which a religious man should dwell upon most attentively, lovingly, and devoutly, so as to be set on fire with God's love	97
XXV.	Wherein is shown how greatly a man is to blame, if he forsakes the aforesaid exercises out of sloth	103

PART III. THE WAY OF UNION.

XXVI.	What the way of union and perfection is; and what conditions the man must have that wishes to arrive at it	107
XXVII.	The things on which a devout monk or religious person should meditate for every day in the week after night prayers, while in this way of union, so that he may climb the six steps which lead to union with God	111
XXVIII.	How to lift up the soul to God by fervent love, even without any consideration of the understanding	123
XXIX.	That he who undertakes these exercises feels and loves more than he sees or understands	126
XXX.	On the effects wrought by little and little in the soul through this love, which perfects us and makes us one with God	130

PART IV. ON CONTEMPLATION.

XXXI.	That great learning is knowledge, but not wisdom, and is by no means necessary for contemplative men	136
XXXII.	What kind of men are the best suited for contemplation	138
XXXIII.	On the difference between learning and wisdom	140
XXXIV.	That a life of contemplation must be begun with the labour of the active life	142
XXXV.	That it is not for all alike to imitate the singular grace that the divine goodness has vouchsafed to some, of living in solitude	143
XXXVI.	That the love of God is the beginning and end of the contemplative life	146
XXXVII.	In what the height of a contemplative life consists; explained by a comparison drawn from worldly love	148

CONTENTS.

CHAP.		PAGE
XXXVIII.	What kind of love of God a contemplative man ought to have.	150
XXXIX.	Concerning two kinds of silence and solitude	152
XL.	Showing that a contemplative manner of life is, in the first place, useful to oneself	154
XLI.	That contemplative men are likewise useful to others	155
XLII.	Wherein is shown, by an example, that it is not pride, as some wrongly imagine, to give oneself to contemplation	158
XLIII.	How far contemplative men excel those who live an active life	159
XLIV.	How greatly contemplative men stand in need of the grace of God.	161
XLV.	How the contemplative soul is raised above the body and becomes one and undivided	163
XLVI.	Concerning divers ways in which holy men have treated of contemplation	166
XLVII.	Concerning the method of contemplation used by St. Bernard at the beginning of his conversion	169
XLVIII.	What contemplation is; its different kinds; and on what subjects a good monk ought to meditate	171
XLIX.	That the contemplative man must 'climb the ladder of contemplation in three ways, making use of the Life and Passion of the Lord	174
L.	On the types and prophecies of Scripture that concern the Incarnation of Christ	179
LI.	On the Annunciation	180
LII.	An abridgment of the Life of Christ for the use of beginners in the school of contemplation	180
LIII.	An abridgment of the Life and Passion of our Lord	185
LIV.	On the Supper of the Lord; and how we should prepare ourselves to receive the adorable Sacrament of the Eucharist	188
LV.	That the devout contemplative man ought not, out of scruples that harass him, keep aloof from partaking of this most health-giving Sacrament	196

CONTENTS.

CHAP.		PAGE
LVI.	That our Lord's Passion contains in itself all the perfection that a man can reach in this life	198
LVII.	Concerning six different ways of meditating on the Passion of our Lord	200
LVIII.	On the Passion of our Lord, divided into six parts; and first, on a brief method of meditating it.	208
LIX.	That the contemplative man ought in every meditation bear in mind the sufferings of Christ, that the fire of his love be never extinguished.	219
LX.	On the resurrection and glorious ascension of our Lord, and on the sending of the Holy Ghost	228
LXI.	That such as wish to gain the height of contemplation stand in need of unwavering perseverance	231
LXII.	Concerning divers hindrances that keep the contemplative man from reaching the summit of contemplation	232
LXIII.	Concerning some other hindrances to contemplation	237
LXIV.	How some are wanting in steady perseverance, and on that account make little way in contemplation	241
LXV.	Of what kind is that knowledge of God which the contemplative man enjoys in this world	243
LXVI.	That God dwells in the soul in a threefold manner.	245
LXVII.	That all men, and above all religious, are bound to strive after perfection under pain of present and future loss	247
LXVIII.	That in certain cases the contemplative man must descend from the height of contemplation, and break off for a time his spiritual exercises	249
LXIX.	Concerning sundry doctrines which the devout man must carefully observe in the matters that have been treated off, and the conclusion of this work	258

THE BOOK OF EXERCISES

OF THE

𝔖𝔭𝔦𝔯𝔦𝔱𝔲𝔞𝔩 𝔏𝔦𝔣𝔢,

IN WHICH A MAN IS TAUGHT THE WAYS OF HOLINESS,
WHEREBY TO STRIVE AFTER AND REACH THE
HEIGHT OF TRUE PERFECTION.

THE AUTHOR'S PREFACE.

As our Saviour said, we must labour not for the food that perisheth, but for that which endureth unto everlasting life. And for this reason, at the earnest wish of some of my brethren, and not out of any rash eagerness of mine, have I been led to put together this book of ghostly exercises. And although, after weighing my own strength in the scales of reason, I find myself without learning and dull of understanding, yet I trust Divine Goodness will fill up what is wanting in me, and that the loving-kindness of my brethren will help me, and my own good and sincere intention plead in my behalf. And since, through God's mercy, I profess the Rule of St. Benedict, I devoutly commend myself to St. Benedict's intercession, asking him to vouchsafe to obtain by his prayers that God may speed this little work on its way for His own glory, making it beget fruits of holiness in all that read it, and work out for me my own reward. Amen.

The zeal of Thy house hath eaten me up (Ps. lxviii.).

PROLOGUE.

DEAREST brethren, in honour of the most Blessed Trinity, and of our Lady the most glorious Virgin Mary, Mother of God, and for the good of such as are eager to try themselves in a spiritual life, we shall in this book set forth how the devout man that useth these exercises ought to exercise himself in three several ways: which are,

> The Way of Purity;
> The Way of Enlightenment;
> The Way of Union.

Moreover, we shall set down how, by the use of certain set exercises, of Meditation, Prayer, and Contemplation, allotting to every day of the week its own share, he may go on climbing step by step until he reach the goal of his wishes—namely, that indwelling of the soul in God which holy men are wont to style true and hidden wisdom.

These three ways of which we speak answer to the three theological virtues—Faith, Hope, and Charity; and by means of them we shall gain the highest top of the mountain—that is to say, of the love of God. For, indeed, the way of purity, as the beginning, answers to faith; the way of enlightenment, because it holds the middle, to hope;

the way of union, being the end, to charity. And, as Gerson truly saith, in his book called the *Mount of Contemplation*, we cannot go from a faulty life to a perfect one, except by steps; nor can a man become excellent and consummate in holiness on a sudden, and, as it were, unwittingly; but this perfection has to be wrought out by us in the way in which Nature is wont to work—namely, by advancing from an imperfect to a perfect state. Thus we see fire begin with smoke, and in the midst of the smoke appears the flame, which after a while burns bright and clear. So when a grain of wheat is sown, it must first turn to rottenness, and then put forth its germ; and afterwards it sprouts up out of the earth, and grows and ripens. Also, when thou wouldst transplant a sapling from a barren soil to a fruitful one, thou must first uproot it, and then set it anew; and at first it droops as if dead, but soon clothes itself afresh in greenness, and in time grows up to its proper height. And the like mayst thou behold in all the rest of Nature's works.

In this manner, therefore, he that would raise himself up to an union with God, and to live a life of contemplation, must not hope to be perfect even from the beginning, but must needs at first send up the smoke of sorrow for the life he has hitherto led; next will follow the fire of love, but as yet not clear of smoke; and lastly, love alone, pure from all such defilement. In our first state our fleshly life turns to rottenness and dies; in the second, it bursts from the earth to newness of life; in the third, its fruit is ripened. And as with plants, so is it with us; for a man must first be plucked up by the roots from the bad and barren earth of worldly living; which cannot be without great toil and pains; next, he is planted anew; at which stage he doth indeed still feel the burden of his flesh, though more lightly now than he did before; until at length he strikes out strong and deep root, and bears fruit in plenty. Whosoever, therefore, shall earnestly school himself in the three ways aforesaid, yearning after the enjoyment of God's love, shall, with God's help, speedily arrive at a holy life; unless, through his own guilt and lukewarmness, he should be unwilling to do so, and should lay aside holy things and go back to his own ill habits and baneful pleasures; concerning which he must labour untiringly to overcome and root them out, as he will otherwise make but little way, according as it is more fully set forth in the book called *The Spiritual Ascent*, which begins thus: Blessed is the man, &c.

PART I.

CONCERNING THE WAY OF PURITY.

CHAPTER I.

That the devout man, who is bent on going onward in the spiritual life, will profit much by seeking the fellowship of good men and shunning that of the wicked.

THE Prophet doth forewarn us, saying: With the holy shalt thou be holy, and with the wicked man shalt thou become wicked. Wherefore, dearest brother in Christ, beware lest the sinful and crafty fellowship of bad men should lead thee astray in thy paths. Put thyself under the guidance of a religious man, singling out one that hath the gifts of virtues, the adornment of prudence, and great learning; a man mature and grave, and firmly grounded in the fear of God, from whom thou mayst at all times hear good words, and such as may cheer thee and bear thee up, and may be worthy to be stored up in thy heart, and carried out in thy works. For as a coal that is not yet kindled, if set nigh to one that is already on fire, doth itself catch fire and burn, so, in like manner, he that is lukewarm or cold doth wax fervent and devout, and reap a harvest of wisdom and goodness of life, if he lives with one already on fire with love and devotion. It befalls them as it did the Apostles, who, by cleaving fast to the Redeemer, became holy men, and were filled with the Holy Ghost. St. Mark likewise, by attaching himself to Peter, grew learned in the Gospel, and became himself an evangelist. And Timothy, the companion of Paul, was from his early youth exceedingly skilled in the understanding of the Scriptures; and being afterwards ordained bishop by the same most glorious Apostle, died at length a blessed martyr for the preaching of the Gospel. So likewise Augustine became a follower of Ambrose, and was by him taught and baptised, and thus came to be one of the Church's brightest doctors, and his fame hath filled the whole world. The holy child Maurus, from having betaken himself to the guidance of our most glorious Father Benedict, deservedly became a most worthy abbot, and shone afar by the light of his holiness and miracles. So also did the devout Bernard, who, after enrolling himself under Abbot Stephen in the monastery of Citeaux, became a bright beacon of every religious virtue to all his order, and shed his light as a shining star over the whole earth, and doth now shine in heaven. We might bring many more examples both from the Old Covenant and from the New, by all which is clearly shown that to keep company with good men availeth much for the good of our souls and for our going forward in ghostly exercises, and that the company of the bad works us great harm; but we forbear, lest we should draw out our discourse to too great a length.

CHAPTER II.

That spiritual exercises are much needed by a religious man for the cleansing of his soul.

DEAREST brethren, it is written in the Book of Psalms that the great Prophet David said, I have meditated at night with mine own heart; I have been exercised, and have swept out my soul. And, in sooth, the religious man who desireth to repair and restore to its former well-being his soul, which was made in the beginning after God's image and likeness, and had afterwards gone down from Jerusalem to Jericho—to-wit, from a calm and peaceful to a wavering and unsettled state—must set before his eyes the example of the same most glorious Prophet, and chasten and cleanse his spirit; and, with the help of these ghostly exercises, free it altogether from ill habits and sins, and from the taint of evil lusts, making it a fitting vessel for God's graces and gifts from above. For it is written: Wisdom shall not enter the soul that wisheth evil, nor dwell in a body under the rule of sin. And since, as Augustine saith, it is order alone that can beget peace and rest in man's soul, and things that are not well ordered cannot last long and are always in disquiet, while such as are well ordered are both lasting and peaceful, and do greatly strengthen the soul, and rendering it dreadful to its foes, as a camp in array of battle, it is well worth our while to lay down a settled plan and allot some fixed exercises; so that, always knowing what we have to do, we may always find ourselves at peace; and by never ceasing to work at them, we may bring our soul back to that dignity which it had in the beginning, and has since lost.

CHAPTER III.

Concerning the fruit to be gathered from settled and fixed exercises.

THE fruit of such exercises as are well ordered is of the greatest value. The first thing we gain by having settled and fixed exercises is, that we are thereby clear of evil and disquieting thoughts and hurtful desires, which often defile us as long as we set no curb on the movements of our hearts, since, as it is written in Genesis, our thoughts and wishes are bent on evil even from our youth. Nor is it possible to bring our heart back from the wanderings of its thoughts, unless it be strongly built on the unshaken groundwork of fixed and duly appointed exercises, and borne up by divine grace. For, as Abbot Serenus saith, in the *Conferences of the Fathers*, man's soul is so made that it can never be idle, but must needs run hither and thither, being carried backwards and forwards by its native fickleness, unless we give it a settled aim, on which it may spend its strength. And holy men say that a soul that hath no such exercises planned out is like a house with four open doors, which men can enter and leave as they please, while the master of the house knows nothing of it; for it is in this way that a man's thoughts deal with his soul, if they find it without a settled employment.

The second good that comes of keeping to a fixed arrangement in our works is, that the soul gains strength for great things from them, and does them with ease; since things we are always doing over again come to pass into our nature, and long-continued usage begets a habit in us. They, on the other hand, who keep no such even tenor in their works have as many counsels to guide them as are the works they see other men do; and they busy themselves to-day about one thing, to-morrow about another, being ever changeful and shifting in their undertakings, as we read in the *Conferences of the Fathers*, and in the book that begins: A certain man went down from Jerusalem to Jericho; wherein we read that such as these never go forward, or at best but little.

A third fruit of this manner of life is the fervour it kindles in us; for he that sees all he has to do laid out in goodly order before him goes to work with more willingness, and would blush to lay aside, through sloth or carelessness, what he had lovingly and in good earnest taken upon him to do. For this reason do holy and religious men allot special good works to stated hours and seasons, that the spirit may never slacken pace in its onward career; and by binding themselves to carry them out, they keep alive and heighten every day their fervour of life. And as, according to holy men's saying, any making light of our ghostly exercises must needs make us grow lukewarm and cold, so by giving ourselves up to them in good earnest, whether they concern the body or the soul, without ever slackening in our fulfilment of them, we come to taste a certain delight in the performance of them, which doth itself grow into a habit.

A fourth fruit thereof is, that by making this suitable allotment of thy duties thou shalt the more easily come to know thyself as thou art; which self-knowledge lies in seeing clearly by how much thou art a gainer or loser, how much thou goest onward or backward on thy way; and by watching the works thou doest to see whether they be done to-day more fervently and carefully, or more coldly and carelessly, than yesterday. For by comparing in this manner one day with the next it will be easy for thee to keep a reckoning of thy gains or losses.

There is yet a fifth gain in this—to-wit, that he who does a few things, but does them in due order and with a straightforward purpose, makes greater way and earns a much richer reward than the man that heaps up a medley of many troublesome undertakings without method or order. And the Saints tell us that one work of a wise man, done as it should be, is worth much painful toil done by a fool.

Bethink thyself, therefore, how plentiful a harvest is shared by such as do carefully work at settled and well-ordered exercises. And since the harvest to be gotten is so plentiful, we will, with God's help, lay down a distribution of holy practices wherein to spend the whole week, according to the three aforesaid ways—namely, the way of purity, the way of enlightenment, and the way of union, concerning which we shall speak at length hereafter.

CHAPTER IV.

Of the conditions with which a man should undertake these spiritual exercises.

BEFORE all, beloved brethren, he that desires to begin leading a life of holiness must cleanse his heart from all its deadly sins by sorrow and confession, since an unclean heart is a vessel that cannot hold within itself the rills that flow from the Holy Ghost. In the second place, he must loathe all the pleasures of the flesh, and shun all lightness of behaviour; for, as St. Bernard saith, heavenly consolations are chary of their presence, and cannot abide with those that set their hearts on other pleasures. Augustine likewise says that if a man's heart be gladdened from without, he must needs be void of comfort from within. The children of Israel did not eat manna as long as the wheaten flour which they had brought with them from Egypt lasted them. Now the wheat of Egypt signifies those works of ours which are according to this world, and which must needs perish, before we can come to taste of the heavenly manna of God's own consolation.

Thirdly, our hearts must be set free from all the cares of outward and unnecessary things that, like empty vessels, we may hold ourselves out to catch the overflow of divine grace.

The fourth condition is, that we do at all times eagerly thirst to go forward on our spiritual journey, as was the case with Jacob while he toiled in thraldom for his beloved Rachel, feeling neither the summer's heat nor the winter's cold, out of the greatness of his love. In such a manner ought a man with burning love go through his allotted task, and do all that we have hitherto laid down, never making light even of the smallest matters; for he that deals lightly with these small things will by little and little fall away.

In the fifth place, let a man be sober and prudent in choosing and fulfilling the works of the spirit, not overburthening himself with too many, lest for want of discernment he should fall short of his mark. For a man should act in one way concerning the end, which is to love God without measure, and to stamp Him on his inmost heart, without ever, if it lies with himself, turning his thoughts from the love of Him, the deep sea of whose love must have no shore; and otherwise must he handle such things as are but means for reaching that end, among which are his godly exercises. Of these we must make that use which will most swiftly bear us on to our wished-for end, of cleanness of heart and love of God, whereof we have spoken; as is written both in the *Conferences of the Fathers* and in the book that begins: Blessed is the man, &c.

CHAPTER V.

What kind of spiritual exercises we ought to choose, and by what rule ought they be measured.

IT doth not befit thee, brother, to follow any exercises thou mayst chance to light upon; but thou shouldst choose and frame them after the examples left us by the Holy Fathers, as it is written: Do all things as it hath been shown thee in the Mount. Now our Fathers followed certain rules in framing their exercises, and thou must abide by the same.

In the first place, therefore, see that they be in keeping with Holy Writ, with the teaching of the Saints, and the examples of the Fathers; for whatever doth not clearly agree with God's Word, how fair soever it may seem, yet must be looked upon with distrust. And since there are in these days many who wrest the right meaning of Scripture to the upholding of their own private devices, thou wouldst do well to lay open the works thou art about to undertake to some holy and enlightened man, and abide by his counsel in all that concerns them.

Thy second rule must be to have these thine exercises meted out with a sparing hand, which moderation must be shown, as holy men tell us, mainly in two things. For thou must neither be too harsh in chastising thy body nor busy thyself about too many things; since too heavy a load of penance laid on thy shoulders will turn thy inward sweetness to bitterness; and if thou busiest thyself with too many things, thy peace of mind goes to wreck. Hence thou must duly temper all that thou doest, and in everything seek to relieve thyself by varying thy employments as suits thee best; and we are told to do this in those words: At one time give thyself to reading, at another to prayer, in due season betake thyself to work, and so shall thy time go by quickly, and thy burden be lightsome. Neither must thou so give thyself up to them as to let them bring thee weariness or illness; for then they could not last long.

The third quality of thy exercises is, that they be chosen and ordered as may best agree with thy state of life, and the habits both of thy outer and inner man; for all things do not befit all men, nor can all find a liking in one and the same thing; but each one should single out such as are best for fighting against his own vices, and wherein he finds the strongest help to grow in the love of virtue. The exercises which do best further this are the best for him; for, as Ambrose saith, a man must in all he does choose what beseems best his age and state and time, and what falls in best with each one's natural bent and liking.

Fourthly, thou must, above all, be careful not to take up these exercises for a season only, laying them down again after giving them a short trial; but thou must steadfastly go on with them to the end. And St. Bernard truly said that we cannot, without great misgivings, witness the fickleness of such as are ever craving for one thing after another, and are led away to-day by one thing, to-morrow by another, standing still nowhere, and always sketching for themselves as many new plans as are the places they meet with on their way, always looking wistfully on what is beyond their reach, while they loathe what they have, and thus reap nothing from either. But he that wishes to see the fruit of his toil must set himself up a fixed aim, and make of all his good works so many means for reaching it, and stick fast to what he begins. Now, as Abbot Moses saith in one of his *Conferences*, and as we read in the book that begins: Blessed is the man, &c., the end of all our ghostly works is to gain a clean heart and a perfect love of God. The latter of these two —that is to say, love of God, or blessedness— must needs be our highest aim; and the former— to-wit, cleanness of heart—a lower mark, and, as it were, a preparation: for it smooths the way for gaining this perfect love or blessedness. And thus must we always keep the eye of our soul on these two ends, doing as archers do when they set up a target and let fly their arrows against it. If we do otherwise, we shall but overwork and wear ourselves out, and not get on.

CHAPTER VI.

On sundry good thoughts which should spur us on in our spiritual exercises.

THE Apostle Paul exhorts us in these words: Be ye in carefulness not slothful; fervent in spirit; serving the Lord. We must, therefore, carefully study the proper way of keeping our fervour alive, since holy men say that the first step towards making a thing our own is to wish for it eagerly; nor can a man ever grow fervent in a spiritual life unless he hath earnestly desired to become so. For, as Bernard says, Whithersoever a man would go himself, thither must the fire of his longing desires lead the way. Now, in order to light this fire of earnest desire within us, we shall point out sixteen considerations, which every devout man should store up in his heart, since without often thinking them over we shall not be able to abide long in a holy life.

In the first place, we must attentively consider how greatly we should love our God, for His own most perfect being—His blessedness, greatness, and loveliness—His boundless might and unutterable wisdom—who is Himself the highest good, and in whom countless perfections are contained. Weigh well with thyself the love thou hast for Him, and thou shalt find how little it is to what thou owest Him.

Secondly, thou shouldst ponder well the many sorrows, the anguish and dread, the harsh chidings and harsher blows, the sharp and cruel tortures He underwent, and how He vouchsafed to die for us on the cross, and yet how little we are willing to bear for His sake.

Consider, next, how many good things He hath promised to give us in everlasting blessedness, when our souls and bodies shall be glorified; and how lukewarm we are in striving after the enjoyment of that most priceless treasure.

For the fourth point, we should dwell upon the many and great good things bestowed on man by God when He created and redeemed him, and on each one of us in our religious calling, and in giving us food and keeping us in life; and notwithstanding so many and such great kindnesses, we make Him no return, but do rather unceasingly offend Him.

Fifthly, call to mind the number and the grievousness of the sins He has forgiven us, and how often we have fallen into them anew; and instead of thanking Him for His forgiveness of them, have laid ourselves under the hateful guilt of ingratitude.

In the sixth place, think well on the height of perfection after which we are bound to strive—namely, to keep God's ten commandments, for the sake of Him who gave them; and, therefore, never to sin grievously, but to love God above all things, and naught else above Him or equally with Him, and to wish well to our neighbour, loving him as ourselves, and seeking his everlasting welfare, which man finds in loving God above all things.

In the seventh place, set before thine eyes the examples shown us in the lives of the holy Patriarchs and Prophets, of the Apostles and of all the Saints, who were indeed but mortal men like ourselves, and yet such is our sloth that it irks us to tread in their footsteps.

Thy eighth consideration should be on the beauty, the worth, and the nobleness of virtue, with the ugliness, foulness, and shamefulness of sin, and how, all this notwithstanding, we do still shun the path of virtue and stick fast to our evil works.

Ninthly, bear in mind how hard the beginning of a holy life becomes for such as put off their conversion to God through lukewarmness; for although the Lord is always at hand to strengthen the wavering of our free-will, yet we never strive to do what lieth in us. And thence it comes that but few begin well, fewer still go on with what they have begun, and very few hold fast to the end; wherefore, brethren, being strong in our hope of God's mercy, it behoves us with earnest endeavour, with our whole understanding and good-will, and with all the means we have at command, to toil manfully after perfection.

In the tenth place, think well how hard it is to win in the strife we have against the world and the flesh, which springs both from our fondness for the good things of this earth and from the evil counsel and fellowship of the wicked among whom we live, and how ill we are able to ward off the cunning and oft-repeated onsets of evil spirits; and while thus surrounded by so many risks, we grow cold and drowsy, as if all were in safety, without ever putting forth our strength to cope with them.

Next, see how few they are that persevere to the end; for even they that begin with eagerness to climb the ladder of holiness often stop halfway up, and do not reach its top. And few, indeed, are they that give themselves any concern about so weighty an affair as is that of their perseverance; which we ought rather at all hours to crave of God, if we wish to be saved, since we know that it is not the man that hath worked hard for thirty or forty years, but he that lives well to the end, that wins the crown.

Reflect, in the twelfth place, on the fewness of thy days in this life, and what a rich harvest of merit thou mayst garner in while it lasts; but when thou hast once gone forth from it, thou canst return no more: and yet how unthriftily thou squanderest the time told out for thee; while at every moment of the day thou drawest nearer to death, void of good works and laden with thy sins.

For the thirteenth point of thy meditations, weigh well the minuteness, the sternness and dread rigour of God's justice; since even one deadly sin for which a man has not duly atoned must assuredly meet with its doom of everlasting pains of body and soul in hell; nor may one venial sin, how small soever, pass unpunished. Hereupon may we well wonder at our own blindness and folly; for although we are able now to turn away the wrath of God and move Him to forgiveness by doing penance, and by our sighs and grief for the sins we have been guilty of against Him, yet we care to do nothing of the sort, and, like men dull of understanding, we are each day nearer to falling into the hands of God's justice.

Next, think on the pains of hell; how bitter, manifold, and everlasting they are; and that he that in this life is fain to taste for one fleeting moment of pleasures that God hath forbidden, dooms himself to undergo them hereafter. And we ourselves, although we believe them to be so many, so cruel and never-ending, are yet careless how to escape them; whilst indeed we ought right gladly undergo for a million years any sufferings whatever that are to have an end, that we might be freed from everlasting pains and tortures; as the Prophet saith: Which of you can dwell with devouring fire? Who of you can dwell with everlasting burnings?

In the fifteenth place, thou shouldst ever keep before thine eyes that unfathomable depth of God's judgments, which He has wrought on several who had lived long in great holiness, and were yet at last forsaken by the Lord for their hidden sins. If we thought well on this, I doubt not but that we should be more troubled about doing our works well. Hence the Prophet's warning, where he saith: Come and see the works of God, who is terrible in His counsels over the children of men. Here we should stop to think on our own salvation, and tremble lest we should lose the grace of God.

Let the sixteenth, and last, of these thy reflections be this, namely, with what earnest longings the blessed await us; how lovingly they yearn for our coming. If we thought well on this, I think we should make haste to be with them; for, as St. Bernard says, The Angels await us to build up again what was cast down among themselves, and the blessed in order to have the fulness of their own glory; God the Father awaiteth us, His children, to set us over all that He hath; God the Son awaiteth us, as His brethren, to bestow on us the fruit of His taking to Himself our flesh, and all that He hath earned for us with His Blood; and so likewise the Holy Ghost, who is love and kindness, and in whom the Father, who doth most assuredly wish for the fulfilment of His decree, hath predestined us from all eternity. Brethren, should we not hasten to any place in the world if our beloved awaited us there? Then, surely, ought we speed onward to the land of everlasting happiness and glory, where so goodly an array of noble citizens look fondly for our coming. This thought should quicken our desire to be set free and be with Christ.

The aim of all these considerations is twofold; for, in the first place, we should gather thence a clear knowledge of our own lowliness. We must next strive to have a burning thirst after higher perfection and greater fervour. Is there any one, unless he has a heart as hard as iron, who does not inwardly yearn for so blessed a life, and will not forthwith try to shake off all his former sloth and carelessness?

The things I have written here I have not set down for thee to read over but once: nay, I would have thee go over them again and again, and have them always as present to thee, and daily turn them over in thy heart, and they will keep it from growing cold; or if it should have perchance grown chill, they will set it on fire anew.

CHAPTER VII.

That our vows, and the holiness of the place we dwell in, call upon us to be fervent in our good works.

It is written in Ecclesiastes: If thou hast vowed anything to God, defer not to pay it; for an unfaithful and foolish promise displeaseth Him. And thou shouldst hold for certain that every vow binds the man that has made it to abide by it. Some learned men say that the bond of a vow is stricter than that of an oath. So that a man sins grievously by breaking his vows, and this sin is even more deadly than if he broke his oaths; and this is according to St. Thomas, in the second part of his *Sum of Theology*. Now, brethren, what is it that we have vowed, if it be not to strive hard by good works to reach the height of perfect holiness? He, then, that shall altogether leave off striving after this must be looked on as a transgressor of his vow; while, on the other hand, we shall not be set down as such, even though we do often fall, so long as we work hard with unflagging zeal to go onward, and tire not in our endeavours to get farther and mount still higher. Let us then, with this good-will, and by a due and orderly fulfilment of our exercises, give to God what we have promised; and we shall have in our turn the reward held out to us. Let us do after the example set us by men of the world, whose dread of breaking their word is so great, that when set free from captivity, on giving their word to return, they fail not to keep the promised day, even though they know that cruel usage awaits them.

The worthiness of the place wherein we dwell is another spur to our fervour. Would that all did heartily consider how grievously he sins that lives a lukewarm, unbridled life within a monastery. Concerning such men saith the Prophet Jeremias: Why is it that my beloved hath wrought much wickedness in my house? For they sin grievously indeed, and this for many reasons:

Firstly, by reason of the loftiness of the religious state, which they debase by not giving to God what they promised Him.

Secondly, on account of the holiness of their dwelling-place, as it is written in Isaiah: In the land of saints he hath done wickedness, and he shall not behold the glory of God; and as elsewhere, Jeremias: Thou hast defiled My holy land.

Thirdly, because they that live in a monastery find it an easy task to live well. Yet it is indeed sad to see our hearts so hardened that we loathe this manna, hungering after the onions of Egypt, which draw tears from the eyes of them that eat them.

In the fourth place, on account of the fellowship of holy brethren; for the wicked man among the good is like Judas among the Disciples of the Lord, and like Satan, who stood among the children of God.

Fifthly, by reason of the loving-kindness of our God, who holds in readiness for us all that we need; since we should rightly account him a traitor that should strive against his Lord, who supplies all his wants. For even dogs are wont to love such as show kindness to them.

In the sixth place, his sin is more weighty with respect to his vows and his profession; since it cannot be held a trifling evil for him who has offered himself to God to turn his back upon Him and give himself up to the devil, swearing a false oath to the Holy Ghost.

Seventhly, he that leads a bad life in a monastery wrongfully fills a place that should be filled by a good monk.

In the eighth place, such an one takes on himself to do things whereof he is unworthy, as when he stands with his brethren in the sight of God, and so forth.

Ninthly, his guilt becomes heavier, for that he makes light of the weighty chastisements which, as it is written, are to be dealt out to such as sin against the sanctity of holy places.

Lastly, because he is not in dread of the evils that must overwhelm him, seeing that he wastes the good things of religion, and sunders himself from their use; being like the blaspheming thief, seeing he descends from his cross in the cloister to the pains of hell. And here I make an end, earnestly begging any one amongst you that feels himself growing cold to say, with blessed Bernard,

Why growest thou cold, O my soul, and dost pine away in sloth? The sufferings of this life are neither worthy of thy past sins, which are forgiven thee, nor of the grace that is now poured out upon thee, nor of the glory to come, which hath been promised thee. Awake, my soul, for what we have promised is, perhaps, great; but what hath been promised us is far greater. Let us fulfil the former, and thirst after the latter. Thou seest that the joy of thy sin doth quickly fade, but its wages are everlasting; the hardship of virtue is but little, and the glory that follows it unbounded. Many are called, and few chosen; yet all receive due quittance, some indeed in glory, others in endless torments.

Watch, therefore, brother, over thy works, and do not sleep at the time of prayer which follows the night-watches;* for when thou thinkest it not shalt thou be called away. Mark well, that such as are always on the watch are called blessed.

Hitherto we have shown how greatly we stand in need of the fellowship of the good for our ghostly welfare; we have spoken of the love of spiritual exercises which we ought to have, and of the usefulness of such exercises as are duly settled and orderly laid down; we have seen what is wanted in such as would fain make use of them, with what measure they should be meted out, and what

---

* Cisneros here alludes to the custom of making the daily mental prayer between Lauds and Prime, usual in Benedictine

wholesome thoughts will be the best for kindling a holy fire in our will. It remains for us now to set forth and declare in what manner a religious man should journey on the three ways aforesaid —namely, of purity, of enlightenment, and of union; and how, by joining these exercises with prayer and contemplation, he may mount up step by step till he gains the end he looked for, which is the union of his soul with God; as Paul saith, He that cleaveth unto God is one spirit with Him. Holy men call the gaining of this object the possession of true wisdom.

CHAPTER VIII.

That our spiritual exercises should be duly fixed and settled, both in respect to the matter of the same and to the proper seasons and hours for fulfilling them.

THE religious man should always use a variety in the food of his soul. For we find on trial that how grateful soever any kind of food may be, yet if it is fed upon day by day, it begets at times a loathing in our taste, and makes us hunger after other meats, although in themselves less delightful. But when many and divers kinds of food are set before a man, he partakes of them more freely and with the greater relish the more he finds something new to his taste. In like manner, when a pious and religious man wishes to give himself to prayer, he must do his best to change from time to time the food of his spiritual banquet; for while the soul is on fire with its heavenward desires, the head and chest and the whole body cannot but feel weighed down by this exertion. And for this reason also we ought to use different kinds of food for our meditations, for even the body itself is thereby relieved. Its first and noblest repast should be placed in devout prayer and chaste desire; wherein the soul thirsts to be cleansed, enlightened, and made one with its blessed and most lovely Bridegroom. For this end beginners, above all others, must in their meditations dwell on the following two points: Firstly, on such things as may strike them with fear; for the soul that seeks to draw nigh to its God must begin by fear to tread the paths of a ghostly life. Secondly, they should often think deeply on the life and sufferings of our Redeemer; for His life, sufferings, and death are the gate through which we must pass to enjoy the love of His Godhead; and it was for this end that His side was opened by the spear, thereby showing us that none can enter in to the love of His Godhead except by the gate of His manhood and His wounds. But when the servant of God feels that he has already taken root in the love of the Godhead he may then for a little time turn his mind away from the thought of the Manhood. For the reason of his abiding in the thought of Christ as Man and of His wounds was, that he might by that means come to love

Him as God. We must, therefore, set down the subjects of our meditation for every day in the week in this manner: to-wit, in the way of purity, we must treat of the fear of God; in the way of enlightenment, of the loving-kindness of our God; and in the way of union, we must praise God for His perfections; and he that thus practises these exercises will have a variety of spiritual meats. And now we have said enough on the subject-matter of our meditations.

Now for that which concerns the laying down of times and hours, we should mark well, brethren, that as it is better for our bodily health, and suits better the cravings of hunger, that we should accustom ourselves to take food only at stated times and without ever swerving from this custom; so likewise the soul that would fain live a ghostly life must have fixed times for being by itself alone, and stated hours for prayer, both by day and by night, that so it may every day eat of the spiritual bread, and drink of the wine of divine consolation. And indeed this food is far dearer and sweeter to the soul than our bodily food is to the body; nor doth it lie according to reason that the soul, the mistress of the body, should be bereft of her own sweet and tasteful food, while the flesh, her bad and sluggish handmaid, hath her own allotted times for taking her meals. Moreover, it can easily be shown how useful it is to have a time set apart for prayer, for the frequent doing of good works begets a habit in the soul, and it comes to find pleasure and delight in what is good; and likewise when times and hours for giving oneself up to prayer are settled, the soul doth at these times find itself readier and less hindered in lifting up the heart with the fire of holy desires. Now the fittest time for prayer is the night; as the Prophet saith: The night shall be my light in my pleasures. And when the servant of God has a stated time for prayer, it must needs be that he will always find himself at that time in a certain manner more ready to pray. And should the time go by without his making his wonted prayer, his heart cannot but be sorely grieved at it, and this, above all, if it has been left out through carelessness or upon some trifling cause; since a soul cannot without sorrow endure to be bereft of its own sweetest food, most goodly refreshment, and of that spiritual joy of which it was wont to partake. To end, therefore, we deem the night the best time for prayer, as it is written in the Psalms: In the daytime the Lord hath commanded His mercy, and a canticle to Him in the night; as if He had bidden us to do works of mercy by day, and in the night to sing His praises. Jerome and Bernard say that the fittest times for prayer are after the night-watches and after Compline, for at these times is the servant of God freer to give himself to his ghostly duties. And now we have said enough on seasons and hours.

CHAPTER IX.

Wherein is shown that for divers reasons have holy men been led to lay down for us times and hours at which we may give ourselves to mental prayer.

THE Holy Fathers, dearest brethren, have not without reason ordained that at stated times of the day and night religious should give themselves to mental prayer; since, according to the devout Bonaventure, it is most needful for every one that wishes to go forward in holiness that he should train his heart to constant exercises of prayer and piety; and that holy religious tells us truly that a man that doth not use this kind of prayer every day is not only wretched and useless, but hath a lifeless soul in a living body. For, indeed, so strong is prayer, that it alone can overcome temptation and the strife we have with evil spirits. And every soul that is unbedewed with the dew of prayer brings forth works that are done but by halves, and are tainted with much loathing and unwillingness. But prayer is of great and untold value for the furthering of all our good undertakings, and for warding off all that might hurt us; and therefore,

If thou wouldst bear with hard things patiently, be thou a man of prayer.

If in thy temptations and hardships thou wouldst win the fight, be thou a man of prayer.

Dost thou wish to tread under foot thy evil passions? Be thou a man of prayer.

Wouldst thou fain find out the wiles of Satan and escape his snares? Be thou a man of prayer.

Wouldst thou live cheerfully in God's work and walk the paths of toil and suffering? Be a man of prayer.

Desirest thou to train thyself to a ghostly life, never dallying with the flesh in its lusts? Be a man of prayer.

And if thou wouldst fain drive off the flies of idle thoughts, be thou a man of prayer.

If thou seekest to fatten the soil of thy soul by good and holy thoughts, and by inflamed and pious longings, be thou a man of prayer.

If thou wouldst ground thy heart on God's will by a manly spirit and unshaken purpose, be a man of prayer.

If thou wouldst root out vices and clothe thyself with virtues, be thou a man of prayer.

Lastly, if thou art fain to climb the Mount of Contemplation, and taste of the embraces of thy Spouse, thou must be a man of prayer. For therein is the unction of the Holy Ghost given to us, instructing our minds concerning all things. By prayer do we lift ourselves to contemplation and taste the things of heaven.

You see then, brethren, how we ought to pray, and what strength and might there is in prayer. Now, to set the seal on all we have said hitherto, laying aside for a while the authority of Scripture, let it be for thee a firm proof that every day we hear and see with our eyes unlettered and simple persons gifted with the gifts aforesaid, and even with many other and far greater ones. Most carefully, then, should all such as long to follow Christ give themselves up to prayer, and above all, religious who have more time for doing so. Wherefore the holy and seraphic doctor above mentioned writes thus to his sister: I exhort and urge thee, as earnestly as I can, to use prayer as thy chiefest exercise; neither ought anything but prayer afford thee pleasure, for thou shouldst rejoice in nothing so much as in dwelling with thy Lord, which thou dost in prayer.

CHAPTER X.

That beginners in God's service must begin by fear, which is the beginning of divine wisdom; and concerning divers kinds of fear.

As St. Anselm saith, in his work entitled the *Book of Doctrines*, all beginners begin with servile fear; but out of this slavish fear comes filial fear. Blessed is the man to whom it hath been given to have the fear of God; for it is written among the sayings of the wise man, that the fear of the Lord is the beginning of wisdom. And, in sooth, it is the gate of our conversion, and, as Cassiodorus says, we do thereby enter into the house of God as by a gateway; and the devout St. Bernard, writing upon the Canticle of Solomon, says, Then doth

God first give to the soul His sweetness when He maketh her fear Him, not when He teacheth her to know Him. And Cassian says, in the fourth book of his *Institutions*, Fear is the beginning and the safeguard of our salvation; for through fear we have both the beginning of our change of life, and the cleansing of our souls from sin, and our safeguard on the way of virtue while we are led on to perfection. Hence we must not forget, as the Master of the Sentences teaches in the 34th distinction of the third part, that there are four kinds of fear, according to which we are in one way or another led on to God, or away from Him : to wit, worldly or *human* fear, *slavish* fear, that fear which belongs to *beginners*, and chaste or *filial* fear.

Human fear, as Cassiodorus says, is when we fear undergoing earthly dangers or the loss of the good things of the world, so as on that account to fall into sin ; and this fear is bad, and comes of too great a love for ourselves and this present life.

The second kind of fear is called servile, and of this we are now treating; and, as Augustine says, servile fear makes a man withhold himself from sin through dread of hell, or else of some temporal suffering or evil. But this slavish fear, as long as it takes not away from us the will to sin, cannot abide with charity ; and he that hath this fear alone cannot be saved ; but when charity comes, this fear is cast out, since he that does what is right only through fear of punishment, and without loving God, is not yet to be reckoned among the sons of God. But we must ever bear in mind that, although this slavish fear doth not abide together with charity, it is nevertheless the way to it, according to the words of Ecclesiasticus, The fear of the Lord is the beginning of love; and again, blessed Augustine says, The fear of God doth pave the way for His love; and when charity begins to take up her abode, the forerunner of charity is driven out to make way for her; and as the one increases, so doth the other decrease; and the greater our love is, the less is our fear; and where there is no fear, there is perfect love.

The third kind of fear is termed filial, or chaste dread, and is that fear which makes us dread to offend our Spouse, lest He should delay His coming, lest He should depart, lest we should be bereft of His presence. This fear springs from the true love of God; and of this the prophet says: The fear of the Lord is holy, enduring for ever and ever.

And for the difference between servile and filial or chaste fear, St. Augustine, on the first canonical epistle of St. John, writes thus: There is a kind of fear which is cast out by charity, and there is a chaste fear which doth abide for ever; for there are men who fear God lest they should be doomed to hell, and this fear doth open the gate to charity. But as it comes, so doth it depart; for if thou fearest God lest He should punish thee, it is not that thou dost love what is good, but that thou avoidest what is evil; and thus correcting thyself, thou dost begin to crave after good things; and when thou hast begun to desire good things thou hast a chaste fear, and dost thereby fear to lose those good things. As if there were two married women, of whom one is willing to commit adultery, but dreads her husband's knowing of it, so that she loves iniquity and loathes her husband's presence; the other loves her husband, and, hating the foulness of adultery, seeks to have him in her company. Both are in fear; but the former fears her husband's coming, the latter his going away. The former saith to herself, 'I am afraid to be condemned;' the latter, 'I fear lest I be forsaken.' From this example we may easily understand wherein that slavish fear which charity casteth out differs from that filial or chaste fear which endures for ever.

The fourth kind of fear is that which is styled the fear of beginners, which holds, as it were, a middle place between the two we have been describing—to wit, that of slaves and that of children —seeing that slavish fear, as has been said, is that which withholds a man from sinning through fear of pain, while filial fear keeps him from sin out of fear lest he offend God; and this fear, which belongs to beginners, makes us shun the guilt of sin on both accounts; that is to say, on account of the guilt itself and of its reward. And therefore St. Bernard says it has two eyes: the right eye, which looks upwards, and fears lest it be sundered from God; and the left, looking downwards, and dreading punishment. It is called *initial* fear, as that which belongs to beginners, who are wont to have in themselves the beginning of filial fear, inasmuch as charity is begun in them, but have not reached the fulness of filial fear, not having yet won the fulness of God's love. And therefore St. Thomas says that initial fear stands with respect to filial fear as that which is already perfect to what is imperfect, these two not differing in their essence, but in degree and state, since some are in the state of beginners, others are already far on their way, and others are perfect.

In this chapter we have described these several kinds of fear, that thou mayst see rightly which of them has its hold on thee, and thus mayst cast off that which is the portion of slaves, and live under the mastery of that which belongs to sons.

CHAPTER XI.

Concerning those things whereof we must always live in fear.

DEAREST brethren, although there are many things whereof we must stand in dread, yet some there are which are more threatening, and therefore to be feared with greater dread. Out of these we shall name the greatest, from which we should more carefully keep ourselves afar.

A man, then, should fear:

The changeful and unsettled fortune of the world, wherein a man can never abide in one and the same state, nor ever know whether he be worthy of love or hatred; since, if once God should forsake us, in the twinkling of an eye the Evil One would lead us astray.

The war, likewise, waged against the Spirit, without any rest, by our own flesh, by the world, and the devil.

Our own helplessness, and the sloth we every day fall into in fighting these battles, in doing penance, and going onwards on our way.

The weight of God's righteous judgments. This we see plainly in the case of Lucifer, who for the guilt of one sin alone was for ever cast out of heaven; how much more, then, shall they who have defiled themselves with many sins be debarred from entering it? So likewise did this rigour appear in the sin of Adam, who for one sin was driven out of Paradise, and the gate of heaven was shut until our Saviour opened it for us by His death. In which death and passion was seen the unbending and dreadful sternness of God's justice, since He left His most Beloved Son in the hands of such cruel men; as was clearly seen by all when He cried out on the cross, saying with a loud voice, My God, My God, why hast Thou forsaken Me? Since the sternness and sharpness of divine justice was shown so highly in the green wood, in One full of holiness and so dearly beloved of His Father, how shall it fare with us, dry wood as we are, barren of good works, and laden with fruits of unrighteousness?

Again did this wrathful justice appear to all

men at the Flood; for then the whole world, saving eight souls, perished.

We must also always fear our doubtful going out of this life, since no man knows where, when, or how he is to die, nor whether he will die a good or a bad death.

The judgment to come, in which the Judge cannot be hoodwinked, nor bent by prayers or bribes; nor shalt thou be able to appeal from the doom He shall have pronounced, nor canst thou in any way flee from its fulfilment.

Next comes the sharpness of the pains of purgatory, which, according to Augustine, go far beyond any suffering of this life.

Then the horrid sight of the devils, and the pains of hell, and its unquenchable fire.

The everlasting separation from the loving fellowship of the citizens of heaven.

The bitter wailing and groans of the damned, bereft of all comfort, who are penned up in hell like sheep, and on whom death shall feed. The sight and burning shame of our own sins, with the hatred of ourselves and of the whole world. The everlastingness of the pains of hell, seeing that in hell there is no redemption. The everlasting loss of that unspeakable glory and of all hope of reaching it; the hardness of the will, since such as are once in hell are hardened in evil, and unable to will what is right; the gnashing of teeth for excess of agony, wherewith the damned are more tormented than can be told in words. The imprisonment and slavery of the damned, unable to come out of hell, which they long to do. The worm of self-reproach ever gnawing at their consciences, by reason of the good they have not done, the scandals they have given, the evil they have wrought.

Let us, then, lift up our eyes to heaven, and pray, saying :
O Christ, merciful Redeemer,
We have been the cause of all Thy toil,
Let us not be lost at that day.

CHAPTER XII.

Concerning the distribution of our meditations throughout the week, according to the way of purity.

THE devout religious man must, above all, in his beginnings, chiefly exercise himself in the way of purity; and in order that, according to what has been said above, he may have settled and duly allotted exercises, the meditations of the way of purity must be distributed throughout the week as follow :

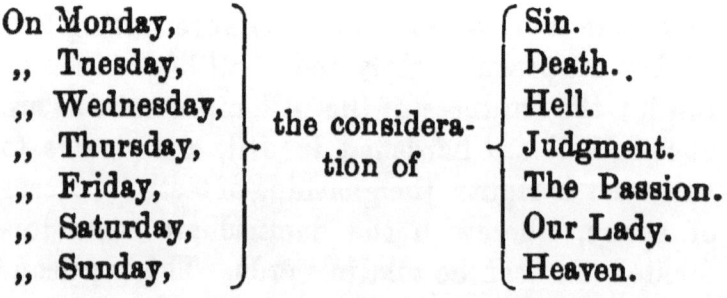

On Monday,   Sin.
„ Tuesday,   Death.
„ Wednesday,   Hell.
„ Thursday, the considera- Judgment.
„ Friday,   tion of   The Passion.
„ Saturday,   Our Lady.
„ Sunday,   Heaven.

On Monday, therefore, we must dwell on the thought of our sins according to the three elements of the way of purity, to wit, first, bitterness of sorrow; second, compunction of heart; third, the lifting up of the soul to God. The exercise of these three should be carried out in the following manner:

Justice and judgment, as the prophet saith, are the preparation of the throne of the Lord. And therefore, whenever a man wishes to mount up by spiritual longings to the fullest union with the divine Bridegroom, and to be refreshed with some crumbs of that bread on which blessed spirits are fed in the glory of heaven, while yet tarrying in the wretchedness of this life's exile, he must needs have at hand three helps, which under God's grace may lift him little by little on the ladder of heavenly contemplation.. For blessed Denis saith, in his book on the celestial hierarchy, that the angels have a threefold office to fulfil, to wit, of cleansing, enlightening, and perfecting. In the first place, therefore, it is necessary for the soul that wishes, while yet in this mortal life, to climb up that lofty height of heavenly blessedness wherein the angels are gladdened with the sight of God's glory, to carefully cleanse herself. Secondly, she must needs be enlightened by the rays of Divine Glory. Thirdly, she must strive, while toiling upwards to the higher grade of ghostly affections, to perfect herself in the deep waters of Divine Love, which may make her one spirit with her God. Wherefore we shall, first of all, speak of the way of purity, or of cleansing, in which the soul passes her time in bewailing her sins and her iniquities against God, in order to gain God's mercy by her sorrow. In this way is a man's conscience cleansed, which, according to what we have set down above, belongs to the state of beginners. In this way a man's heart is made straight and fitted up anew without earthly teaching, but giving itself up to the study of heavenly doctrine alone. And indeed, how simple and unlettered soever be the man that devotes himself to this practice, he will without fail be lifted up with the Light of God, not to any theoretical science, but that which bears on actual practice. Hence, before the Uncreated Wisdom can find its resting-place in a soul, making thereof its throne, according to what is written : The soul of the just man is the seat of wisdom, judgment and justice must fill that soul. I speak first of judgment; because, just as the soul hath by mortal sin turned its back on its Maker, making light of Him and forsaking Him, and hath given itself to creatures by an unhappy and wretched love for them, so ought it now to humble itself so fully as to draw down God's mercy and pity by its very lowliness, as much as it had before called forth by its rash deeds the avenging justice of the Most High Judge. Next, the soul should be prepared by justice; for the soul that has bartered the most amiable sweetness of its Creator for the loathsome delight it has found in creatures must chastise itself with such sharpness of sorrow as to make the satisfaction offered to the offended Majesty of God at least what would be looked on as a due measure if weighed in the scales of men's justice.

Now, brother, since we do really wish to work out in ourselves both judgment and justice, on Monday, after Matins, at the appointed hour for prayer, coming to the appointed place, kneel there, and signing thyself with the sign of the cross on forehead, lips, and breast, say this antiphon: Come, Holy Ghost, fill the hearts of Thy faithful ones, and kindle in them the fire of Thy love. And then say three times this verse: O God, incline unto my aid; O Lord, make haste to help me. And then, withdrawing within thine own spirit, look on thyself as a guilty man; and standing before thy God with great fear, as before a severe judge about to condemn thee, thou must exactly recall to mind and deeply consider how much God is offended by every sin. Thus, in order to pierce and rouse thyself up to devotion, according to the first element of the Way of Purity, which we have elsewhere called bitterness of sorrow, let thy heart at the beginning of thy prayer be wounded by the thought of thy sins; and thus, sharply reproaching thyself under the pricking of these thorns, say to thyself as follows:

O my soul, bethink thyself now most carefully, and strive with all thy might to feel how much even one sin is displeasing to God. See how pride cast down Lucifer from heaven, disobedience drove Adam out of Paradise; Sodom and Gomorrha were burnt for luxury, and the whole world perished by the Flood.

Think how the Son of God, thy Redeemer, underwent for sin a most bitter death that sin might not be unpunished, and God's justice might be duly satisfied. And again, in thy inmost heart remember that God will judge thee according to thy works alone. Remember that God is that justice which cannot be blinded, can never err, which none can flee from; as righteous in the chastisement of the wicked as in the glorification of His chosen ones. Hence He will reward thee according to thy works.

Turn over likewise in thy mind the sins thou didst commit before thy conversion; how manifold they were in thought, consent, delight, by word and work, and indeed they are so many that thou canst not reckon up their number.

Think how shameful they were, and above all the sins of the flesh, on the thought of which thou shouldst not stay long, lest thou shouldst be caught taking pleasure in that thought from which thou art fain to reap sorrow. See how weighty they are, since thou hast offended God and crucified Christ afresh by them.

Then think of the sins committed since thy first coming to God, and how thou lived so many slothful, lukewarm, and fruitless years.

Look on thy sins one by one, and confess them in God's sight; and when thou hast examined them, ponder well in thy heart the following things: how little thou hast done to make amends for thy sins; how little thou hast grieved for them; how few good works thou hast done in satisfaction for them. Know for certain that in this life or in the next thou must pay even to the last farthing. And therefore St. Bernard says, thou shalt pay a hundred times over what thou mightst have paid but once. When therefore thou, being a sinner, and above all if thou art a beginner, hast dwelt on all these things within thyself, and dost feel the arrows of fear in thy heart, and thy soul filled with grief, not through the fear of the hell thou hast deserved, but because thou hast wronged thy most loving God, bow down thy soul, rest thy head on thy hands, thinking thyself unworthy to look up to Heaven, and, turning thy heart towards thy God, say, with bitter sorrow: O most loving Father, I am that prodigal son who have committed all these crimes against Thy boundless Majesty, and have been so thankless to Thee. Thou hadst made me innocent; and I have defiled, crippled, and torn myself with countless sins. Thou, O Lord, wast for me crucified, wounded, and trodden down; and I have with all my might

striven to lift myself up. Thou hangest naked on
the cross; and I am clothed with vain and luxurious garments. To Thee, Lord, they gave gall
and vinegar to drink; and I have delighted in
rioting and drunkenness. Thou, O Lord, art full
of many toils; and I am languid and idle. What,
then, shall I do, O Lord? Shall I despair? But
what doth the prophet say? I wish not the
death of a sinner, but that he be converted and
live. Rusty bronze and tarnished mirrors may
be cleansed; and I, in this cleansing way, shall
strive to polish myself with the file of contrition,
confession, and satisfaction. And as I have
lifted myself up, so may I now become the offcast
and scorn of men. To overcome covetousness, I
shall renounce worldly possessions. Against the
lusts of the flesh, I shall never cease from chastening myself with fasts and watching, with hunger and thirst, and shall work hard to cleanse
myself by these three means, to wit,

1. By tearful prayer.
2. By the way of Thy Passion.
3. By the fire of Thy Love.

When, therefore, thy soul hath been after this
manner tried in the first part of the way of purity,
and is full of bitterness and grief at the painful
thought of her sins, let her pass on to the second
step—that is to say, to compunction—and say with
lively feeling, O my Lord, I grieve

That I have lost Thy friendship;

That I have set Thy Majesty at naught;

That I have yielded to my evil passions, and have in many ways lived a sinful life;

That I have thrown away my time and my strength both of body and mind,

And have trespassed against Thy commands and those of my superiors.

I am sorry, moreover, for my slothfulness in resisting sin, in doing penance, and going forward in virtue.

For neglecting my daily work, prayers, meditation, and ghostly reading.

For my evil habit, custom, and oft-renewed intention of committing sin.

For that I have sinned against Thee more than words can tell by the most foul sin of unthankfulness; for whilst Thou hast very often granted me forgiveness of my sins, I confess that I, over and over again, times without number, have fallen into them.

For that by my countless sins I have quenched in myself the life of my soul, Thy Love.

And that I have cast away the fear of Thee by the weightiness and abomination of my crimes.

And when thou hast after this manner humbled thyself with shame and compunction of heart say this prayer:

O Lord Jesus Christ, my God, I am that unhappy man, of all sinners the vilest and most wretched, who have done so many and such great crimes against Thy boundless Majesty, that I am

not able to number them; for they are even above
the sands of the sea, the number whereof no man
can tell.

And when thou hast prayed thus, or in any
other wise, as thy devotion or the sorrowing of
thy heart shall move thee to do, try with all thy
strength to put forth sighs and groans from thy
inmost heart; for even as a file cleans iron and
brightens it up, and takes away all its rust, so do
heartfelt sighs and groans clear off the rust of our
sins and vices, and wash them quite away with
the dew of divine grace. Say therefore with heartfelt sighs: Whither, O my Lord, shall I fly from
the sight of Thy Majesty? If I go up into heaven,
Thou art there; if I descend into hell, Thou art
there. And then go on and pray thus: Lord,
what shall I do? Shall I kill myself? Not so, O
Lord; for I know Thy loving-kindness towards all
who turn to Thee in truth, and that Thy mercies
are above all the works of Thy hands.

And if not even thus art thou able to move
thyself to sorrow, do not therefore cease from
running through the foregoing points every night
in thy meditation. For God is satisfied if we try
to do what we can. And, besides, our Lord oftentimes waits for the end of our works, and leaves us
a while to ourselves, granting us neither compunction nor any other consolation, to try our faith and
patience, and to give greater sorrow for our sins
after they have been tried.

Now when thou hast schooled thyself well in

compunction of heart, despair not of God's mercy, but rouse thyself to hope, which lifting up of thy heart is the next part of thy work. With great confidence, I say, lift up thy head, which hitherto thou hadst held on thy knees; and rest a little while, recall thy thoughts, and with sweetness of soul lift thyself up to praise the Lord, imploring His mercy, considering His greatness and nobleness, pronouncing at the same time these five words, which will kindle great devotion within thee: Good, beautiful, sweet, merciful Lord.

For in order to have God's grace, without which thou canst not find His mercy, thou must do like courtiers dwelling at the court of great kings, who first praise the king in many ways, and then ask for what they want; so, like a spiritual courtier, praise thy Lord and ask from Him forgiveness of thy sins. And as God is so excellent that no human tongue can give Him that which belongs to His being, we name Him by His works; and by these we extol His greatness and excellence: firstly, as He is the beginning and source of all creatures, saying as above, O Lord; to wit, O Thou, Maker of all things. Secondly, we call Him good, as indeed He shows Himself to His angels and saints in everlasting blessedness; as if we had said, O Thou, Fountainhead of Goodness, whom the angels and blessed spirits gaze on face to face in unspeakable happiness. Thirdly, we call upon Him by those names which express how He stands with regard to creatures, rational and irrational, declaring the might wherewith He controls them all, and extolling the loveliness wherewith He has clothed them. Thus: O Thou loveliest One, loveliness of all those things which Thou hast made. O Thou most sweet One, sweetness of the just. O Thou most merciful One unto all poor sinners, have mercy on me a sinner, and grant me forgiveness of all my sins.

And when thou hast praised the Lord on these five heads, thou mayst securely ask pardon of all thy sins. And after this manner are we taught to pray in the Canticle of Solomon, wherein the Spouse says to His beloved, Thy voice is sweet and thy face is beautiful; assuredly by reason of the scattering of the darkness which had formerly obscured her. The heavenly Spouse may be specially invoked under any one of these names, which do so much good to the devout soul that she should always be turning them over in her heart. And thus whenever thou wouldst pray, there is no need that thou shouldst go over a great number of words, but rather, collecting thyself within thyself, and without wandering in thy mind through outer things, thou mayst pray, saying: O good, beautiful, sweet, and merciful Lord, deal in Thy mercy with this sinner, whom Thou hast bought with the precious Blood of Thy Son.

And while saying these words let thy only thought be to obtain forgiveness of thy sins. And since it is very meritorious and very pleasing to

God to pray for others, therefore thou mayst in these same words pray for all conditions of men, whether faithful or infidel, saying : O good, sweet, lovely, and merciful Lord, be merciful to all sinners, and bring all unbelievers to the knowledge of Thy holy Catholic faith. And at times it is well to begin thy prayer in this manner. After this thou shouldst likewise implore thy Redeemer's pity, and seek thine own pardon by placing between thyself and God His priceless passion and death, saying thus :

O my Lord, by the blessed passion of Thy most beloved Son, who for me was immolated on the cross, be merciful to me a sinner. Or else : By the most holy incarnation; or, By the birth of Thy most beloved Son, &c., according to the mystery of the life of Christ that occurs on the day of the week. Again, thou mayst offer thy prayer through the intercession of the saints, and, above all, of our Blessed Lady, thus :

O most gentle Virgin, Mother of our God and Saviour, thou that art the most holy, the most humble, and most loving of all the Saints of the Court of Heaven; thou that dost ever incline thine ear to the prayers of thy servants, and art ever ready to help us; if thou, my Queen, wilt deign to pray before the Majesty of God for me, who am so great a sinner, full of pride, and worse than all sinners, the whole court of heaven will pray together with thee, and will say : Incline, O Lord, the ear of Thy mercy to the prayers of Thy most holy

Mother; for it is most meet that when Thou seest her intercede Thou shouldst, for her love, show favour and mercy to the lost one, grant health to the sick, and forgiveness to the wretched criminal. O most kind Virgin, if I am unworthy, thou art most worthy. If I am proud, thou, Lady, art most humble. If I am unclean, thou art most pure. If the stench of my sins doth offend Heaven, thou art the sweet-smelling fragrance of Paradise. I am carnal, but thou art a most pure Virgin. I am the most guilty of sinners, but thou art most holy. Therefore with my whole heart I beseech thee, by all the sorrow which thou didst endure with burning love for thy most sweet Son, that thou would deign to intercede and pray for me, who am most wretched and forsaken by all. By thy flight into Egypt, I beseech thee. By the three days' loss of thy dear Son, when He disputed in the Temple with the doctors; by the grief that wrung thy heart when He foretold to thee in Bethany His death and passion; by the word to thee most bitter, which He spake on the cross, Woman, behold thy son; by His bitter drink of gall and vinegar; by His sweet side pierced by the point of a cruel lance; by the laying down of His beloved Body into thine arms, —may He forgive me all my sins, and give me His grace in this world and His everlasting glory in the world to come!

Next, invoke the Saints as follows:

On Monday commend thyself to all the angels

in general, and to thy guardian angel in particular, whom thou shouldst always love and revere, and say some devout prayer to him daily, as well as to the saint whose feast is kept on that day.

On Tuesday invoke our Lady and all the holy patriarchs, prophets, apostles, and disciples of the Lord, and choose one of them for thy chief advocate, together with the saint of the day.

On Wednesday honour the Blessed Virgin and the holy martyrs.

On Thursday commend thyself to our Lady and all holy confessors.

On Friday to our Lord's painful and most bitter passion.

On Saturday to our Blessed Lady and the whole choir of virgins.

On Sunday adore the Most Blessed Trinity, and call to thy aid the almighty power of the Father, the wisdom of the Son, and the goodness of the Holy Ghost, and contemplate the boundless infinity of God and His marvellous counsels concerning the children of men. And after thou hast thus implored His mercy, enlarge thy soul to adore Him, to magnify and thank Him for the favours thou hast received of Him, and chiefly for such as thou hast received on that day, for the grace of sorrow and devotion, and all His other gifts, and say:

O God Most High, my soul doth adore, magnify, and thank Thee for such and so many benefits which I have received from Thy overflowing kindness. With my whole heart do I devote myself to the love of Thy goodness. Then strike thy breast three times and say, O Lord, be merciful to me a sinner. And then rise up, and, standing, say with great reverence the Psalm, 'Praise ye the Lord in His Saints;' or, 'Praise the Lord, O my soul;' or else, 'Bless the Lord, O my soul,' as far as the words, 'Thy youth thall be renewed like the eagle's;' with *Glory be to the Father*, and an *Our Father* and *Hail, Mary*. Then say, O Lord, hear my prayer, and let my cry come unto Thee. And end with the prayer of the Blessed Trinity: Almighty and Everlasting God, who hast given Thy servants in professing the true faith to know the glory of the Everlasting Trinity, and to adore Thy Oneness in the power of Thy Majesty, we beseech Thee that by the might of that same faith we may be ever defended from all harm.

Or else the prayer: O God, to praise whom worthily, &c. And in this manner is ended the Exercise of the Way of Purity.

Lastly, understand aright that although each of these three ways has its own peculiar name and its own peculiar way of proceeding, yet it may be well if a man while going through one of them should, by God's inspiration, be able to exercise himself in all three, that is, in the Way of Enlightment and of Union, as well as that of Purity, by confessing his own misery, giving thanks, and lifting up his soul to adore and magnify the Lord. And be careful not to let thy thoughts get scattered as soon as thou hast ended the said exercise; but strive hard to keep thy heart in its strength and vigour, and not to let it lose them in vague and restless thoughts or dissolute mirth, otherwise the soul must forfeit what it had gained in compunction, and be filled with hollow and unsettled imaginations. Rather work hard to ground thy heart firmly on the life of Christ, according to the meditation of that day, or on some other holy thought that may kindle devotion within thee.

CHAPTER XIII.

On the subjects for meditation on Tuesday morning.*

WHEN thou hast entered the place of prayer, dear brother, and made the sign of the cross on thyself, recall thy thoughts, as we said above in our instructions for Monday, and meditate upon death after this manner.

Bethink thyself how suddenly it will come, and how like a thief; when thou dost least expect it, when thou art least prepared, when thou art most confident of long life, and hast arranged many things to be undertaken.

Next, turn over and over again in thy mind the manner in which we draw nigh to death; and think as if thou wert about at once to die, and thus shalt thou more deeply feel what follows.

* *Post matutinos;* after Lauds, the hour set apart by St. Benedict in his Rule for Meditation.

How a cruel sickness will be the forerunner of thy death, and how all other sicknesses are as messengers to warn thee thereof.

Think on the pains of thy last illness, and on the natural dread that will make thee struggle with death for dear life.

Next, when thy going forth from this life is certain, and thou knowest from thy physician, or feelest within thyself that thou art dying, how will thy conscience cry out against thee, and how great will thy remorse be, since, when thou wert able, thou didst not prepare thyself! All thy sins will then come before thy eyes.

Then shalt thou be tortured with great sorrow for each evil passion thou hast not laboured to conquer.

Wert thou thus at the point of death, and encircled by thy vices and passions, reflect how earnestly thou wouldst long for one year or even one hour of health.

Consider, moreover, how short in that hour will past time seem compared to that eternity to which thou art about to go. All thy life will look like a dream; and all thy days will seem to thee but as if thou hadst walked a mile or so.

O, how greatly wilt thou grieve in that hour, that for a moment's trivial delight thou didst forego joys everlasting and unspeakable!

Think how bitter it will be to tear thyself away from those things which here thou hast so guiltily loved; from those honours and that high estate to which, with all thy strength, thou hast clung; from the pleasures thou hast so greedily fed upon; and so on with the rest.

Think on the appearance of a dying man; how the body turns black, how the eyes grow fixed and glazed.

How the devils stand by, like lions eager for their prey, lying in wait for the soul.

How the unhappy soul, the moment of its going forth being now come, will begin fearfully to peer into the unknown land whither it goeth, and to see the fiends in wait for it. With what a struggle it leaves the body, and how it longs to come back, were it but possible; but cannot return, since the gates of its senses are all shut, and so it is forced to go out, and pass through the ranks of the evil spirits that await it.

And then the evil spirit of each vice will beset it, each seeking his own prey; thus the spirit of pride, the spirit of uncleanness, &c., will claim every one his own portion.

Lastly, reflect how the soul, on quitting the body, will forthwith stand before the judgment-seat, and in that moment will hear the doom that shall never be recalled; and where the tree once falls there shall it lie for ever.

Then shall thy dead body be given up to the grave and to everlasting forgetfulness. Thou hast been as the guest of a night in this world; and now that thou art gone, all memory of thee has vanished from the earth.

Turn now to the thought of the death of a just man. When he sees that his time has come to leave the world, the testimony of a good conscience fills his soul with gladness, and the thought of being freed from the sufferings of this life makes him cheerful; nor does it grieve him to go hence, since he is bound by no fetters of carnal or other vices.

And when thou hast thought over these things, or at least some of them, according as thou thinkest it enough to excite thee to compunction and devotion, take upon thyself the person of a slave or a guilty criminal who has offended his lord; and with deep feeling of humility and sorrow, utter a prayer from the depth of thy heart, as was said above, and confessing thine own wretchedness, cry out for mercy, and say: O most kind, beautiful, sweet, and merciful Lord, &c., have pity on this sinner, whom Thou hast redeemed by the precious Blood of Thy Son. And when thou hast said this prayer, implore the mercy of our Saviour, placing between thyself and God His precious death and passion, saying, as above, O my God, most kind, beautiful, sweet, and merciful, by the sacred passion of Thy most precious Son, who was immolated for me on the wood of the cross, be merciful to me, a sinner. And after this, turn the eye of thy soul to our Lady, and ask her help; and then do the same for the saints of that day of the week, as above, and especially pray to the saint whose feast is being kept on that day.

Finally, adoring and magnifying God and giving Him thanks, thou shalt conclude thy exercise in the manner described for Monday.

CHAPTER XIV.

On the subjects for meditation on Wednesday morning.

On Wednesday morning, after coming to the place of prayer, signing thyself with the sign of the cross, and collecting thy thoughts, as we have said above, make thy meditations on the pains of hell as follows:

Think, brother, on the pains of hell and on hell itself, according to those similitudes which holy men have described.

Imagine it to thyself as a dark abyss, a place beneath the earth, a pit of fire. Again, as an immense and most horrible city, all on fire with gloomy, dark, and fearful flames, whose citizens with fearful cries howlingly tell the greatness and number of their pains, which no man's tongue could ever express. By these and such like figures mayst thou express the unutterable excess of those pains. For, as blessed Augustine says, our fire differs from the fire of hell, as a painted from a real fire. In like manner think on the stench of hell. The gnashing of teeth, the groans, howls, and blasphemies declare the agony of their pains. Next meditate on the variety of those tortures, on the harrowing inextinguishable fire, the intolerable cold, the stench, the darkness that may be felt, the ceaseless torment of every sense. The eyes are tormented by the horrible sight of the devils; the ears by sounds of wailing, by the groans and howls of the damned.

Think on the wretched companionship and the fierce cruelty of those ruthless executioners, who neither grow weary of torturing, nor can ever be moved to pity, but cry out insultingly to the tortured: Where is now the splendour of your nobility, the loftiness of your state, your pride, your delights?

In all their members will the damned be tormented, but in those most cruelly wherewith they have sinned.

Now meditate on their inmost pains, or the gnawing conscience, and the worm that never dies. What mind can understand aright how great is the pain of the damned? who, while living in this world, might have shunned those most bitter and everlasting pains by the slight and almost momentary sufferings of this life, and yet cared not to do so.

Think how their evil passions will tyrannise over them. Rage and envy will tear them like ravenous dogs; they will think over their past sins and the delights they once enjoyed, and wailing, will say, What hath our pride availed us, our lust and avarice, the glory of this world, and the pleasures of the flesh?

And of these torments there shall never be an end. Ponder the eternity of pain; how they will not end after a million of years, seeing that in hell there is no redemption.

Therefore, most beloved brother, when thou hast awakened the sting of thy conscience by these meditations, turn towards thy Lord, saying in thy heart: O the depths of the wisdom and knowledge of God, how incomprehensible are Thy judgments! O God, how many for one sin only are tormented in hell! And I, who have so many and such great sins, of what punishment am I not worthy? Most righteously do I deserve everlasting damnation, worthy as I am of every torment, and unworthy of any mercy. And after uttering these or such-like words from thy inmost heart, bow down thy soul before the Lord, in whose sight thou standest. For whenever thou givest thyself to prayer, thou must firmly believe that thou art before thy Lord; and the more intensely thou dost condemn thyself, as worthy of everlasting death, and dost bow down within thyself, the more speedily shalt thou be acquitted, and the higher shall be the state to which thou shalt be lifted up. So first pierce thyself through with sorrow, and then raise thy soul to hope, and to the confidence of gaining mercy; utter a fervent prayer in the depths of thy heart, taking upon thee the person of a sinner; and remembering thy misfortunes and unhappiness, with humility and fear call upon God's mercy, and, thinking on His loving-kindness, give thanks to Him, as we have said elsewhere.

CHAPTER XV.

In what pious thoughts the devout man should exercise himself on Thursday morning.

ON Thursday morning go to thy praying place, and arm thyself with the sign of the holy cross; and collecting thy thoughts, as we have said above on the Monday, meditate as follows on the Last Judgment. Reflect what terror there will be when sinners shall hear the archangel's trumpet and shall see the terrible signs of the tempest that will accompany it. Their terror and horror will be greater than can be told in words.

How the wrath of the just Judge cannot be turned aside: He comes to punish those who have offended Him; and at His coming what must be the dread of the reprobate!

Think on that most bitter separation, when the humble and mild shall take their place on the right, and the proud, envious, and lustful on the left—never more to meet.

What trembling, terror, and wonder shall the proud and haughty then feel, when they shall see themselves humbled and cast off—poor, wretched, and a laughing-stock; and those whom they thought most vile they shall behold in glory, at the right hand of Christ; whence they say within themselves, sorrowing: These are they whom once we held up to scorn. And on the other side the righteous shall stand in glorious unbroken array, over against those who dealt hardly with them.

How an account of every deed and thought must there be given. There shall Jerusalem be examined with lighted lamp; that is to say, the works of those who now appear holy shall then be laid open; whatever lay hidden within them shall be brought to the light of day; angels and devils shall be the witnesses, and shall set before our eyes the wrongs we have done, and the place and time of our misdeeds. And our own sins and the whole world together will bear witness against us.

How Christ will then show the marks of His Passion, and will reproach the wicked with the fruit of His being made flesh, which they have slighted.

Think next on the terrible and irrevocable doom, when He shall say, Depart from Me, ye cursed ones, into everlasting fire. On the delicious feast of that eternal Supper, to which the righteous shall be invited in those loving words: Come, ye blessed of My Father, receive the kingdom that hath been prepared for you from the beginning of the world.'

Remember how much God is pleased with works

of kindness and mercy; since these alone does our Redeemer seem to remember at the Judgment.

How the good shall go into everlasting life, and the bad into eternal torments. And these two places, to-wit, heaven and hell, shall for ever remain separated by the immense abyss between them.

Now, brother, when thou hast roused thy conscience by the foregoing meditation, turn thy heart to the Lord, and say, O God, who will be able to flee from that day of doom, so just and yet so fearful? Enter not, Lord, into judgment with Thy servant, for no man living shall in Thy sight be found just. And in these or such-like words form thy prayer, as above.

CHAPTER XVI.

Subjects for meditation on Friday, after the office of Matins.

On Friday, after going into thy praying-place, and strengthening thyself with the sign of the cross, calling thy thoughts together, as we have said above for Monday, bethink thyself for thy meditation how our Redeemer prayed in the garden; and, as if thou wert there present,

Thou must consider how, when the supper was ended, which He ate in Jerusalem, in that supper-chamber on Mount Sion, He went out with His disciples into the garden.

With what loving-kindness He spoke to them, saying, Watch ye, and pray, that ye enter not into temptation.

How He tore Himself away from them, and, knowing all that was to come upon Him, He fortified Himself with the armour of prayer.

How, when He entered on His agony, the pain and horror in His sensitive part was so great that drops of bloody sweat gushed forth from His whole body, showing by this sweat the greatness of His innermost grief and sadness.

How many and how great were the pains, and how sharp the swords of grief that pierced His Heart, and what were their causes; for the cause of all these were the sorrows of all the elect, past, present, and to come, which He saw more clearly, openly, and distinctly than anything can be seen by human ken.

How He satisfied His Father for wrongs done to Him; atoning for each and every one of His elect, offering Him an everlasting atonement, by enduring an ocean of pains and sufferings for every offence done to His Father.

How at that time were laid open before His eyes all the sins of men, one by one, even to the smallest venial sin; and what great pains He took upon Himself for each one of them; satisfying His Father most abundantly for thee.

Consider the causes from which such immense suffering proceeded.

The first cause was that He was the Son of God, and therefore felt most keenly all offences against His Father.

The second, that He was the Mediator of peace

between God and men; and as much as He loved peace, so much did He grieve for the enmity and wrath of God against man, which sin drew down upon us.

Thirdly, He was the Spouse of souls, and loved their beauty with a burning love, whence its loss filled Him with sorrow.

The fourth cause was that He was the Restorer of grace, which had perished through sin.

The fifth, that He was the Redeemer of all mankind; and it behoved Him not to leave one sin unatoned for, but that He should pay the debt of all to God's justice.

Next think on the sharp swords that pierced His Heart.

Think first how He saw the kingdom of His glory robbed of its citizens by sin; and how few in number they should be that would enter it.

Again, He saw His grace in divers ways wasted in men's souls, and that His most sacred Passion would be of use to but few. For, since He was grace itself, He grieved for sins as His own destroyers.

Thirdly, on account of our ingratitude, whilst He beheld the sins of such as, after having known their inestimable ransom, do not blush to return to their sins, crucifying Him anew in themselves.

Fourthly, because He saw the open gates of hell, and all the reprobate that were then damned, and would be lost, until the end of the world.

Fifthly, because He saw with clear, distinct,

and open vision all the pains, the scoffs, and mockings which He was then about to undergo.

Sixthly, all the sufferings of His Most Holy Mother and of all His followers, all the torments of His martyrs, and the labours of all His chosen ones were then laid open to His eyes; and whatever was to be undergone for His sake until the end of the world was a sword to pierce His heart.

Consider the keenness of His sorrows on account of the liveliness of His faculties, and how these sorrows went beyond all measure, being far more and far greater than we are able to understand.

Think on His infinite mercy in our behoof, and how plentiful a ransom and satisfaction was given to God.

O, most hardened heart of man! how ill will it be for thee at the last day if thou canst not be broken at such tokens of love, and art not able to melt with love, and canst not be cured of thy hardness by so many bonds that draw thee to love.

Now therefore, brother, that thou hast roused thy conscience by the foregoing meditation, turn to the Lord the eye of thy heart, falling down at His most blessed feet; and craving forgiveness of all thy sins, and of the thanklessness and coldness thou hast hitherto borne, and resolving to heat thyself for the future at so great a fire of love, say with the Prophet: Remembering I will remember, and my heart shall pine away within me at the thought of those things that have been here told me. And lying prostrate at His feet, let Him not depart till He bless thee; and then do as on other days of the week.

CHAPTER XVII.

On the subjects for meditation on Saturday morning.

ON Saturday, entering into thy place of prayer, and signing thyself with the sign of the cross, recall thy thoughts to thyself, as we explained for the Monday, and then make thy meditation on the sorrows of our Lady.

Take heed, therefore, that if thou wishest to be her child, and to have her for thy advocate, thou must stay with her in her sorrows, since the whole of her life was filled with sorrow, anguish, hardship, and affliction, so as to be one continued and cruel martyrdom.

Think what pain she underwent when she saw her blessed Son in the manger, wailing for the sharpness of the weather, and not having wherewith to cover Him from the cold.

So likewise at the circumcision, and when Simeon foretold to her that a sword was to pierce her very soul; at the flight into Egypt, and for the three days after which she found Him in the temple; and throughout the whole of her life, seeing Him harassed by hunger and want, and not being able to help Him.

How often she saw Him weeping, and how she herself wept with Him.

She saw Him wearied with walking, worn with hunger and thirst, laughed at when He taught, abused and blasphemed, and watched by His foes that He might be ensnared. Were not these for her the sharpest of sufferings? Assuredly they were. Often and often she heard Him speak of His passion; and if it was even so sad for Peter and His disciples to hear Him talk of His passion, what ought we not to think of His Mother, who loved Him so tenderly?

What were her feelings when she knew that He had been sold by Judas, seized by the Jews, and forsaken by His disciples.

When she saw Him led from one judge to another, and bearing His cross on His shoulders under sentence of death.

When she saw Him on His cross, and, with heart pierced through, listened to His voice, and saw her dearest Son in His agony and death. And when she saw Him taken down from the cross, lying dead upon her blessed knees, and gazed on His cruel wounds. And when she saw Him laid in the earth no tongue can tell the depth of her woe.

And when she stayed in the supper-chamber, with John and the Marys and the disciples who joined them afterwards, think how sad and sorrowful they were, thinking on yesterday's events, on the death and passion of the Lord; and, as if thou wert there with them, look on attentively, and see how sad it is to behold the Queen of the universe and the royal princes of the army of God shut up thus in a humble dwelling, filled with fear and bitterness and mourning.

How they talked on these things together, weeping and sighing.

How full the disciples were of shame and sorrow, seeing they had fled from Him; and Peter, who had denied Him above all the rest, and all, striking their breasts, besought of our Lady to intercede for their pardon.

And then she consoled them with words of kindness, and, encouraging them, would say: Our gentle Master and faithful Shepherd has left us, and here we are as orphans, but firmly do I await His speedy return. You know how kind my Son is, and how He loved you; and fear not but that you will be easily reconciled to Him, and willingly will He forgive you all your offences. Had you stayed with Him, you could not have helped Him, so great was the fury of His enemies, and so powerful, by His Father's permission, was the daring of wicked men against Him; so you must not now be troubled. And then Peter modestly said, Truly, O Lady, it is even as thou sayest, for even I, who trusted so much in myself, was overwhelmed in the court of Caiphas by such excessive dread that I thought I could never have escaped; and so I denied Him, and I remembered not His words, and how He had foretold me this, until He looked upon me.

Now, brother, having awakened thy conscience by this meditation, turn to thy Lord, and ask pardon of Him for all the sins with which thou hast denied Him, thinking how often thou hast sinned against Him; and, as we said in the beginning, draw near to our Lady with all the other Saints.

CHAPTER XVIII.
On what subjects should our meditation be made after the office of Matins on Sunday.

ON Sunday, when thou art come to the place set apart for prayer, and hast shielded thyself with the armour of the saving cross, recall thy thoughts, as above, and make thy meditation, as follows, on the glory of heaven:

Contemplate that wondrous place and the marvellous light that fills it, under those similitudes and images which holy men have made use of in describing it, to help our understanding.

That place is as a noble city, marvellously built of gold and precious stones, and each of its gates of one precious stone.

Within that city is a most lovely garden, adorned with the beauty of all the flowers that can be thought of; its lilies and roses are of such a fragrance as no tongue can express; its flowers can never fade.

The bloom of summer, the fragrance of all perfumes, abide there for ever.

Therein is the abode of everlasting delights, of one bond of love without any dissension, in which the Saints live for ever, and that contains in itself all that can afford delight.

What joy will there not be there, to gaze for ever on the Most Blessed Trinity, in which the source of all beauty, sweetness, and goodness shines forth; in which thou shalt know all things that can be known, shalt possess all those that can be wished for, since in that vision thou shalt find thy blessedness.

Think how great is the happiness the blessed do there enjoy, since they rejoice there in the perfect and clear contemplation of the brightness of God, and sweetly rest in the delicious enjoyment of the Divine Goodness, gladdened for ever by the tranquil possession of the Majesty of God, since they have no fear of ever being bereft of it.

So likewise shall they feast on the sight of the Manhood of our Redeemer, seeing how He who was once in this exile reckoned as poor, lowly, and a castaway, shall there be seen as the Most High God and as true Man. What will not be thy own joy at the companionship of all the Saints, of our Queen the Blessed Virgin Mary, and of all the apostles, martyrs, confessors, and virgins; for thou shalt rejoice at their happiness as if it were thine own.

Meditate on the qualities that will give to thy body its own blessedness, on its immortality and impassibility, its agility and brightness; and on the ornaments of the soul, the fulness of knowledge, of justice, and of gladness.

How many other great and unspeakable good things will follow these chief gifts: security from all fear of losing them, freedom from all temptations, most perfect liberty, health, delight, friendship, honour, and peace; and, to say all in one word, thou shalt have whatever thou willest, and shalt not have whatever thou wouldst not.

Therefore, brother, when thou hast stirred up thy soul by these stimulants of love, grieve from thy heart that by thy sins thou hast wandered far from this marvellous dwelling-place; and, reflecting on thy sins, turn to the Lord with thy whole heart, and say, O Lord, draw me after Thee; I shall run after the fragrance of Thy heavenly perfumes. And then turn likewise thy prayer to our Redeemer, and to His Mother; and after imploring their mercy, and returning thanks, make an end of thy exercise, in the manner we have already laid down for the Monday.

CHAPTER XIX.

For how long a time a man should remain in the way of purity, and how he may know that he has succeeded in purifying himself.

WE have hitherto dealt with that course of purification whereby the new disciple of Christ is disposed towards the obtaining of the desired end, which is, to ascend step by step towards the union of the soul with God, in which is true wisdom; and we have said that a man should study to accustom himself to it. But after he has been at work in this kind of exercise for the space of one month, as Henry de Palma writes in his *Mystic Theology*, let him go a step farther, and give himself up to the love of the things of heaven; and this is done by means of the exercises of the second way, which is called the way of enlightenment, because it enlightens the heart by the careful calling to mind of God's works of goodness. And however great a sinner he may be, let him not fear to ask of the Lord this fire of His love, since in so doing there is no sin of presumption. For after he has, for the aforesaid space of time, been employed in kissing the feet of his Saviour, by the bitter recollection of his sins, he may worthily approach to the kiss of His hands, by the consideration of the divine benefits; that is to say, if he has so carefully watched over his own life as to have nothing more that requires his constant efforts to wash it away. And in order to know whether he be perfectly cleansed, let him diligently consider whether he has obtained these three gifts; to-wit,

>Against sloth—alacrity;
>Against concupiscence—self-control;
>Against ill-will—kindliness.

For when these three virtues are possessed, a man's conscience is good, pure, and upright. And that the nature of these virtues may be the more readily understood, we must here give their definitions, laid down by St. Bonaventure, in a work entitled *Parvum Bonum*.

Alacrity is a certain vigour of the soul, that excludes all negligence, and disposes it to do good works, with *wakefulness, confidence,* and *neatness.*

Self-control is a certain healthiness of soul, bridling all concupiscence, renewing the soul's vigour, and making it a fervent lover of whatever is *harsh to oneself, poor,* and *lowly.*

Kindliness is a certain sweetness of soul, excluding all ill-will; that is to say, all *anger, envy,* and *sadness;* and making it *benevolent, forbearing,* and *cheerful.*

And this is the end and term of the way of purity, according to the path of mental prayer; for every pure conscience is gladsome and cheerful. When these three things have been mastered, the soul is ready for its upward flight: and by these may we know that we are at the end of our purifying trial.

PART II.

THE WAY OF ENLIGHTENMENT.

CHAPTER XX.

That the man who wishes to begin the way of enlightenment must be first purged and cleansed from his sins in the way of purity, that he may be able to bear the splendour of the divine light.

UNTIL now we have dealt with the way of purity, in which the soul gets its cleansing; and what we have been saying is more easily felt in the heart than it can be taught by word or writing. Now may the soul without delay climb the higher way of enlightenment, the end of which is to shed light from above on her steps, as the Prophet saith: Blessed is the man whose help is from Thee; in his heart he hath disposed to ascend by steps in the vale of tears, in the place which he hath set.

Here it should be noted that by the tears and sighs of the way of purity the soul is cleansed from the rust of its ill-deeds, and forthwith rises to that brightness in which it is lit up by the rays of the Divine Light. And this is agreeable to the nature of the soul that receives them in herself, as we may see by daily experience, in any mirror, that if it be spotted by rust or any other impurity, the face of him who views himself in it does not appear distinctly, as it does when it is bright and polished. Now the soul is likened to a mirror; for were it to behold itself clearly, it would see Him to whose image it was made. And whenever we rub off whatever darkens it, in a moment that spiritual Sun lights it up with the brightness of His grace and goodness. And, which is still more, just as the rays of this sun of ours, striking upon a window, if they find it closed, do not turn aside, but, as soon as it is opened, enlighten the whole room which before was in darkness; so likewise the true Sun of Righteousness, of whom our sun is an image, keeps on knocking at the gate of our conscience, and awaiting naught else but that in some way or other we may open it, and give Him admission, that He may peacefully rest in our soul. And in this manner the soul receives its ghostly light. Since then our soul has to be lit up by the divine effulgence, it must be duly fitted and prepared for it, so that it must be first cleansed by the way of purity from the darkness and stains of sin, and become like a spotless mirror, that it may receive the rays of the the increated Light. And since we have already laid down the exercises wherein we should employ ourselves in the morning while in the way of purity, which is intended to cleanse the soul; we have yet to speak of the exercises of the way of enlightenment, the best time for which is in the evening, after Compline, according as St. Bernard says, that at this hour a religious should examine his conscience, and return thanks for favours received.

CHAPTER XXI.

How the man who takes up these exercises should examine his conscience before beginning the way of enlightenment.

GOING out from Compline, it is not well for thee to remain long outside thy cell or allow thy thoughts to wander by signs or talk. St. Bernard says that a monk ought not speak from the end of Compline till after Mass of the following day without weighty reasons. At the aforesaid hour, therefore, enter thy cell, and, either on thy knees or standing, after thou hast shielded thyself with the sign of the cross, collect thy thoughts, and call upon the Holy Ghost, saying the following antiphon : Come, Holy Ghost, fill the hearts of Thy faithful, and kindle in them the fire of Thy love. Then say the whole psalm, *Deus in adjutorium*. Whoever does not know by heart the said antiphon and psalm may say thrice the verse: O God, incline Thou to my help ; O Lord, hasten to help me. After this, call thyself diligently to chapter,* and examine thyself on thy sins of

Sloth,
Concupiscence,

---

* In allusion to the custom in our order of accusing ourselves of our faults in chapter.

Uncharitableness.

Under which heads all other sins may be reckoned.

With respect to sloth, examine thyself on these nine heads :

If thou hast been slothful on that day,

1. In keeping watch over thy heart, concerning which thou must examine thy thoughts, words, and deeds.

2. In the employment of thy time.

3. In the right intention of thy works, which should always be to the honour and glory of God, to which end all things should be directed.

4. In thy prayer; seeing how that thou hast on that day fulfilled the work of God, with lukewarmness or with fervour; whether thou hast left out any canonical hour or any of thy accustomed pious works.

5. Concerning devout reading.

6. Concerning thy good works; for with these three last-named tools must thou till the soil of thy heart, to make it bear good fruit in due season. And one of these three, without the other two, is not enough to excite thy sorrow for sin, to cope with temptations, and to advance in virtue. For thou needest all thy strength to bewail thy sins, to drive back the Evil One, and to go forward in holiness.

With respect to concupiscence, thou must examine if there still lives in thee .

The concupiscence of pleasure,

> The concupiscence of curiosity,
> The concupiscence of worldly vanity.

First examine thyself on voluptuous concupiscence, which assuredly lives in thee if thou art ruled by the love of what is sweet, of whatever is soft, of carnal pleasures; to-wit, if thou seekest after

> Delicacy of food,
> Refinement in thy apparel,
> Lustful delights.

And concerning these last, it is not only sinful to consent to them, but even if thou dost not repel the first motions of them.

2. Examine thyself concerning the concupiscence of curiosity; whether it has lived or does still live in thee, and this mayst thou know if thou desirest to

> Know hidden things which concern thee not;
> Feast thy sight on beautiful things;
> Possess worldly goods.

For herein lies the sin of avarice and curiosity, most unworthy a religious man.

3. Next examine thyself in the concupiscence of vanity, which failing lives in thee if thou nourishest the love of

> Favour,
> Praise,
> Honour;

all which are mere emptiness, and make a man a lover of vanities, and are as much to be abhorred as carnal pleasures. And concerning all such things thy conscience should smite thee. And take special heed concerning these sins of concupiscence.

With respect to uncharitableness, examine carefully if there live or have lived in thee the vices of

    Anger,
    Envy,
    Ill-temper;

all which make a man uncharitable.

1. First of all must be considered the uncharitableness of anger, which consists in the heart, in signs, and in words.

2. Secondly, we must examine into the uncharitableness of envy, which

    Repines at another's happiness,
    Rejoices at his misfortunes,
    Is hardened against his want.

3. Lastly, thou must examine thyself on the malice of bitterness, whence arise

    Evil suspicions,
    Blasphemous thoughts,
    Unjust detractions.

All malice in this kind is peculiarly hateful. And when thou hast thus examined thy conscience, if thou findest thyself guilty, grieve before God, and wash away the filth of thy sins; cleansing thy conscience by tears, and resolving, if thou findest anything weighty, to confess it. And mark well this method of examination, which we have set down at length, in order that it may be of use to thee for the confession of thy sins. For it would not be well always to go through such a lengthy examen after Compline, especially if thou hast kept good guard over thyself during the day; but rather see briefly how thou hast spent the day, and ask forgiveness of God, making thy confession in a general form, and saying a *De Profundis* for thy faults. And thence pass to a minute and diligent consideration of the benefits God has done thee. In which meditation thou wilt be enlightened with heavenly splendour; and when thou findest thyself in this light, with kindling affection give thanks to God. And in order that thou mayst more fully and perfectly go through the loving-kindnesses of thy God, I have thought it best to divide them among the days of the week, as will be seen in the following chapters.

CHAPTER XXII.

On the way of enlightenment according to blessed Dionysius.

WHEN the mirror of the inner man has been well cleansed and brightly polished, as we have already explained, it becomes better fitted for God's love, and more enlarged to receive it; so that now it is able to go on to the way of enlightenment, wherein the soul gets the first glimpse of its Beloved, on whose Face, until now, it could not fix its gaze, by reason of the rust of its sins. But now the soul begins to ask itself, Who is my well-beloved ? And it answers itself, and says, My Beloved One is He who has given me such and so many good things, whose praises, were it possible, I should never cease from uttering, but should be ever giving Him thanks.

The Prophet in the psalm was proceeding by this way when he said : Bless the Lord, O my soul, and let all that is within me bless His Holy Name. Yet we must understand that God is not to be loved chiefly on account of His works of goodness, but on account of His own boundless Goodness, and for Himself. For as light is not the end for which sight is ordained, but only the means to see with, so the way of enlightenment has its name because it kindles, draws, and enlightens men to love God. Hence St. Bernard saith : God has done me so many good things that, had a poor man done them for me, I must needs have loved him. What then shall I give my Divine Lover for His loving-kindnesses ? I shall return Him thanks, and never grow weary of thanking Him. And do not run on hurriedly through many different subjects ; but that thou mayst more at leisure dwell on the divine mercies, attend to what we have said, in the *Directory*,* concerning the hours of Prime and Terce.

* See the last part of this volume.

CHAPTER XXIII.

On the order in which the devout man, for the enlightening of his soul, should ponder the works of God's goodness according to the days of the week, and how he should give thanks for them.

On Monday, after Compline, think diligently on the benefit of thy creation, saying at the end of each of the following points of consideration, I give Thee thanks, O Lord, my God Most High.

That Thou didst from all eternity predestine me, and hast loved me with everlasting love.

That in Thy own good time Thou didst create me as one of Thy noblest works—to-wit, a man; and that I was not made a senseless creature.

That Thou gavest me a body, gifted with integrity of organs, free from many miseries, and able to serve Thee.

That Thou didst create my soul to Thy own image and likeness, immortal and capable of Thyself; adorning it with many natural gifts and powers.

That from the time I was created Thou didst allot an angel to be my keeper, who has done me countless benefits.

That Thou gavest me Christian parents, and didst make me a Christian—not allowing me to be a Jew, or a pagan, or an infidel—and that Thou gavest me to be born in Christian times.

And when Thou hast after this fashion completed thy task, and given thanks according to this way of enlightenment, end thy exercise by adoring and giving glory to God with the deepest reverence, and say, O God, be merciful to me, a sinner; and the canticle *Benedicite* or *Te Deum*, or the psalm *Lauda;* and at the end of the psalm say, Let the name of the Lord be blessed, from henceforth and for ever. O Lord, hear my prayer, and let my cry come unto Thee.

Prayer.

I thank Thee, O holy Lord, Father Almighty, Eternal God, who hast deigned by Thy holy mercy to watch over me during this day; grant me with cleanness of mind and body so to pass this night that in the morning I may be able worthily to serve Thee, through Christ our Lord. Amen.

And then, with strict guard over thyself, lie down to rest, and joyfully say in thy heart, Most zealous lover of my soul, my glory and my love, my Father and my hope; when shall I love Thee as a son ought? When shall I cling to Thee with all my heart? And if thou sayest over and over again these words, with heartfelt love, thou wilt learn by experience how much it will profit thee, and how high it will enable thee to soar. So take thy rest joyfully, repeating within thee the above or other such-like words.

But remember that in this exercise of the way of enlightenment, thou must not get hurriedly through thy meditation, with a view of leaving nothing out; but thou must halt at each article, and let thy soul get inflamed with the fire of love until it fixes its admiring gaze on God's goodness. And should the allotted time of prayer be only enough to meditate on one article, do not trouble thyself about the rest, unless it be to run through them in thy mind, but bring thy exercise to an end. And this same rule shouldst thou keep in all thy other works; for it is never well done to run through with thy meditation in a hurry; but if, in the beginning of it, God favours thee with compunction or devotion, shut thyself up within thyself; and keep quiet, not allowing the grace thou hast in thee to be lost, and letting thy heart swell with inflamed thoughts of love. In this way spend thy whole prayer-time, without wandering elsewhere, since if thou wishest to pass to something else, either from a desire of finishing off thy exercise or for any other motive, the feeling of devotion will straightway vanish; nor canst thou have it again at will. And shouldst thou feel thyself on fire with love and devotion, do not on that account go through prostrations or discipline thyself.

On Tuesday, after Compline, meditate on thy calling to grace.

I thank Thee, O my God,

That Thou didst deign to make me acceptable to Thee in Thy Beloved Son, not sparing Him, but giving Him up for me as my ransom, as my example, as my brother.

That Thou hast given me Thy Holy Spirit as

a pledge of my adoption, a privilege of Thy love, and the seal of my soul's union with Thee.

That Thou hast given me Thy Sacraments; giving me first of all Thy Holy Church as my place of refuge, where I may be safe from the deluge of sin, as Noah was saved in the ark.

For the grace of Baptism, whereby original sin was blotted out, innocence restored, and righteousness granted.

For the Sacrament of Confirmation, the grace of which many have not obtained, through which Thou hast bestowed many gifts on me, and kept many evils away from me.

That Thou hast called me by Thine own Name, to-wit, a Christian, to show that I have been received into Thy favour. And thus, in memory of Thee, dost Thou make me Thy son and heir to the kingdom of heaven.

And having thus ended thy exercise for this day, do everything else, as has been said above on the Monday, according to the way of enlightenment.

On Wednesday, after Compline, meditate on the grace of thy vocation.

I thank Thee, O my God,

That when, after so many kindnesses received from Thee, I had slighted Thee, Thou didst bear with me so patiently; and though by so many sins I still turned aside from Thee to creatures, Thou didst wait for me so long, and didst not condemn me, nor allow me to die in that state.

For that Thou hast in divers ways recalled me to Thyself, from whom I had so often and in so many ways gone astray. At one time by internal aspirations, at another by other men's counsel, again by warnings of Scripture, sometimes by conferring Thy benefits on me, then again by promises of reward, by threats of chastisement, and in other wondrous ways.

And that Thou didst deign to soften the hardness of my heart, giving might to Thy voice, and giving me a good will, chiefest of Thy gifts, and hast turned aside the hindrances to my conversion.

That as often as I strove to turn to Thee, like the prodigal son in the Gospel, Thou didst gladly receive me, encircling me in Thy loving embraces, and with Thy kiss gavest me back the robe of innocence and the signet-ring of my baptism.

That Thou hast not only led me forth from the world, but has gathered me to a holy and well-disciplined brotherhood, and hast kept me aloof from an unbridled one; holding out to me the precious season of repentance, and giving me grace wherewith to gain merit, and blotting out, at my profession, as in a second baptism, all my sins.

Conclude thy exercise as above on Monday.

On Thursday, after Compline, make thy meditation on the grace of Justification.

I thank Thee, O Lord my God,

That Thou hast deigned so to change my will, that works of penance, once bitter, should become sweet to me, and the things that were once tasteful should become tasteless for me; and that Thou hast vouchsafed me the noble gift of continence.

That Thou hast given me a steadfast and persevering purpose, without which none can be saved, since many who began well have not persevered to the end.

That Thou didst give me strength not to faint in the beginning, with hope of pardon, grace, and glory; and didst comfort me by many kinds of inward consolation, and giving me grace to go forward, with loathing of my past ill deeds, and a longing to do good in future.

That, lest I should faint on the way, Thou didst prepare for me a table at which I might be refreshed with food, giving me the most precious Sacrament of Thy Body and Blood as the sustenance of my wayfaring, as a sacrament of union and the sacrifice of my redemption.

And that I might with even greater fulness be justified and cleansed, Thou hast given me all needful things, Thy Holy Scriptures and holy books as a looking-glass wherein I may see my failings and kindle my desires.

I thank Thee likewise for bestowing on me the adornments and exercises of virtue wherewith to cover the shame of my sins. And lest I should give way or grow lukewarm in righteous works, Thou hast set before my eyes the examples of Thy Saints, that I might by them be taught and spurred on to virtue.

Conclude as above.

On Friday, after Compline, meditate on the singular gifts with which God has adorned thee.

I thank Thee, O Lord my God,
Because Thou hast given me,
Out of the gifts of nature, understanding and memory.
Out of the gifts of fortune, strength and beauty.
Out of the gifts of grace, a pure faith and ardent desire of imitating Thee.
Because Thou hast bestowed countless other good things on me,
By leading me back when I had gone astray.
By teaching my ignorance.
By raising me when I had fallen.
Because Thou hast granted me the singular grace of meditation and spiritual exercises, enlightening my understanding, kindling my will, co-operating with my endeavours.
Because not only hast Thou taught my understanding by meditation, but, which is more, Thou hast drawn my will by Thy sweetness and devotion, and hast cheered me on by inner consolation, giving me a pledge of life everlasting.
And that I might not lose all these graces, Thou in wondrous ways hast saved my feet from slipping by removing from me the occasions of sin, giving me strength to resist, and a healthy will to persevere.
And when Thou didst allow me to be conquered by temptation, yet Thou hast raised me up

again to greater strength, giving me power more firmly to resist, and laying Thy hand on me that I might not be altogether shattered.

When Thou hast ended this meditation, add in what we have above arranged for the Monday.

On Saturday, after Compline, meditate on God's loving care and guidance as follows:

I thank Thee, O Lord my God,

That Thou hast hitherto preserved me in being, giving me my daily bread, with health and happiness, while I of myself am nothing.

That from my earliest childhood to this day Thou hast so lovingly freed me from so many perils, illnesses, and enemies, and many other evils.

That Thou hast given me food and clothing in plenty.

That Thou hast bestowed on me all other needful things, giving me a dwelling to shelter me and a bed to sleep on; and not only things needful, but even such as serve for pleasure and use hast Thou lavished on me.

And not only hast Thou been my guide, but Thou hast preserved and governed all other creatures for my good, arranging the succession of seasons, and bringing forth divers kinds of fruits for my gratification.

Nor hast Thou been with me in prosperity alone, but likewise in my hour of sorrow; doing me much good, cleansing me from my sins, adding to my good deserts. And yet more than this, that Thou hast so watchfully cared for me and lovingly guarded me, as if I had been Thy only care. And Thou art ever at my side, considering all my works.

End this exercise as on Monday.

After Compline on the Sunday meditate on God's providence concerning thy future glorification.

I give Thee thanks, O Lord my God,

That Thou hast promised me the joys of heaven: to-wit, *above* me the enjoyment of my God and Redeemer, and the sight of His Mother. O God, what delight will it not be to see the King of Heaven in all His beauty, and my Queen, the Virgin Mary, gloriously as it were transformed in God! *Around* me, to enjoy the most delightful fellowship of the Saints, lovely and glorious, full of charity, and countless in numbers. *Within* me, shall I rejoice in all blessedness of body and soul by reason of the fourfold gifts of glory which shall encircle me, of deathless life, and splendour above that of the sun. *Without myself*, shall I feast my eyes with the sight of a most lovely and beautiful place, filled with all that can give pleasure, with all fragrance, with everything grateful to the taste, with radiant splendour, immense and replete with loveliness and light.

And many other joys wilt Thou bestow on me, according to Thy plighted word; for not only shall I find delight in things above, around, and within me, but even in such as are below me; seeing that I have by Thy help and might overthrown my wrathful and deadly foes, and through Thy mercy blotted out my sins with tears, and escaped such dreadful torments.

I thank Thee for the many other good things that Thou wilt heap upon me, countless in number, measureless in greatness, priceless in value.

I shall be gladdened by the absence of all evils and the fulfilment of all my wishes, having all I can wish for, and nothing I could abhor.

Conclude as on Monday.

As we have said above, at each one of the points just laid down thou must proceed leisurely and not hastily. And, moreover, when calling to mind each individual benefit, thou shouldst make use of some ejaculations fit to lift up thy heart and kindle thy affections; as, for example: O Supreme Goodness. O Most Sublime Eternity. Majesty beyond comprehension. Most ardent Lover. Most sweet indweller of the soul. Most delightful sweetness. Most noble King. Most wise Master. Most generous Pastor. Most bounteous creditor. Most careful Guide.

O Lord, when shall I be able worthily to thank Thee for so many kindnesses, gifts, and mercies?

And after this manner shouldst thou utter ejaculations, not only in these exercises of the way of enlightenment, but in other exercises likewise.

Besides, whilst dwelling on the aforesaid

divine benefits, it is well to take some texts from Holy Scripture suitable for lifting up the soul; as, for example: Blessing, glory, wisdom, thanksgiving, honour, might, and strength be to our God for ever and ever. Amen.

And again: To the King of Ages, to the undying and unseen One, to the only God, let there be honour and glory for ever and ever. Amen.

Or else: Bless the Lord, O my soul, and let all that is within me bless His holy name.

And remember that even in our other exercises we ought to give thanks. For prayer, in order to be perfect, should have three parts, to-wit:

> Confession of sin,
> Imploring for mercy,
> Thanksgiving.

And from any one of these mayst thou begin thy prayer; for it is not necessary always to begin by meditating on our sins, but each one should do according to the state of his own soul; that is to say, let beginners start from the meditation of their own wretchedness, those that are already proficient from acts of thanksgiving; and such as are perfect from loving sighs and longings after union with God; yet from time to time descending to dwell on their own misery, and on such things as may beget fear.

CHAPTER XXIV.

How the way of enlightenment receives its rays of brightness from divers sources, but above all from the Lord's Prayer; which a religious man should dwell upon with great attention, love, and devotion, so as to be set on fire with divine love.

As the planets receive from the sun their brightness, so likewise doth the way of enlightenment receive the effulgence of its light from that Sun of Righteousness our Redeemer; to-wit, from His most holy life, example, and teaching; for the life of our Saviour is nothing else than an emanation from that Eternal Light for the enlightenment of our souls. And it will therefore be well, if thou wishest to be abundantly enlightened in ghostly matters, often to think over the life, example, and teaching of the Lord. Again, this way of enlightenment hath a stream of light from the lives of the holy Fathers, which have been wisely set before us as models to be copied. So is it likewise increased by a prudent consideration on creatures, by a careful reading of Holy Scripture, by often hearing the Word of God, by unceasing prayer, and, above all, by the Lord's Prayer. And to the end that thy understanding may be more brightly illumined, and thy heart burn more intensely, we shall now explain the Lord's Prayer in a spiritual or mystic sense, according to its seven petitions, as follows:

Our Father. O dearest Father, who dost beget us, Thy children, by diffusing through our hearts

Thy sweetest love, to quicken us into life. If, therefore, O Lord, I am indeed Thy child, teach me truly to love Thee, and with my whole heart to embrace Thee. Thou art indeed our Father, and over all such as love Thee Thou pourest forth Thy goodness; and if I truly loved Thee I should receive some drops of the dew of Thy grace and love. Give me, O Lord, to love Thee with all the fire of my heart; for if I love Thee with all the strength of my will, the riches of Thy loving-kindness would be seen in me.

This is what is meant by the spiritual unravelling of the *Our Father;* and by this way of meditating we shall little by little kindle the fire of our love. For as wet flax in a fire is first dried, and then catches the blaze; so will our heart become all on fire, and be lifted up to God by the foregoing meditation. And so the devout soul may go on with it after this manner:

Who art in heaven. O my wretched soul, when wilt thou become clear and transparent as the air of heaven, and when shalt thou be decked out with divers virtues as with the stars of heaven? Then, dear Father, shall I know that it delighteth Thee to dwell in me, when I shall embrace Thee with most burning fire of love, and by the flames of Thy love shall be freed from the dregs of my sins. Then in truth shall I behold Thee, when Thy grace shall overshadow me, and Thou shalt vouchsafe to take up Thy abode in the temple of my soul, made whole from sin.

First Petition.

Hallowed be Thy name. Most Holy Father, Thy name shall then indeed be hallowed in us, and the knowledge of Thy name shall be in us undimmed by stain of earth or worldly love, when Thou shalt be beloved by us above all else in the world. When I shall have gone thus far, no fleshly desire shall have a place in me, but Thou alone, most loving Father, by Thy grace and love, shalt dwell in me.

Second Petition.

Thy kingdom come. Alas, an unhappy sinner am I, since vain-glory, gluttony, and the lusts of the flesh are ever striving to win me over, while I wish none to reign in me save Thyself alone, my Father, who art in heaven. And then shalt Thou reign in me in very deed when I shall love Thee with a most ardent love. When, therefore, shall I have Thee, O my Lord? when shall I be bound fast to Thee with the bonds of love, so that Thou alone mayst begin to reign in the kingdom of my will, as yet filled with the darkness of my sins?

Third Petition.

Thy will be done on earth, as it is in heaven. Thy will, indeed, shall begin to be wrought in me when, wretched worm of earth that I am, I shall give myself up to Thy will, as much as human weakness can, after the manner of those blessed spirits who gaze upon Thy majesty face to face in heaven. But O, my sweetest God, what will make me give myself up to Thy will unless it be the fervour of Thy love, which makes even hostile wills to be at one, and makes like to Thyself him who loves Thee, and in wondrous ways transforms him from brightness to brightness? When, therefore, shall I love Thee with my whole heart, O good Jesus, O my Lord and Saviour? When shall I be one with Thee, unless when I shall cleave to Thee by the might of Thy love?

Fourth Petition.

Give us this day our daily bread. O Bread of angels, when shall I be able to be filled with Thee, sweetest Bread of heaven? On Thee, living Bread, that camest down from heaven, do the angels and blessed spirits feed in Thy kingdom, and cleave fast to Thee, dear Father and Redeemer, with winged desires of love. Let me then, in this mortal life, be nourished by that food on which the angels feed in the glory of heaven, and let me feast at the table of the everlasting blessedness. O Eternal Father, give me ever to eat of this bread, since my heart is overcharged with restlessness, until it be filled with Thee, Bread of Life, that comest down from heaven, since the bread of Thy love is indeed our daily bread; and the more ardently we love, the more eagerly we crave after it.

Fifth Petition.

Forgive us our trespasses, as we forgive them

that trespass against us. O gentle creditor, sweet Jesus, my Redeemer, when and in what manner can I tell that my sins have been forgiven me? If I really loved Thee, O my Lord, assuredly should I know, by a taste of internal sweetness, that my sins are forgiven me; as sin made me Thy enemy, so if I cleaved to Thee by love, it would move Thee to forgive me my sins, and would make me dear and pleasing in Thine eyes. Therefore, O Lord, my Saviour, when shall I be reconciled to Thee by love, so as to learn by experience that my sins have been forgiven me, and that Thou hast become mild and gentle towards me?

Sixth Petition.

And lead us not into temptation. And this I ask of Thee, O my Father and Creator, trusting in Thy goodness, hoping to be linked with Thee by bonds of love never to be sundered. I know, dear Lord, that if the sweet-smelling odour of Thy love makes me run after Thee, I shall indeed be bound to Thee by such bonds, and shall make light of all else, and never more be torn from Thee. Who will give me to find Thee, and fold Thee in a never-ending embrace? For Thou alone art the welcome guest of my soul, and Thou alone canst make me Thine, and free me from all that can stand against me.

Seventh Petition.

But deliver us from evil. Not only from the

evil of the pains of hell, but also from the evil of
temporal suffering. I ask not, dear Father, to
escape torments, but that I may not long remain
in purgatory, that I may not be kept from the fulfilment of my desire; to-wit, from the sight of
thy Majesty, which the holy angels and blessed
spirits are ever longing to gaze upon. And if I
truly loved Thee, that love would eat up all the
rust of my sins; and my spirit, being cleansed in
the fire of inflamed desire, would without hindrance fly to Thee at the very hour of my death.
When, therefore, O Lord, shall I love Thee so
ardently that my love may suffice to set me free
from everlasting pains and the bereavement of Thy
sight? This wilt Thou effect, O Lord, who livest
and reignest through never-ending ages. Thou,
O Lord, in whom there is no change or shadow of
change, art able to bestow on me, Thy useless
servant, Thy holy virtues; Thou, who fillest all
with Thy good things. Thou art, O Lord, the increated Wisdom, who enlightenest with the rays of
Thy brightness the angels and all the citizens of
heaven, since it is Thy might that quickeneth
every living thing. Increase the number of those
who love Thee, O Lord, and take from them the
love of earthly things, and bring them to the knowledge and love of Thee, defending them against
every assault, and drawing them nigh to Thy
kingdom and to heavenly truth. For Thou, our
Redeemer, gatherest together into Thy temple of
everlasting light the true sons of Israel, who go

wandering hither and thither among the concupiscence of things of earth.

End with this prayer:

O good, sweet, and lovely Jesus, gentle and merciful One, have pity on all sinners, whom Thou hast bought with Thy precious Blood, and through such great and so many pains. Who livest and reignest with God the Father and the Holy Ghost, God for ever and ever. Amen.

CHAPTER XXV.

Wherein is shown how much a man is to blame if he forsakes the aforesaid exercises out of sloth.

THE holy Abbot Ephrem, in his book on *Contemplation*, sharply reproves those who, though dedicated to the divine service and even called to the religious state, and to whom the Lord has granted so much leisure and convenience for attending to ghostly exercises, and keeping close to God by prayer and meditation, yet are so taken up with useless employments, so reckless, slothful, and sluggish, that they do not choose to employ themselves in prayer. Against such men he brings the followings reasons:

First, such as these disobey the command of God, who says, Enter into yourselves, and see that I am God; thereby warning us that He should be the special object of our thoughts, employment, and meditation—our Lord and God, who above all others is worthy of our love. And thus, when a religious man makes light of these exercises, he is plainly disobedient and a breaker of the aforesaid commandment.

Secondly, it appears from this that such a man loves God but little, and less than other things; seeing that he neglects that which concerns the habit he wears and his religious state. And while he is believed to be a special friend and worshipper of God, and is ever reading or listening to sacred Scripture, which is an image of God, and chanting the divine Office, which is speaking with God, and is yet insensible to all these things, it is a great sign that he loves God but little, and has but little part with Him. And it would have been better for such a man that he had never come to religion.

Thirdly, the more lukewarm and slothful such men are in serving God, the less sure they are of being in His grace; and because they do not seek Him, He shows them no sign of His love. Whence it happens that, to their shame, He often shows greater signs of His love to people living in the world, and to simple and unlettered men who worship, love, and seek after Him more faithfully and earnestly.

Fourthly, men of this kind show very clearly that they have very little worth in them, because, living in a more excellent state of life, they are duller, colder, less devout and hard-working than those who live in a humbler state, and therefore are they worthily cast off and despised by God, and they become the scandal of others who live in a less exalted condition.

Fifthly, God gave them greater means for a holy life than other men, and has freed them from the employments of the world that they may give themselves up to Him. And because they waste in delicate, slothful, and careless living the time allowed them for giving themselves to God, it is not to be wondered at if God gives them no taste of Himself and no delight in His love.

In the sixth place, God has set them as His mediators between Himself and His people, and wishes them to eat the sins of the people, which indeed they do; and notwithstanding, they do not strive to keep with God by constant prayer, contemplation, and the practice of good works. Whence it comes to pass that by slighting Him they make Him angry with them, and so make themselves unworthy of being mediators between Him and His people, and of receiving the alms which on that account are given them by the people.

The seventh reason why prayer and contemplation are more necessary for religious is because these make them stronger in temptation, and greater haters of sin, and an example to others, and holier and more fervent in healing others of their sins. And for all these reasons, Abbot Ephrem exhorts every religious to employ himself only as óbedience bids him; and to give himself to prayer and contemplation above all other works.

Lest we should be lengthy, we leave out many useful hints that might be added on this subject. So, having done with the way of enlightenment, let us speak now of the perfect way of union.

PART III.

THE WAY OF UNION.

CHAPTER XXVI.

What the way of union and perfection is, and what conditions he must have that wishes to reach it.

WE have now spoken of the way of enlightenment, which gives light to the mind, and have seen how a monk by meditating may reach the wished-for goal, and cling fast to God by love; and now we must pass on to the way of union and of perfection, which links the soul with God and perfects it. And this is the embracing of true wisdom, according to what holy men tell us.

Wishing to define the way of union, we may say that it is the stage wherein a soul, being thoroughly cleansed and enlightened, is united to its Creator, exulting over His blessedness and yearning to please Him alone; while gladly and piously it magnifies, praises, and admires Him, and languishes with His love; so that it can cry out, in the words of the canticle, My soul melted away when my Beloved One spoke to me; and again, Prop me up with flowers; tell my Beloved that I am fainting for His love.

And this love with which thou goest in search of thy Beloved should be most pure; that is, it should be chiefly on account of His goodness; as the psalm saith, What have I in heaven, and without Thee what do I wish for on earth? that is to say, I love Thee purely, neither on account of heavenly nor of earthly gifts, but on account of Thy great goodness, and on account of Thyself.

Whence we must take note that in this way of union a man lifts up his mind to God, shutting out all empty things; that is to say, all creatures; and turning aside his love from every creature, he fixes it on his Creator, saying to himself, I saw everything under the sun, and behold all things were vanity and affliction of spirit. Therefore, dear brother, do as the bird doth when soaring aloft, that, if it meets with flies, it heeds them not; so do thou likewise pass on, saying, My course is towards the sun, towards Christ my Saviour, the true Sun of justice, who alone is holy, who alone is Lord of all, God the highest; and therefore I ought not fill my heart with earthly vanities.

This way of union is gained by internally recalling thyself from outer things, from the lowest to those above, from things of time to those of eternity.

Again, remember that, in order to gain ground in this way,

Firstly, a man must be rooted in virtue by habit and grace; must take no pleasure in feelings of vain-glory, in the desire of riches, in the concupiscence of the eyes, and in gluttony.

Secondly, he must live in a silence of the inner man; troubling himself no more about things seen or heard than if they happened to him in dreams.

Thirdly, he must abide in a certain loving union with God; listening with utmost reverence to all His words, deeds, and teachings.

Fourthly, he must seek for nothing, but look upon his Beloved as more than enough for him; giving Him a place in his heart above all else; loving Him above all that can be seen, heard, thought of, or imagined, since He is most lovely, desirable, and faithful.

And here take heed that He whom thou wishest to love perfectly can neither be seen nor heard, tasted, touched, or in any way reached by our senses, but yet is above all worthy of thy love.

Know for certain that He whom thy love seeks after hath no limit, shape, measure, change, or idea to which thy fancy might liken Him; and yet is all thou canst desire. Again, He whom thou lovest cannot be pointed out or defined, nor His lineaments traced or His value weighed, nor His footsteps tracked for thy understanding, yet is He all thou mayst wish for.

Fifthly, thou must often bring the divine perfections back to thy mind, and dwell on them with joy. And although the divine perfections cannot be numbered, yet three there are concerning which thou shouldst stir up thy heart, and say,

O my Lord and my most Beloved One, I rejoice that Thou art most mighty, not for my own convenience nor because I seek my own good therein as my highest end, but because Thou hast this perfection, and fearest none, lackest naught, and none can overcome in strife with Thee, none can withstand Thy might, be he spirit or being of flesh and blood, and therefore do I rejoice.

Secondly, O Lord, I congratulate Thee that Thou art most wise, and that in Thyself Thou viewest most clearly and transparently all things, to-wit, both good and evil, past, present, and to come, real and possible, temporal and eternal; changeable things Thou seest unchangeably, things to us uncertain Thou knowest without fail, and all this on account of Thy perfect nature, because none can deceive Thee, nothing can be hidden from Thee.

Again, I rejoice and am glad that Thou art infinitely good and most perfect; that Thy goodness can undergo no change; and that nothing better than Thee, nothing more worthy, nothing loftier can our understanding frame.

In the sixth place, it is useful for a beginner to have some short utterances or words wherein he may express his longing desire, speaking, as it were, face to face with his Lord in prayer, as we said at the end of the way of enlightenment, and as we shall explain in the next chapter on the way of practising the present stage.

CHAPTER XXVII.

On those things on which a devout monk or religious person should meditate every day in the week after night-prayers, while in this way of union, so that he may duly climb the six steps of the ladder which lead to union with God.

WHEN thou hast entered the place set apart for prayer, thou shalt first, for thy defence, make the holy sign of the cross; and then, gathering together thy thoughts, thou shalt take on thyself, with loving feelings, the part of a son or spouse, and meditate on the divine perfections and praises, learning to taste therein how sweet the Lord is, as follows:

On Monday think how He is the source or beginning of all things.

On Tuesday, how He is the beauty of the universe.

On Wednesday, how He is the glory of the world.

On Thursday, how He is all love.

On Friday, how He is the ruler of all things.

On Saturday, how He is the ever tranquil guide of all.

On Sunday, how He is the most bountiful giver.

On Monday, therefore, bethink thyself at thy leisure that God is the author, the Alpha and Omega, the beginning and end of all, and that on His will all things mortal and immortal depend, and that He alone has given all things their being.

He it is that makes and restores all things, that creates and governs what He has created; to whom it is the same to will as to do. Nor canst thou even imagine God as not existing, for were He not there would be nothing, since He has His being from none, and whatever is hath its being from Him.

Meditate how there is nothing so ready to spread its goodness abroad as He is, and the more widespread His goodness the more perfect it is.

How none can be so readily appeased as God, and how there is none so lovely, delightful, and loving as He is.

How He is the great universal cause of all things, whom even the Gentiles adored as the first cause.

How in Him, from Him, and through Him all things have their being; how He fills heaven and earth, and everything exists by His might; and He is everywhere, through whom all things were made, and without Him nothing was made; who can be neither heard nor seen, yet Himself hears, sees, and knows all things without fail.

Now when thou hast dwelt on all these things in thy inmost heart, rejoicing in praise of the goodness of thy Beloved One, pour forth thy prayer, and with sighs and burning desires lift up thy mind to God, and thus lovingly hold converse with Him in thy heart.

O Lord, Thou art my love, my glory, my hope, my safeguard, my life, my end, my guide, my teacher, my delight. I seek naught else, O Lord, I wish for naught else; let nothing be spoken in my ears, or held out to my choice, but Thyself, O my God; for Thou art enough for me, father, brother, food, guide, keeper, most lovely, desirable, and faithful one.

Who is there so generous as to give himself?

Who so loving as to die for so wretched a sinner?

Who so lowly of heart as thus to bow down his majesty?

O Lord, who despisest no one, nor forsakest him that seeketh after Thee, that hatest no one, but dost forestall and goest forth to meet such as run after Thee. Thy delight is to be with the children of men. What hast Thou found in me but the filth of sin? and yet Thou wishest to abide with me until the end of the world. Was it not enough that Thou didst die for me, and hast given me so many sacraments and angels to watch over me? And though I have always been thankless to Thee, yet dost Thou still wish to be with me. Most loving Father, Thou art so good that Thou canst deny Thyself to none. Let us therefore exchange, and as Thou thinkest on me, so will I ever think on Thee; and do with me as Thou knowest best and Thou willest, for I wish to be Thine and Thine alone. Grant, O Lord, that I may think on Thee alone, and may love Thee alone, that I may ever burn with Thy love, may wish for nothing but Thee, and give myself up to Thee without ever seeking to take back what I have offered.

O fire that inflamest me! O love that dost burn me! O light enlightening me! O rest, refreshment, and hope! My treasure and my life! O love that dost ever burn and canst never be quenched!

O Lord Jesus Christ, my King, kindle in me the fire of Thy love, of longing desire for Thee, of Thy gladness and peace, of Thy piety and mildness, so that being wholly filled with the sweetness of Thy love, and made partaker of the flame of Thy charity, I may love Thee, most sweet and beautiful Lord, with my whole heart, with my whole soul, and with all my strength, with all the intenseness of my love, with all sorrow and burning tears, with utmost reverence, fear, and trembling; having Thee ever in my heart and everywhere before my eyes, so that no private love may enter my soul, but I may be wholly transformed into Thy love, and may deserve to be one spirit with Thee.

And when, with the help of divine grace, thou hast for some length of time trained thyself after the aforesaid manner, being now an adept in the art of love, and having mounted the six steps of the ladder of which we shall shortly speak, thou mayst, without any meditation to begin with, and without any exercise of thy understanding, raise thy mind lovingly to God a hundred times a day.

And should any one, through ignorance or dulness, not know how to go through this exercise, then let him ground himself on the virtue of faith and be sorry for his sins. And if he knows not how to meditate on Sacred Scripture, let him do his best to love God with his whole heart, and often say over and over again in prayer the following words:

O Lord, when shall I be able to embrace Thee with unshaken and undivided love? O most ardent lover, when shall I love Thee as Thy true child?

And if he does this, however simple and unlettered he may be, yet from sorrow and compunction for sin, as if from the kiss of the divine feet, and from the memory of God's loving-kindness, as from the kiss of the hand, shall he rise to the kiss of the divine lips, namely, to the intimate union of love, even as Solomon says in the canticle, speaking in the name of the spouse, that is to say, of the devout soul wedded to her Redeemer: Let Him kiss me with the kiss of His mouth. Nor should a man be thought proud or presumptuous for seeking this kiss of the divine mouth when he has already practised and accustomed himself to the kiss of the feet and of the hand, by sorrow for sin, and the thought of the divine benefits, as we said above in the nineteenth chapter, speaking of the way of purity. And this is enough said on the exercises for Monday, which indeed consists mainly in loving sighs after the Beloved.

On Tuesday, after coming to thy praying-

place, and making the sign of the cross, take on
thyself the person of a son, and with a loving heart
meditate as follows:

First of all, see how thy Beloved One is Himself the beauty of the universe, and has clothed all
things with loveliness.

He is the one whose beauty the sun and moon
admire, and on whom the angels long to gaze.

From this, thy Beloved, the stars of heaven,
the roses and lilies, the flowers of the field,
and all creatures have the bloom of their loveliness.

From Him the ears of man drink in the sweetness of music, the song of the nightingale and
lark, the melody of all singing-birds.

From Him is the sweetness of honey, the deliciousness of fruit and of wine, and of all kinds of
food.

He peopled the sky with stars, the air with
birds, the earth and sea with countless tribes of
living creatures.

All things doth He uphold, and were His arm
withdrawn all things would come to naught.

He is the spring of wisdom, and from Him
gush forth in streams all the treasures of wisdom
and of knowledge, since He is the everlasting
wisdom, stretching in His might from end to end,
and yet disposing all things in sweetness. He it
is who sitteth on His heavenly throne, and looks
into the deep, weighing the mountains in His
scales and grasping the earth in His mighty palm,

laying down the law for the waters that they go not beyond their shores.

And when thou hast slowly turned these things over in thy mind concerning the might and the beauty of thy Beloved, then from thy inmost heart, kindling with love, form thy prayer as we have said above for Monday, and say,

Thou, O Lord, art my love, my glory, my hope, &c.

On Wednesday, after coming to thy praying-place, and signing thyself with the sign of the cross, take upon thyself the person of a spouse, and with intensest yearnings of love meditate as follows:

Behold how He whom thy heart pants for is the glory of the universe, whom the angels and archangels adore, before whom the powers of heaven tremble, and whom all creatures obey.

All things made by Him sing praises to Him, and He is our hope, our salvation, our honour, our glory, our last end, and our expectation.

He is the everflowing source of all good things; the earth and the fulness thereof is His; glory and plenty are in His abode. If the man that possesses gold is called wealthy, what must He be called who made gold and precious stones and all the wealth of the world?

Thy Beloved One exceeds all comprehension, and concerning Him is it written, Great is the Lord, and exceedingly worthy of praise, and of His greatness there is no limit.

So lofty is He that none can fully understand His greatness; neither angelic natures nor any creature whatsoever; since all created beings are finite, but thy Beloved is infinite, and between finite and infinite there is no proportion.

And when thou hast with joy of heart duly pondered over the glory and riches of thy Beloved One, with heart overflowing with love, make thy prayer as above on Monday, saying,

O Lord, Thou art my love, &c.

On Thursday, after coming to thy oratory, and signing thyself with the conquering sign of the holy cross, take on thyself the same person as before, and with burning love meditate after this fashion:

Contemplate how He whom thou lovest is all love, and whoever abides in Him abides in love; and as it is the nature of fire to kindle and to heat, so doth it belong to love to create and spread abroad, to inflame and set on fire, to save and ransom, to guard, set free, and enlighten.

How He whom thou lovest is not in any place, as if circumscribed, but yet is everywhere; for if thou goest up into heaven, He is there; if thou goest down into hell, He is there: as St. Bernard says, God governs everywhere, and rules everywhere. His Majesty fills all things, for even in hell he doth the works of His justice; and it is folly to say that He is absent from the place wherein He acts.

How this Beloved of thine is the reward of the

Saints, the joy of angels, the mirror of all the elect, the expectation of patriarchs, the corner-stone of apostles, the diadem of martyrs, the bright light of confessors, the glory of virgins.

When, therefore, thou hast gratefully meditated thus on the love and greatness of thy Beloved One, pray as above, saying,

O Lord, Thou art my love, &c.

On Friday, coming to thy oratory, and signing thyself, take on thee the person of a child or spouse, as above, and then lovingly meditate as follows:

See how He whom thou wishest so ardently to love is the rule and model of all things, and the nearer a thing is to Him the nobler must it be.

How some things have being without life; others, both being and life, and these latter excel the former; others, again, have being, life, and understanding, and these are above both; and others, besides all this, have the gifts of purity and holiness, and these last are nigher to God than the rest.

How by reason of His unmixed goodness He has in Himself the type of all things made, the source of all moral goodness, and the will to make others partake of His goodness.

How thy Beloved One is Himself the ordainer and the disposer of all things, who allots to everything its place, higher or lower, according to its condition and deserts, as a wise painter arranges his colours, bright or dark, light or shade, so as to give beauty to his work.

And He for whose love thou dost thirst is Himself most perfect, and without shade of imperfection, standing in need of none, since He hath all in Himself, than whom naught can be or be conceived better or more worthy, nobler or more excellent.

Whatever the creature has of goodness or worthy of praise in any degree, the Creator has in its highest degree.

And when thou hast by ardent darts of love ended thy meditation of the might of the Beloved, shown in stamping the image of His goodness on the things He governs, make thy prayer as above on Monday.

On Saturday, entering thy place of prayer, and disposing thyself as above, meditate after this manner:

Reflect how thy Beloved One is ever most tranquil, ruling the world by His fixed decree, giving motion to all things, Himself unmoved.

How He is the beginning, the ruler, the guide, the path, and the term of all things.

How He is the last end and peaceful rest of the just, ever still and unchanged, since He is everywhere and cannot move from one place to another, there being no place which He does not fill.

He is the delightful refreshment of all, as He said, Come to me, all you that toil and are burthened, and I will refresh you; and how the soul that is firmly rooted in the love of her Beloved finds refreshment and repose in Him as in her centre, and the soul that is not so rooted is troubled and worn out with empty fancies.

After thou hast carefully turned these things over in thy mind, till thou hast begun to find some taste in them, rejoice in the repose, stability, and refreshing power of thy Beloved One, and make a prayer of love as before.

On Sunday, after entering thy place of prayer, and strengthening thyself with the victorious standard of the cross, and taking on thyself the person of a son or spouse, with a loving heart meditate as follows:

In the first place, call to mind that He whom thy love seeketh is the fulness of all things; and whoever has Him has all things, and He who has Him not is beggared and poor, since all else beside Him gives no strength, or if it gives any, it is not enough; and even were it enough for a time, it lasts not for ever, and leaves much to be longed for; but whoever has Him has his fill, because he has his last end, and has nothing else to seek after.

Reflect that thy Beloved excels all that can be seen or heard, all taste or fragrance, and all that sense can reach; how He has no limit, shape, or measure; and is above that can be circumscribed in space, all that is subject to change or that can be conceived by human thought; and in His height cannot be reached by mortal ken, cannot be defined or described, nor can His footsteps be traced by the understanding of man. And yet He is most worthy of love, praise, and desire.

He is thy safest treasure, and where thy treasure is there shall thy heart be; and whatever thou losest, still, if thou hast Him, thou hast enough, since He is the one thing necessary, as He said to Martha.

He is our highest reward; and if the whole world casts us off, yet His goodwill is enough for us, seeing that He is our whole desire and sufficiency.

He is the life in whom all things live, in whom we move, live, and have our being, since of Him is it said, From Him, through Him, and in Him are all things.

Reflect how thy Beloved is named Christ; that is to say, Anointed; and is indeed that precious balm which gives sweetness to all the things of this world.

In His elect He is the balm of grace, in the damned the balm of justice and the avenger of unrighteousness.

How He whom thou lovest is the Creator, Ruler, Redeemer, giver of righteousness, of reward, and of glory. Therefore, rejoicing in these perfections of thy Beloved, and giving Him thanks for them, let thy soul melt with love, and sleep and rest in peace in Him, and say, Do not awake me till I wish to burst forth in His praises. And though I cannot worthily praise Him, yet I will not hold my peace, since He is the sweetness of all taste; and whosoever tasteth of Him is overcome by His sweetness, and may even die for love. O my most lovely One, Thee alone do I love. Where dost Thou abide? Where dost Thou wish me to seek Thee, that art all sweetness? Delightful guest of the soul, be Thou my guest, and I will abide with Thee for ever.

And when thou hast thus at length dwelt in thought on the abundance and sweetness that is to be found in thy Beloved, with sighs and longings from thy inmost heart pray as above.

CHAPTER XXVIII.

How to lift up the soul to God by fervent love, even without any consideration of the understanding.

WE have described above how our understanding is to be lifted up to God by thinking upon and praising the divine perfections, and how the fire of divine love is to be enkindled in our hearts by words and inflamed desires of love; now we must show how the spirit that has already had some exercise after this fashion may be raised to God without any labour of the understanding, and cleave fast to Him by an inflamed love which holy men call true wisdom; for, as blessed Dionysius writes, This wisdom is known by means of our ignorance, since no human reasoning of the mind, no wisdom of man is able to lift the soul to this loving union; but it is the work of God alone, who vouchsafes without any help from our own understanding to communicate a knowledge of Himself to the soul. Wherefore the soul at this stage, as far as the intellect is concerned, is rather passive than active; for sense has no place where love alone reigns. This is the wisdom concerning which St. James says that every perfect gift is from above, coming down from God. Nor is any effort of the understanding able to beget this wisdom within us in the way knowledge is got by man's own effort; but the exercise only of those inner affections of which the Prophet spoke when he said, My soul hath refused to be consoled; I was mindful of God and I rejoiced, and my spirit fainted away; that is to say, the soul which drives away all worldly and fleshly delight is exhilarated by the touch of God's sweetness and lifted up on high, and thus faints away; because the tongue cannot utter what the soul now feels towards its Beloved One. Philosophers never reached this kind of wisdom; nor do those reach it who employ their minds on corporeal and fantastic objects. And it excels all supernatural and infused gifts, as far as concerns the manner of the lifting up to God, which is by means of love, for in nothing else does the soul find such true repose, nor has she herein any regard to her own advantage or pleasure, but to God alone; who alone is worthy of being loved above all things, whom alone she seeks, and runs after and loves, because she feels Him to be the supreme Good, far removed from all want and wretchedness. And as the same blessed Dionysius says, in the seventh chapter of the book on the Names of God, this wisdom reaches its Beloved One by means of love, in such a manner as not to speculate or reflect on Him with subtle considerations, which do not awake love; as when a man wishes to discover some subtle truth, and studies hard on the Trinity, or the generation of the Eternal Word, or the creation of the world, wherein the might of God is displayed, he certainly is not moved to love. But the wisdom of which we speak only attends to such considerations as may touch the heart, so as to lift it up and kindle in it an ardent love of its Maker, knowing Him without the aid of corporeal similitudes, and understanding Him in a way that cannot be told, so that, against the usual course of nature, He is beloved before He is known. How He is loved and known by means of this seraphic wisdom may well be felt, but can never be told in words; for being wholly spiritual, nothing bodily can give it any help, but God does it of Himself alone.

Wherefore any man, however simple and unlettered he may be, a peasant, or an ignorant countrywoman, may in an instant become a learned scholar in this school of wisdom, according as God

Almighty may vouchsafe them the gift of wisdom in a low or a high degree, which He will do according as the disciple has prepared himself; for he that doth not prepare himself by doing what he can on his own side will never come to possess this kind of wisdom.

CHAPTER XXIX.

That he who undertakes these exercises feels and loves more than he sees or understands.

DAVID the prophet confirms the sentence at the head of this chapter, where he says: Taste and see that the Lord is sweet. Here he shows us that the devout man doth always, in the first instance, taste God by love; and later on begins to know with the understanding what he had tasted with the palate of the soul. And this is likewise proved from the fact that many contemplative and devout people have more love than knowledge or understanding, as is the case with the unlearned or simple, who are often more devout than schoolmen. Such men as these have more love than knowledge, and their love goes beyond their understanding, and is not wholly based on any previous knowledge. Nevertheless all such love requires the light of faith, and the presence of grace and charity, as Dionysius says in the beginning of his book on *Mystic Theology*; and this lofty wisdom, of which we are speaking, belongs only to him who is a true follower of Christ and friend of God.

Whence we may take note that, although this love is granted to pious persons who have not received any previous enlightenment, because the light of faith is enough to root it in the soul, yet it is not granted to all with the same abundance; and, therefore, they who are beginners in contemplation, and have not yet reached the fulness of this love—which is the last end of all contemplation—must apply themselves to deep thought, and to the consideration of creatures, and of the works of God, in the same way as the man that wishes to climb to a high place stands in need of a ladder. The Psalmist insinuates this where he says: Fire shall be kindled in my meditation. As if he had said, Before the soul is set on fire with the flame of divine love, an attentive consideration of God's works in creation must go before, by which, as by a ladder, the soul may mount up on high. But with perfect and well-tried souls, without a thought of anything that is not God, and even without any foregoing thought of God Himself, the superior part of the soul in one moment mounts up to God by the fire of love; and, lest any one should tell me what Augustine says—We can love things unseen, but not things unknown—I say that, according to holy doctors, the meaning of Augustine is, that some kind of knowledge is wanted for every sort of contemplation, which is true; but this sublime love, of which we are now speaking, concerns God Himself, as He is the highest Good, and is a singular gift of God, and can nowise be had except by His gift. And so it really does presuppose the knowledge of God which the light of faith affords us, which is itself a virtue, infused by Almighty God. But in no other way is this love begotten in us; neither by means of any study or labour or art of men, nor is it like that natural love which arises whenever the soul of herself inclines to any beloved object.

And, to make what we have been saying still more plain, be it observed that, as an individual drawing near to the fire may well feel its heat before he sees its light, so a perfect contemplative man feels the warmth of divine love before he is able to tell what it is he feels—at least, in this life; for in our true country it will be otherwise when our soul shall be closely united with that everlasting light of glory, to-wit, God Himself. And that man will more swiftly reach the love of which we are speaking who doth oftenest repeat, with sighs and groans of his heart, those utterances of love which we spoke of for Monday's meditation; for example: O Lord, when shall I love Thee? when shall I be fast knit to Thee? when shall I see into the inmost depths of my own being? &c. A man of this kind will soar aloft to loving and longing after God much more speedily than if he were to contemplate the hidden depths of God's fathomless eternity, or of the divine processions; for he who harbours these speculations only for the sake of knowledge, and not that he may be set on fire with divine love, can make but small progress, love being the last end of all the thoughts of a man whose soul is rightly ordered. And since neither the greatest philosophers nor many divines of our own time have done this, it follows that, although keen reasoners, they are yet far from God, and from His love and fear, and are steeped in many and great sins.

St. Paul, speaking of this high and glorious wisdom, says that none of the wise men—that is, of the so-called wise men of Greece—could understand it. And, concerning the same wisdom, he writes thus to the Corinthians: Our own spirit, when it has become one with the Spirit of God, judges aright of the things of God; and this is the wisdom which we speak of among perfect men, of which our Redeemer said to His Apostles before His ascension: Ye shall be clothed with power from on high. This is symbolised by the priest putting on the vestments before the altar; beginning from the head, he puts on the amice, next the alb, and lastly the chasuble; because this divine wisdom must come from above, and none can teach it but God alone.

CHAPTER XXX.

On the effects which this love, making us one with God and perfecting us, doth little by little work in the soul.

THE works or effects which this love of God, and this spirit of heavenly contemplation, brings about by little and little in the soul, as holy men tell us, are these six degrees: enlightenment, inflamed love, sweetness, desire, fulness, and rapture.

And these may be looked upon as expressed by the six steps whereby Solomon ascended his throne, which was raised on high; and by these six steps doth Christ Jesus ascend to the higher part of our soul, which is called its summit; and when He hath firm possession of it, He is said to be seated thereon.

The first step to be ascended, and the first fruit which divine love begets in the soul of the contemplative man, is called enlightenment; for when a man has once been on fire with this seraphic love, it leaves behind it in the soul a certain experimental knowledge of God. Herein the soul sees God to be the source of all goodness, grandeur, and beauty, worthy of all honour, glory, reverence, and praise; and he finds himself in His sight more wretched, vile, contemptible, and hateful than human tongue can utter. And then, comparing God with himself, he sees how sweet and full of pity God is, since He has vouchsafed to store up such priceless riches of wisdom in so poor a storehouse; that is to say, in man's heart, filled with all kinds of defilement and sin.

The second fruit—which is likewise the second round of this ladder of love—of this loftiest portion of the contemplative life, may be called inflamed desire; for the soul that has been once enlightened, and knows by experience the loveliness, sublimity, and dignity of God, is so inflamed with the fire of his love as to think of nothing and delight in nothing else, and to wish never to speak of or give heed to aught else. And then the soul loathes all bodily delight, from what side soever it may come.

The third effect or degree consists in a kind of sweetness or pleasure; for, now that the soul has been lit up and set on fire with the love of God, there springs up within her a joy such as words cannot tell of, as far removed from all the delights of this world as is the sweetness of honey from the bitterness of gall, so that even a particle of that sweetness refreshes the soul of man more than any delight that this world has ever offered or ever will afford.

The fourth degree is a spiritual hunger or desire; for when the spirit of the contemplative man has received the joyful light of its God, as we said above, it yearns so strongly after the possession of God that it would rather undergo all kinds of pain and torment than miss even one hour of those pleasures which it has found in its Beloved.

Hence all other pleasures it holds as death, and abides unceasingly in that burning and eager desire of those delights which it enjoys in the company of its most amiable Father and God.

The fifth degree is called *fulness* or satiety; when the soul is so filled with the aforesaid taste of God that it neither seeks nor wishes for aught besides, but rather finds death in everything else; and all other wishes, all other joy and love, seem lulled to sleep within it; and it seems to enjoy God, and in Him to have all things, seeing that nothing exists without Him, and that he who has God is king over all things that are or that can have a being.

Lastly, from all these five degrees which the aforesaid seraphic fire begets in the heart of a true contemplative there proceeds the sixth, which is named rapture or excess of mind; not that it must needs make a man behold any real or imaginary visions, but a man must find himself so enlightened, inflamed, refreshed, and elevated by love for his Creator that what he hears and sees cannot be told in words, by reason of its height, goodness, loveliness, purity, and nobleness; and the reason of this is, that this rapture is an effect of the grace of God, who, by His immense goodness, wishes to raise that soul in a way in which nothing else could raise it, since that elevation is far beyond all created might; and, since this rapture is something spiritual, our intellect, weighed down as it is by the burden of the flesh, cannot abide in it any length of time, but, like a captive, is no sooner lifted up than it forthwith falls back on itself. Moreover, our understanding during these ecstasies is like the eye of our body while gazing on the sun's rays, and unable for a length of time to look fixedly on the sun, but yet looks for a moment, and can no longer bear the dazzling brightness of its light, but immediately closes itself, and then again opens, and yet cannot stand the light of the sun. Something like this happens to our intellect, during contemplation, while it strives to look steadily on the Sun of Righteousness; or it is like an arrow shot upwards, which comes down at once by force of gravity; or like a fish leaping out of the water and falling back into it at once.

Learned men add to the aforesaid six degrees the two following:

The first of these two is called security or peacefulness, because when a soul finds herself so dearly beloved by her spouse Jesus Christ, and by Him enlightened, inflamed, filled with delights, and lifted out of herself, she receives from Him and in Him such peace that no pains of this life, no earthly hurt, not even death itself, would she fear to undergo; in short, she is free from all fear. And such firm trust hath she in God's everlasting goodness, which she has tasted and proved, that she does not fear to be ever sundered from it; but rather holds for certain, and without any doubt, that she will live with Him for ever. O, what happiness dwells in such a soul, which already feels and foretastes that gladness on which its certain hope reposes.

The second of these two degrees is perfect tranquillity; for since no trouble nor harm nor dread of this world can strike fear into such a soul, she must needs be in absolute peace, and in such repose that no tongue can express it. Whence Richard of St. Victor says on this point, in his *Contemplations*, O Christian soul, since thou hast it in thy power to ascend to this heaven, and find thy rest in this true life, sell all that thou hast, sell all thy knowledge, and buy this pearl; and let it not seem dear to thee, for Christ is the seller thereof, and He offers it to all who wish to purchase it.

And here it must be noted that we can never in this life fully perfect ourselves in any of these three ways of enlightenment, purity, and union; but by exercising ourselves in them we can gain purity of heart and charity, as far as it is possible so to do in this world.

In the first way we seek God, and indeed find Him, but not as He is found by fervent love.

In the second, or way of enlightenment, we offer victims and sacrifice of praise and inflamed desire, with hope and eager longing after everlasting blessedness.

In the third, or way of union, we find Him whom our soul loves and thirsts after.

So that in the first we bid farewell to the lusts of the world; in the second our understanding is enlightened; in the third it finds a peaceful rest in God. And yet we must never think to cleanse ourselves in this life from all our concupiscences, since not even Paul was able to reach this, as Augustine and the author of the treatise *Beatus vir* teach us. Nor is it in our power to direct all our affections in such a way as never to come down again to earth, for our dwelling on earth weighs down the many desires of our heart, and we cannot here below gain such cleanness of heart as to be at all times closely united to God with bonds of love, because as long as we live in the body we are wayfarers and afar off from our Lord.

So far, then, have we set forth these three ways, and have shown in what manner, by means of them, and by earnest application to prayer and meditation, we may step by step journey onwards to the wished-for goal—to loving union with God.

And now having done with the way of union, we must at least in a few words say in what manner we may reach that seraphic union by means of contemplation.

PART IV.

ON CONTEMPLATION.

CHAPTER XXXI.

That great learning is knowledge, but not wisdom, and is in nowise necessary for contemplative men.

ALTHOUGH many Saints and many enlightened doctors have written very learnedly on contemplation, as St. Gregory in his *Morals*, St. Bernard on the *Canticle*, Richard of St. Victor in his book on contemplation, and many others, whose works may be consulted by the learned; yet, for the benefit of the unlearned, we shall now briefly say something on contemplation, notwithstanding that we have often spoken of it above. And before all, we say that great learning is not wanted in order to be a contemplative man. For although letters and science and the knowledge of the divine law and of Holy Scripture are a great help to such as wish to climb to the summit of contemplation, yet they are often a drawback to many, not indeed of themselves, but by reason of the puffing up to which they give occasion. Now no man can climb the true ladder of contemplation except by the steps of humility; as the Apostle says, If any man among you seems to be wise according to this world, let him become foolish, that so he may be wise indeed. That is to say, let him bend his understanding by humbling himself, and look upon himself as foolish with respect to the wisdom of God, and as one unable to understand God's judgments and works. Hence it is that nothing has so much closed the gate of contemplation against the wise men of this world as their disdaining to humble themselves, by making their intellect a captive and bowing down before the hidden things of the redemption that Christ Jesus hath wrought, and before His works of lowliness and the examples He left us. And yet he that will not enter by this humble and lowly gate is a thief and robber, and strives in vain to enter, as the Lord hath said. In the emptiness of his own conceit, while he walks with uplifted head—to-wit, with a high opinion of his own understanding and of his own knowledge—and while he scorns to be humbled and become as a little child, he will never be able to pass through that lowly gate, but will stumble and turn back, as some of our Lord's followers did; concerning whom it is written, that they left Him and went back, because they could not understand Him. And we know that the same thing has often happened to learned men, for whom it were well indeed if they had not had so much learning, but had remained simple and unlearned as their own mothers were; not through the fault of learning itself, which is useful and of great profit to such as use it with humility and are in the grace of God; but this evil effect arises from the inroads of pride, as the Apostle says, that pride puffs a man up. And this, moreover, happens according to the difference of men and their natural dispositions. For we know by experience that wine does harm to such as are in a fever, and a sword is a bad weapon for a madman, who might kill himself with it. And so in like manner we see that light is painful for weak eyes, which yet is most pleasant, sweet, and delightful for healthy ones. The same holds good of knowledge; good as it is in itself, it does great mischief to a man that is indisposed, and that uses it ill owing to the bad state of his soul.

CHAPTER XXXII.

What kind of men are best suited for contemplation.

BLESSED Gregory says, in the sixth book of his *Morals*, that there are some men, naturally or through bodily habit or custom, so strongly inclined to exterior things and worldly employments, that they cannot raise themselves up to contemplation, but are much better suited to an active life; and if these men were to give themselves to contemplation, they would fall into great errors and blasphemies, because the more leisure they have for their own thoughts the fiercer do the storms of their hearts grow. And such men as these should employ themselves in active occupations.

Others have so calm and peaceful a soul that, if any active work takes up their time, they give way under it at once, but yet can live very happily in the thought of God, and of a heavenly life; and while dwelling on these things, and meditating with great humility on their own salvation, they withdraw their minds as far as they are able from the laboriousness of excessive toil; and oftentimes men who could contemplate with calmness have fallen when overwhelmed with work. And such as these, if they employed themselves in exterior occupations, would be certain rather to ruin themselves than to do any good.

Others there are who, either out of custom or by their strength in contemplation, or from their great love of God, or perhaps by a disposition inherited from their parents, have a vigorous mind, and, as it were being able to use the left hand as well as the right, are able to employ themselves in one or the other way of living; and such men as these are fit to govern others.

As to those of the first kind and condition —that is to say, who, on account of natural disposition or through custom, are suited for exterior occupations—such men will often go astray if they give themselves up to deep meditation, and neglect exterior work and employment. And it often happens that there are simple and unlettered men of the second condition, and these may with safety live in solitude, and think over their eternal salvation without outer employments. Hence it is plain that simple-minded people are not to be kept away from contemplation, as if they were unfit for it. For we have seen, and do often see by experience, among holy hermits, and even among devout women, that some make greater progress in contemplation than many learned clergymen and religious men. Gerson gives a reason for this in his *Mount of Contemplation;* which is, that this contemplative life is better gained by a good, simple, and humble way of living than by great learning; even as Solomon says, that God's wisdom walks with the little ones, and His conversation is with them. And therefore are we elsewhere thus commanded: Seek God with a simple heart, seeing that He is Himself most simple and is found by the simple.

CHAPTER XXXIII.

On the difference between learning and wisdom.

THE doctors of the Church say that there is a great difference between learning and wisdom; and among them, St. Bernard in particular says that knowledge gives us the understanding of things, but that wisdom carries them into effect. Hence some etymologists used to say that the Latin word for wisdom, *sapientia*, was derived from *sapida scientia*, and means a knowledge that can be relished; and this relish is a thing that belongs to the affection, desire, will, or appetite of the person that possesses it; and on this account a man may have great knowledge and learning who has yet little or no wisdom. The reason of this is, as Gerson says, that such a man has no relish nor love for the object of his learning; and he explains this by some examples. A man may know the nature of honey from having heard people talk about it, or because he has read about it in books, without having ever tasted its sweetness. Again, physicians know the nature of diseases, and oftentimes better than the sick man himself; but as for the feeling of pain, the sick man knows his illness better, not from learned reasonings, but by reason of his own experience. Likewise a man may have an intimate knowledge of a person without having any great feeling of love or hatred, of pleasure or displeasure, in his regard; and, on the other hand, one may have a great love and complacency for a person he knows little about.

Thus we can well understand that great wisdom may be without much learning, and great learning with little wisdom. And from all we have said it is plain that devout and simple men, though unlettered, are far more fit for contemplation than learned men without piety.

CHAPTER XXXIV.

That a life of contemplation must begin with the labour of the active life.

The first step, which belongs to the state of beginners and to such as are imperfect, is humble confession with penance, whereby a man is able to mortify in himself the love of the world with its wicked concupiscences, and all unlawful movements and evil habits. To such a man it belongs to chastise and subdue his flesh, so that it rise not against the spirit, but be kept under it; and this end he obtains by fasting and watching, by abstinence, affliction, tears, and sighs, and by such bodily labour as his superiors shall lay upon him. Should any one, before undergoing this penance, and without such previous work and self-training, wish on a sudden to lead a perfect and contemplative life, he would deceive himself, and would be like a man wishing to gain the top of a high mountain at a single jump. And on this account St. Gregory and other Saints say that the active life, with its labour and corporal austerities, must be practised before the contemplative, as a means of preparing the way for the latter. And this was prefigured in Jacob, who served seven years for Rachel, in whom was the type of a contemplative life, yet was first offered her sister Leah, by whom is signified the active life. And here we should note, with Gerson, that young men, still full of temptations of the flesh and evil habits, and great sinners who have spent a great part of their lives in sin, cannot and ought not all at once give themselves up to a contemplative life; for while they would be thinking that all their thoughts are on God, and that they are offering up pure and secret prayers to Him, very soon they would find themselves thinking on those things to which their evil inclinations lead, and thus would become worse than before. And for this same reason Seneca advises that a man should not be long alone, and all holy men and philosophers alike condemn idleness. Nevertheless, Seneca himself and these same holy men extol solitude, and the leisure of contemplation in such as are well schooled to it, that they may serve God with greater freedom, as the holy hermits did, and many other devout men besides.

CHAPTER XXXV.

That it is not for all alike to imitate the singular grace that the divine goodness has vouchsafed to some, of living in solitude.

By a special gift of God it has been granted to some to give themselves, even from their youth, to solitude, and to living apart from men. Thus we read that St. Benedict did; yet in his Rule he did not counsel others to do so, imitating in this other holy hermits and learned men, who have always been wont to dissuade men from rashly

attempting to undertake that kind of life; for
this reason, that a special favour given to one
man must not be heedlessly imitated by any one
else; and they who have at times dared to do
otherwise—namely, to seek after solitude and the
tranquil life of the desert—without having first
worked hard, and been taught and been accustomed to the company of their brethren, have been
unhappily beguiled in their hope. The aforesaid
Gerson gives a reason for this, and says: They
strove to fly before they had wings, and to engage
in warfare with a formidable enemy before overcoming their other lesser foes—to-wit, the world
and the flesh. And he adds that, on that account,
he did not believe too much in certain hermits of
his own time who were loud in boasting of their
own advancement; and he thinks the same of
women living as recluses. And, writing to his
own sisters, he says, You know, my beloved
sisters, how necessary it has been for you hitherto
to work much; and without doubt some of you
stood greatly in need of it before you were able
to live alone and in solitude, and give yourself up
to meditate on God after the manner of hermits
and recluses; for we can find a true hermitage
not only in woods and deserts, but wherever a
place can be found to escape from the world,
and turn aside from its noises, its turmoil, and
anxiety.

Wherefore we see, in well-governed religious
orders, that novices and beginners are heavily

burdened in learning their duties, and busily employed in work, in watching, fasting, and chanting, so as by these means to remove the thoughts which otherwise solitude might raise in them; although others, well accustomed to such penances, and skilled in overcoming temptations and bad thoughts, would be able to live without difficulty for a long time in solitude. Hence it happens that there are some who need such strength for overcoming and conquering their temptations by means of hard work, that they are not fit for the perfect and contemplative life, but must be constantly engaged in active labour; and of these there are not a few. On the other hand, there are some for whom active life is a heavy load, and who are wonderfully kept back by it.

It likewise sometimes happens that a man is of such an excellent natural disposition, or has received such a grace from God, that in one day's contemplation he will gain more than another in a whole year. Yet I do not mean to say that a man should so give himself up to one kind of life as never to try the other, for a longer or shorter time, according as he sees it to be most useful for him; neither must he give himself so wholly to an active life as not to think from time to time of God and of his conscience, in order to confess his sins and do penance for them. Nor must he entirely employ himself in contemplation, so as never to do any work; for which reason, in one and the same person we must always find Martha with Mary, and Mary with Martha, more or less, as we have said, and his manner of life will take its name from that kind of exercise to which he mainly devotes himself.

CHAPTER XXXVI.

That the love of God is the beginning and end of the contemplative life.

THE root and principle of the contemplative life must be the love of God; that is to say, it must be for His love that the contemplative man bids farewell to the life of this world, and it must be to give himself up to God that he flies its cares and businesses; and whoever does otherwise deceives himself, and oftentimes will not reach the wished-for end, unless by doing penance he put himself again into the right way. So there are many who enter religion or devote themselves to study, not for the love of God, but out of sloth, to escape a laborious life in the world, or to gain their livelihood, or through vanity and pride, wishing to be thought great and holy religious, or out of mere curiosity and thirst of knowledge, as has been the case with great philosophers. Moreover, the love of God ought to be the end of a contemplative man; that is to say, that out of love for his God such a man should do his best to go forward in goodness, and keep clear of all other business and worldly employment, at least if it be of such kind as to be a notable hindrance to contemplation. For I am well aware that at times a moderate amount of employment is useful, and even necessary, as a help to contemplation, and to ward off excess of sadness and slothfulness.

The Apostle bears witness that the love of God is the highest aim of contemplation, when he says, Love is the fulness of the law. Wherefore, in the divine law, which is rightly named wisdom and divinity, that man should be deemed the better master and teacher who loves God more; for a man lives a more perfect life, and is in a higher state, when he loves God more ardently and with greater purity. And since for such as are well prepared a contemplative life is a great help for loving God, because it is a kind of school wherein this art of divine love is more speedily and easily mastered; therefore is this kind of life so highly spoken of and extolled in Scripture and by holy men, and above all by the true God of love, Christ Jesus, when He said: Mary hath chosen the better part. And what is the better part of which He spake? This, and no other, that she sat at our Lord's feet, and listened to His word, and while she listened was set on fire with His love.

However, it must be allowed that oftentimes one man, in the course of an active life, loves God more than another who is a contemplative; and the former is a more perfect man, albeit in a less perfect and more lowly state than the contemplative, and the active life of the one is more perfect than the contemplative life of the other, though his state be otherwise. Hence we may see the mistake of such as think that the end or aim of a contemplative life lies in the knowledge or finding out of truths. Rather it is the chief end of contemplation that we should learn to love God, and taste how good and sweet He is. Yet, indeed, that taste or sweetness or spiritual feeling of pleasure is itself a certain manner of knowledge, for love itself is knowledge. As blessed Gregory says: This knowledge is such and so hidden that none can know of it except the man who hath it; nor can it be conveyed to us by words or teaching, just as we are wont to say of any severe illness, that no one can know what it is unless he undergoes it.

CHAPTER XXXVII.

In what the highest point of a contemplative life consists; explained by a comparison drawn from worldly love.

BEFORE we go further we must explain in what the perfection of contemplative life consists. Although we said in the foregoing chapter that the love of God is the end of contemplative life, nevertheless, as Gerson says, it may be truly said that all our works ought to be referred to that end —to-wit, to the love of God. Wherefore I must here lay down some conditions of contemplative life, not that I myself understand them fully; but I write on these things as a blind man on colours, saying over again what holy men have left us in their writings, and leaving many things to them that have experience in these matters. And that we may the more easily be able to see of what kind that love of God should be which is worthy to be called the perfection of contemplative life, I shall try to unravel its mazes by means of its opposite; namely, by means of earthly love, because we know and feel the latter much better and more intimately than we do the love of God. Let us see, then, what the love of this world is able to do in a man that is over head and ears in love, whether it be the love of gold and silver, of honour and dignity, or of the delights of the flesh. A man taken up with such love first begins to pine away with the longing wish of grasping what he loves, unwisely indeed, but too well. Next he fixes his mind, his whole heart and understanding, with such vehemence on the beloved object, that he can think of nothing else but that. And then he forgets himself, lays aside all shame, and soon there is nothing that can keep or withdraw him from the things he loves: neither toil nor suffering, nor peril nor death, nor the fear of God nor the dread of His judgments. Sleeping, he dreams of it; waking, he cares not to hear or speak of aught else; so that he loses in this matter the use of reason, and becomes like a madman or a drunkard. Nothing can any longer withdraw such a man from his love; and there is nothing that he would fear or refuse to undergo, as long as he can gain what he burns and longs for with this raging and worldly love. Moreover, he forgets all other good things, both of this life and of the life to come. Hence if a man were, in his hearing, to speak of heaven, or hell, or death, it seems to him a dream or a play. Nor can he for ever so short a time conceive or retain a spiritual thought, because his carnal or worldly love drives it out in a moment.

CHAPTER XXXVIII.

What kind of love of God a contemplative man ought to have.

CARRYING out the simile we have just set forth, we may reflect that the love of God in a man ought to be such and so great as to make him altogether despise and forget the world, and ought to be so enkindled and powerful and rooted in his heart as that he may neither have the power nor the understanding to give a thought to anything else of his own free will or inclination; and may fear no contempt, no shame, nor threats, nor persecutions, nor even death itself, through the fire of divine love; and that all the sights and sounds of the world may be to him but as a dream or a scene in a play. For God's honour and glory he should make light of all these things, and be such as the world would set down for a madman or a drunkard, laughing at all the things of the world, and rating them lower than the things of God and heaven are rated by men plunged in worldly love.

This, I say, would be that perfect love which a truly contemplative man ought with all his might endeavour to reach; and a man living in such a state of love would rightly be said to be dead and crucified to the world, since naught that it has can now bind him down, and to live to God; and such a man would be asleep to the vanities of the world and awake to the good things of life everlasting, and would have his sight dulled and dimmed to the doings of worldly men, and open to the delights of the Saints. And holy doctors say that this was foreshadowed in Moses, who, when he wished to speak to God, entered into clouds and darkness; so, in like manner, whoever wishes to reach the highest summit of God's love, must enter into a total forgetfulness of worldly things, foreshadowed by that cloud, so as neither to see nor to hear nor to be moved by them.

But now let us set forth in what manner we are to acquire the love of God we have been describing.

For this, and no other, is the aim of a life of contemplation; and whoever has reached this love has climbed the summit of the mount where Christ was transfigured before His three disciples, like

Moses when he received the law, so doth such a man speak to God, and is lifted up in spirit, or rather above his spirit, and his conversation is in heaven. A man like this lives on love, and walks in happiness and delight, without any darkening of smoke or vapour. But yet, brethren, how sad it is that this grace is granted to so few, and lasts so little, as long as we tarry in this our place of banishment.

CHAPTER XXXIX.

Concerning two kinds of silence and solitariness.

ACCORDING to the several varieties of states and conditions of men, each one may single out for himself a secret hiding-place, where he may abide in peace and silence; yet it is nevertheless true that our chief resting-place ought to be rather within than without the soul; that is to say, the soul ought to drive far away from the abode of man's heart all human and worldly care, all foolish and dangerous thoughts, and everything that can hinder it from reaching its proper goal.

For at times it happens that a man while alone and severed from the companionship of his fellow-men doth none the less undergo tricks of fancy and sad thoughts, but is rather forced within himself to put up with a most irksome and burthensome company, which begets in him storms of imaginations, and much talking and chattering, and brings first one thing and then another before his mind's eye; leading him sometimes into the kitchen, at others to the market-place, setting before him unclean and carnal pleasures, dances and beautiful sights, alluring him with voices of singers and other phantoms, in order to throw him headlong into sin, as St. Jerome humbly bears witness of what took place in himself; who, while he had no company but scorpions and wild beasts, often found himself in thought in the midst of Roman dances.

Again, thoughts rise up in the mind which provoke the solitary to anger, and make him quarrel with an absent enemy, and heap words of insult on him as if he were present. At other times he will be counting out his money, and trading with his capital. Often will his thoughts carry him beyond seas, and sometimes lead him about through foreign lands, and place him in exalted dignities. And thus the poor soul, although alone, is often filled with fancies and follies. Wherefore she is not really in solitude nor alone, although she may seem so as to outward show. Yet, to say the truth, the devout soul when in contemplation ought never to be said to be without a companion, for she is never less alone than when alone. But the company that fills these two kinds of solitude is far from being the same; the devout contemplative soul hath the excellent, profitable, and sweet fellowship of God

and His Saints, with whom she abides by means
of holy desires and devout thoughts; the other in
her useless wanderings hath companions who avail
her naught and do her great harm.

CHAPTER XL.

Wherein is shown that a contemplative manner of living is, in the first place, useful to oneself.

FOR three reasons are people most apt to wonder at a man who gives himself up to contemplation. Firstly, because contemplative men seem to live for themselves, and for no one else. Secondly, because they seem to wish to find out and understand more and fly higher than is good for them. Thirdly, because many are thereby led astray, and grow moping and stupid. Which three reasons, if indeed they deserve the name, Gerson overthrows, bringing forward holy and learned men who have entered into this matter with copiousness, subtlety, and depth of reasoning. Before all, he says, that a man who employs himself in contemplation is far more useful to himself and nearer to God, and pleases God better, than if he led an active life; and this is enough said, for there is naught after God I ought to love more than myself, not even the whole world put together. Hence I ought to embrace what is most pleasing to God, and undertake the kind of life He wishes, and by so doing I shall please Him better, and gain some little merit; whereas if I were to try to gain over others I might lose myself, and bring about my own damnation.

What I have just said holds good when a man is so fully his own master that he is able at his choice to give himself either to this or to that kind of life. And I add this, for the sake of such as have public duties, superiors and others placed in authority, which obliges them to attend to active work. And the like holds good for married women, as far as regards their children and the government of their household, and for such as are bound to provide for their parents. If, therefore, such as these were to employ themselves in contemplation when they ought to be minding their own business, they would deceive themselves; and this would be a cunning and dangerous temptation; to-wit, that they should please themselves in contemplation while despising or putting off the things they are bound to do, and should thus do harm to themselves and their neighbours also. But it is otherwise with such as are not bound by reason of their state to serve other men.

CHAPTER XLI.

That contemplative men are likewise very useful to others.

WE must next show that contemplative men are of no small use, not only to themselves, but to others likewise; chiefly because they afford other men the example of a holy life, showing forth in their own works that God is to be loved above all things, and that all things else are hollow and contemptible. And this manner of teaching is one that should not be undervalued, being all the more excellent because it is well known that facts are less likely to deceive than words. Again, men of contemplation do good to all mankind by their holy prayers; and it has often happened that God hath bestowed through their merits, even upon guilty men engaged in worldly business, great gifts, such as peace of mind and the like; because we can do no good without God's special grace, and this grace is more easily got at God's hands by contemplative than by active men.

What our eyes are to our body, contemplative men are to the Church, shedding a guiding light on all the works of her other members; and although the eyes do not work like the hands or feet, yet neither hands nor feet can say that the eyes are useless to them. And thus it belongs to men of prayer and contemplation to guide and offer up to God the works of other men, who have not the like ghostly enlightenment and elevation; for those who keep their hearts ever uplifted to heaven, even though dwelling in the world, understand well how to turn to God as to their last end, whatever good works they do. However, I do not deny that a contemplative man ought now and then to lay aside his contemplation, in order to help the wants of others. But could a man be found able to live perfectly both kinds of life at one and the same time, like St. Gregory and St. Bernard, such a kind of life would be better than either. And he that considers how far our soul and spiritual things go before the body and worldly goods cannot but see clearly that the prayer of one single contemplative man is of greater avail towards helping other men, throughout the whole Church, in their temporal need, than are the prayers of two hundred of such as, of their own accord, and not out of obedience, devote themselves to the employments of an active life; and that it is far more profitable to give oneself to contemplation than to live in the world under colour of helping others, but in reality for one's own convenience, and oftentimes with other people's harm.

I say, therefore, that when a man feels himself bent or moved towards a contemplative life, as by a movement of the Holy Ghost, he should judge of this with the counsel of some ghostly man, not trusting himself, since he might easily be led astray, and be welcoming Satan himself instead of an angel of light; and after this he may indeed, without casting any slur on the active manner of living, give himself up to a life of contemplation, and in so doing will deserve praise. And his heavenly reward for this will be great, unless perchance he were bound to do otherwise by his Superior's command, or to take on himself some public office, or help any one in a case of urgent or extreme need; and we call a need urgent whenever any one is likely to perish, either in body or soul, unless he were to afford them such help as he is able.

CHAPTER XLII.

Wherein is shown by an example that it is not pride, as some wrongly imagine, to give oneself to contemplation.

As Gerson reasons, it cannot be rightly said, as in the second of the aforesaid objections, that he who gives himself up to that contemplation whereof I have spoken—to-wit, to loving God above all things, and with his whole heart—is aiming too high, or striving rashly, but rather a man who is fit for it, and hath been gifted with such a grace from God, would be found wanting, and would do wrong if he made no use of God's gift, above all if he were an ecclesiastic or religious, whose life ought to be rather contemplative than active; and were it otherwise, as our opponents would have it, ecclesiastics and divines would reap little good and great harm from their knowledge, and would become puffed up and grow vain, hollow, and proud.

To make this plain to everyone's understanding, let us suppose that in a royal palace there were, we will say, a man working in the kitchen, whom the king, out of kindness, should appoint to be his chamberlain, deeming him fit for such an office, and because it so pleaseth him, assuredly, were the wretched hireling, out of sloth, faint-heartedness, or gluttony to refuse the office, and to say he had rather stay at his work in the kitchen, he would be worthy of great blame. In like manner, he that is able to serve God well in an exalted office, and yet chooses to busy himself with trifles, cannot look for an excuse in humility, but his so doing must be set down to self-deceit and lukewarmness; and I add that the reason why such as in their contemplation seek to fathom things too deeply fail and go astray, is because they lack that humility which is the keeper and foster-mother of charity.

CHAPTER XLIII.

How far contemplative men excel those given to a life of action.

Now, as concerns the third objection—to-wit, that some contemplative men come to grief, and turn out half-witted and sad—the aforesaid Gerson replies that in active life many are likewise led into error for lack of the discernment they need to fulfil what they have undertaken. Neither is the grace of contemplation granted to all men, for sundry reasons, as declared by the Apostle; for example, that each one hath his own gift from

God, one after this and another after that fashion; and, again, because if in the body all the members were eyes, where would the hands be? &c. It is true, notwithstanding, that worldly men easily imagine contemplative souls to be foolish or gloomy, because they do not live like themselves, and because they make no account of what men of the world love and doat on; but the latter do not see the great joy, the holy works, and the ghostly riches which men of prayer gain by despising the world; and whilst they drive away all covetousness, anger, envy, and all that vanity which brings so much heartbreaking to the lovers of this world, they live in great and untroubled peace of mind—a boon so great that naught can be compared with it; and instead of those worthless and earthly pursuits which men run after within the narrow bounds of the earth, and for a trifling gain, these men of prayer find their home in a vaster and loftier realm, and their employment in a nobler sphere—to-wit, in God Himself. And what I would fain tell in words is known to such as have tried it. For it cannot be doubted that the life of the rational creature consists rather in acts of the understanding or of reason than in anything else; that is to say, we live by thought, and by the love of what our free-will has chosen. Hence they alone can be truly said to live who live on such food and drink, and not those who strive no more than brutes to lift up their souls and their lives to things above; for these latter do but eat and drink, make merry, and laugh over light and fleeting amusements, and wear out their bodies therein, as if they were but sheep or cattle. They may say they do good to other men by their work, but the horse and the ass do so likewise, and sometimes do it better. Still, if a man who can do nothing higher serves other men by his toil, and does it with a right intention and good end, that he may serve God and help his neighbour, such a one is worthy of praise. And, again, I even allow that contemplative men may be less wise and foreseeing in worldly business than active men. The reason is, as the aforesaid doctor declares, that they do not use their talents and efforts about such things; whence it comes that they are held as simple and unwise. But concerning these things they care nothing, seeing that, according to the Apostle, they have been called to this; and to this they strive with all their might, that they be looked on as fools, that so they may be truly wise.

CHAPTER XLIV.

How greatly contemplative men stand in need of God's grace.

WE have elsewhere pointed out that there is a twofold silence—one without the soul, and the other within; and the aim of a man of prayer must be rather to have the interior kind of silence and solitariness than that which is without. To obtain this we must needs keep to the retirement of our cell; for, as St. Bernard saith, the Spouse of our soul, Jesus Christ, is shy in His love, and does not like to visit His Bride when a crowd is present, but seeketh to be alone. It doth therefore behove the soul to drive out all other employments and thoughts, and to be eager and concerned only about welcoming her Spouse; for since He is single and one, He wishes to be sought after in simplicity and singleness of heart. Now a heart that is worried about earthly things is not simple and undivided, because it is shared between many human, vain, or unlawful cares.

But alas, brethren, in what a depth of misery hath this noble soul been sunk by sin! seeing that in its state of primeval innocence it had been created to gaze upon the beauty of its Creator, and dwell among spiritual things; and now, weighed down by the load of its own corruption, it can scarce fulfil its task, even though with pain and toil. And this is well known to such as attempt it. O my God, what is there left to bear the soul aloft and gather it unto Thy Oneness, and lead it back to its own singleness, and save it from sinking amid the stormy and wild billows of this sea of countless bewilderments and changeful fancies, and of this whirlpool of evil thoughts? Naught but the might of Thy grace can do this, and can still the waves of the wide and mighty deep that rage within us.

Thou, O Lord, dost lift up the needy one that lieth covered with the mire of vain thoughts; Thou raisest the poor man from the dunghill of disordered pleasures, placing him on high, and making him sit with princes, that is, among Thy Angels and Saints, that his converse be in heaven. But on those alone is this gift of Thy grace in very deed bestowed, who yearn after it with burning love and dispose themselves to receive it.

CHAPTER XLV.

How the contemplative soul is raised above the body and becomes one and undivided.

We ought not to think that the soul forsakes its body while engaged after its wont in contemplation: but it is at such times said to be where its heart and desire are; for, according to St. Augustine, the soul is more truly where it loves than where it quickens—meaning, in the body, to which it gives the breath of life. I say, therefore, that the lifting up of a devout soul out of the world, and above bodily things, unto itself, or even unto the fellowship of the angels and of its own Creator, than whom it can go no higher, is brought about by earnest and holy meditation, or by the flame of love. And this earnest and holy meditation and burning love have such strength that they make it forget and shun all other thoughts and fancies; as if it were in perfect repose and in a sweet sleep; and though those other workings do not cease altogether, yet they cannot hinder that deep meditation and burning love by reason of the strength of the latter.

Moreover, the soul must be wholly absorbed in this kind of meditation and love, and reckless for the time being of aught else, without more than glancing at other things, and must by no means tarry in them or stop long over them. And that this can easily be done in lesser matters we see from everyday experience. Aristotle shows this where he says that it sometimes happens that a man's thoughts are so taken up with his employment that, with his eyes open, he sees nothing of what passes before him; and often those who are in his company will do or say things without his knowledge; and so vehement is his abstraction, that he acts like a man in his sleep. Hence comes that common saying: He is dreaming of his love. Men of science sometimes undergo this kind of loss of sense while thinking over some subtle point. Painters and other artists are at times carried away by something of the sort.

There is a story about Archimedes, a skilful mathematician, that he was wont to plunge deep in thought about the contriving of military engines for the defence and storming of fortresses; and that when the city in which the philosopher lived was stormed, the besieging general gave orders that the philosopher should not be killed. It so happened that a soldier found him at his studies, and asked his name; but he, fixedly intent on his own thoughts, neither understood nor answered what was asked him, except by a sign of dislike at being disturbed, and so lost his life. Here we see how keen this man's application was, since he was neither aware of the taking of the city, nor heeded the enemy who took his life.

Another philosopher, Neades, when sitting at table, was often wont to forget his food; and his servant had to see that he ate, otherwise he might have died of want, concerning whom Valerius, who tells the tale, says that he lived for the sake of his soul, which was shut up in the body as in a useless outward prison.

These examples we have quoted to show that the soul can drive out from herself thriftless fancies and cares, and so be able to soar aloft to higher and more profitable things; and in this manner be led back to her native oneness and singleness, striving only to reach her Creator, who is her dwelling-place, her home and love, although it is harder and more toilsome to do this, as we see from the examples given, because we have to give ourselves to ghostly meditations, and to dwell on high and unwonted thoughts.

CHAPTER XLVI.

Concerning divers ways in which holy men have written on contemplation.

RICHARD of St. Victor wrote a book divided into five parts, wherein he discusses the subject of contemplation with depth and keenness, and distinguishes six kinds of contemplation. Two of these, he says, are lodged in the imagination, two in man's reason, and one in his intellect. Hence he goes on to say that the soul is as it were encircled by heavenly spheres, since she may fix her thoughts and meditate either upon those bodily objects which fall under the senses, or upon herself, or upon the angels and their state, or upon Almighty God Himself. And in the fifth book in particular Richard of St. Victor shows how contemplation may be formed or diversified in five different ways. Sometimes the soul is herself in a certain manner enlarged. Sometimes, on the other hand, the soul raises her understanding to a higher sphere. At others, a kind of wandering and forgetfulness takes hold of the understanding itself. And he shows how this comes to pass, with examples drawn from Holy Writ. For indeed this may happen, either out of intense wonder, or out of an inflamed love, or even for very excess of gladness and spiritual delight. But since I intend to go into no subtleties, but to talk plainly and briefly, I must say but little on these things; partly on account of their difficulty, which makes them a fit subject for learned divines alone; partly because they are too high for my own understanding. We shall, therefore, only set down here those grades of contemplation which can be easily grasped and understood even by the unlearned, and which holy men, who had made trial of them, have spoken of for our instruction in their works.

St. Augustine, in his book of *Confessions*, speaks of a certain way of meditating which he exercised once when in his mother's company, not long before her death, seated at a window that looked into her garden.

Moreover, St. Gregory, in his book of *Morals*, talks at great length on contemplation, and shows both its dangers and its advantages, but does not give us any special method for beginning it or abiding in it.

St. Jerome, writing to Eustochium, lays down for her, among other things, a certain method of praying; namely, that she should think on the hour of death, and what a reward she would then receive; and how the Virgin Mary, with her Son our Redeemer, and with the holy angels and virgins, would come forth to meet her, chanting the song that Mary, the sister of Moses, sang after the children of Israel had crossed the Red Sea: Let us sing to the Lord, for He is gloriously magnified, &c. And St. Jerome says of himself that, after grievous temptations and cruel beatings of his breast, and after he had with tears and weeping long besought God's help, it seemed to him as if he were present amid the throng of angels, owing to the excess of the peace and spiritual joy of his conscience which God sent him from heaven to crown his suffering and penance.

All learned men are agreed on this, that every man should meditate on the fearful pains of hell, the joys of heaven, his own sins, and the vanity of the world. But because we have said enough on these subjects, in the ways of enlightenment and union, we shall now seek out another kind of contemplation. St. Bernard, in almost all his sermons on the Canticle of Canticles, treats of one manner of prayer, to-wit, of the spiritual wedding of God with the soul, in which he is followed by another holy doctor, in a work on the same spiritual wedding, called the *Clock of Eternal Wisdom*. And this manner is, to say the truth, hard and subtle, and not without danger; above all, for any one who should try it at the beginning of his conversion. Gerson, as a reason for this, says, that these novices, unskilled in spiritual things, if they began to meditate on this spiritual union, would easily fall into thoughts of the flesh, and would lose the very cleanness of heart they were aiming at.

CHAPTER XLVII.

Concerning the method of contemplation practised by St. Bernard in the beginning of his conversion.

BLESSED St. Bernard tells us of himself that, in the beginnings of his conversion, he saw that he needed good and meritorious works; that he could not have them of himself; and therefore strove to possess himself of them out of the merits of Christ our Redeemer. And from that time he began to think most diligently on the whole course of the life of Christ, from His conception to His ascension, and to make up for himself a bundle of myrrh out of all His suffering and bitterness, and to keep it ever in his breast by never forgetting it, and by heartfelt sorrow. Whence I conclude that St. Bernard began his contemplation and the climbing of the mystic ladder from the life of our Lord, which he was ever meditating; just as we read of St. Cæcilia that she kept the Gospel ever hidden in her breast, that is to say, by frequent meditation on His life; and that, neither by day nor by night, did she leave off speaking with God and praying. And the seraphic doctor, Bonaventure, treats of this matter in his work entitled the *Pricks of Love*, and speaks in particular of the passion of our Lord and Saviour Jesus Christ; showing how all good things are to be found therein, and that it is the gate of this way of contemplation, and whosoever wishes to enter by another opening doth beguile himself.

And the aforesaid doctor confirms his saying with the words of our Lord, who saith, I am the way, the truth, and the life; the way in which we have to walk, the truth that sheds its light on our path, and the life that doth refresh, uphold, and reward us. We often meet with some who have no method in their meditation, except such as they have learned from some pious book, and are wont to read the life of a saint, or something of the sort, to kindle their devotion, according to what they meet with in their reading, and such as these always stand in need of books. Wherefore this method is not sufficient by itself, unless they must get accustomed to carry it out even without having books at hand. There are others who endeavour, while saying the Divine Office in church, to learn and exercise themselves in meditation; but I think this must be very hard; and on account of the fatigue of chanting, no one can in this way perfect himself in contemplation unless he has beforehand in retirement accustomed himself to it.

Now, that we may not go to too great a length, passing over many different ways which devout people have used in exercising and training themselves to contemplation, we shall add a few more words of our own on the subject.

CHAPTER XLVIII.

What contemplation is; its different kinds; and on what subjects a good monk ought to meditate.

As Richard of St. Victor says, contemplation is a fixed gaze of the soul on the things of God; or, according to the blessed St. Augustine, contemplation is a light let in upon the soul, drawing it with a wholesome sweetness towards the unseen things of God. And according to Master Hugh of St. Victor, contemplation is a clear sight of the understanding; and he to whom it hath been given beholds all things with clear undimmed eye, as it is written: The Spirit searcheth all things (that is, maketh us search them), yea, the deep things of God. Now before we divide contemplation into its several kinds, we should consider, as the above-mentioned Richard tells us, that the contemplative man may go forward on his journey by three different paths. First, by his own industry; and this, as he thinks, may be of the greatest help to him. And he ought to be most earnest, with the help of divine grace, to ascend higher. The second path is by the learning and skill of other men; and in this way he may study and carry out those teachings of the Saints which we have already quoted and others likewise. The third means is by some particular gift of God; when He chooses He raises a man to the knowledge of His own hidden things.

This being laid down, we must note well that

contemplation has three parts, or is of three kinds. The first is called enlargement of the mind, and is when the soul that contemplates is by human efforts enlarged and extended beyond the object of its meditation. The second is called the lifting up of the understanding; and is when the understanding of him who contemplates, lit up by the divine light, seizes on those things which mortal endeavours cannot reach. And though the mind is thinking on things above man's reason, yet the understanding is not lost nor doth it wander; and the soul sees that she remains within herself, though not as she was wont to do. The third kind is called ecstasy of the mind, where the soul gazes on heights too lofty for human strength to scale; and in this vision the contemplative soul goes out of herself and of her wonted habit of understanding, so as not to know where or how she is, nor whether she is in the body or out of the body, and this is called rapture; and we have mentioned it elsewhere when speaking of the way of union. And take heed that the first of these three kinds, that is to say, the one we have called enlargement of mind, is helped by our own skill, by constant exercise and great diligence. The second—to-wit, elevation of mind—is helped by light from heaven, which the soul gets above the measure of its own strength, yea, at times above its own understanding, and even above its nature; and after this manner were the prophets lifted up on high, so that they saw and told of things past and to come, and of the hidden depths of the hearts of men, yet without being rapt or estranged from their senses. The third kind, that is to say, when a man is bereft of his senses, otherwise called rapture, happens either through excess of devotion arising from a most inflamed love of God, or through excessive admiration of something that appears marvellous to man, or on account of the greatness of delight and joy which we feel for some favour received from God.

And we further remark that, as the aforesaid doctor teaches us, a man who feels himself cold at the beginning of his meditation ought to seek spiritual warmth by his own industry, that he may the more speedily mount up to God in prayer, taking up some point that is wont to kindle his devotion and fervour, like those we have laid down above while describing the three ways of purity, enlightenment, and union. But because, according to the seraphic and excellent doctor St. Bonaventure, whom we have quoted above, the gate for entering contemplation is the life and passion of our Lord Jesus Christ, and whoever thinks to enter elsewhere misleadeth himself, we shall now in few words speak of our Lord's life up to the time of His last Supper.

CHAPTER XLIX.

That the contemplative man must in three ways climb the ladder of contemplation, making use of the life and passion of the Lord.

THOU must know that Christ Jesus, God and man, and the mediator betwixt God and man, is the way by which thou must climb to the knowledge and love of the Godhead. For, as Augustine says in his *Confessions*, book vii., Christ took to Himself our flesh for this very reason, that since we were unable to know God according to the spirit, we might ascend to spiritual knowledge and love by means of the Word made flesh. Set forth for thyself, then, in Christ's life and death a threefold plan of contemplation by means of devout exercises.

Let thy first exercise be to cleave fast to Christ with a certain gentle and heartfelt love, though as yet after a manner an earthly one; live ever in Christ's company, ruminating on His life and death, and sweetening thy exercise by the thought of His presence. In this first step of love thou mayest in sundry ways vary thine exercise, as in Christ's own lifetime many followed Him, one drawn by one motive, another by another. For the Apostles at first followed Him for the sole delight of His company, for the cheerfulness of His conversation, and His sweet and winning ways. And do thou likewise and in this way begin to follow Christ, and abide in His company.

Think how lovely His presence was, how graceful and beautiful the face of Him who was the Beautiful One above the sons of men. Hearken to the music of His voice, the sweetness of His doctrines; see how He acted, and how kindly and gently He spoke. See what He was within, how mild and loving and kind. Hearken to the wisdom of His words, and look upon the loveliness of His face. In Christ's heart we behold the depth of wisdom, in His speech the sweetness of eloquence, all that is noble in His nature; and this it was that drew the Apostles to follow Him.

Others there were who followed Christ to be healed from their ills. Do thou likewise; and from time to time follow Him after this manner, and, lying humbly at His feet, adore Him and say, 'Lord, if Thou wilt, Thou canst cleanse me;' and 'Jesus, Son of David, have mercy on me.'

Others followed Him by reason of His miracles. And do thou in like manner admire His might in His wondrous works, for He changeth natures, exchangeth elements, putteth devils to flight, and healeth all kinds of sickness. In these things mayst thou see that He is God Almighty, who in the beginning gave to the things of this world their natural powers, but hath ever kept them under the control of His word, even for the working of things above nature; and after this fashion thou mayst vary thy prayer and thy affections in this first contemplation.

But observe, that although this is a very useful practice for a spiritual man, to-wit, that he should employ himself about the life and person of Jesus Christ our Lord, yet, as far as gaining His love is concerned, it is not enough, and of itself is not worth much. What did it avail Judas, Pilate, Herod, or the Pharisees that they saw Christ in His bodily presence and in His works, and yet would not follow Him? Therefore, thy aim in this first manner of contemplating the life and passion of the Lord, according to St. Bernard where he writes on the Canticle of Canticles, must be that, as the Apostles, being drawn after Him in this way, forsook riches, relations, and all they had; so thou likewise must abide fast in this stage until that sweetness hath filled thy heart, and weaned it from all love of the flesh and of bodily delights. In a word, a man, while in this degree, should open his heart to the love of Christ's manhood, so that all his tastes and affections be transferred to the sweetness thereof. This first step of contemplating Christ belongs properly to beginners.

The second way of contemplating the life and passion of our Lord is a little higher than the foregoing. In this second way a man does not limit himself to the manhood alone, but, as St. Bernard says, finds God in man, although he neither beholds God alone nor man alone, but Christ God and man, and loves and adores Christ both as God and as man. It would afford thee much fruit in dwelling on Christ's life and passion, if, whenever thou readest or rememberest Christ's having done or suffered this thing or that, thou wert able to form such an idea of Christ as might bring clearly before thy eyes the God-man, and might show thee One Person who is both God and man; so that whatever thou readest and hearest that Christ did, as in raising the dead to life, or in His other wondrous works, thou mayst understand that it was done by man. Again, when thou readest that Christ's hands were pierced and His feet nailed, believe firmly that God bore all this, and this by reason of the One Person in whom Godhood and manhood abode unmixed in their natures. Every true Christian believes this; but the more clearly a devout man conceives it, the deeper is his love for Christ's life, sufferings, and miracles. Think on Christ as man, and thy feeling will be one of sweetness, of love, and firm hope, seeing that He is most mild and gentle, noble and gracious, all-beautiful, sweet, and lovely; and hence it is easier for thee to think on Him, and thou hast a greater trust in drawing nigh to Him and adoring Him, as it is easier for us to conceive His human nature, whereof we have the stamp in ourselves, than His divine nature, by reason of its remoteness from ourselves. But if we set before our eyes Christ as God, His words and deeds, His miracles and conduct awaken rather our fear and terror, our dread and wonder. Thus if thou canst imagine and conceive both things at the same time, thou will gather thence great devotion, love, and hope, mingled with awe and reverence. And this second degree belongs to such as have made progress.

The third manner of contemplating the life of our Lord is to raise ourselves by means of His manhood to a spiritual love, gazing on Christ with our mental eyes as through a glass in a dark manner, and through His manhood reaching the knowledge and love of His Godhead. By means of this gaze and of this fast cleaving to God and transforming of oneself into Him, a man begins in a certain manner to be one spirit with God, to quit himself and look upon the very Face of Truth, and prepare himself for that divine union. Hence Augustine says in the seventh book of his *Confessions*, And now I have been bidden to withdraw within myself; and with Thy help I have entered into my inmost being, and because Thou didst become my Helper I have been able to do so; and with the eye of my soul, such as it is, I saw above me, and above my own mind, the never-waning Light of God; not this common light, which all flesh beholdeth, nor was it a light of the same kind, but of greater intensity, as if our light had grown in brightness and filled all space; not such, but something differing far from all this. He that knoweth truth hath seen it, and he that hath seen it hath known the Everlasting One; and it is love that hath known it. Eternal Truth, true Love, and beloved Eternity, Thou art my God; after Thee do I sigh day and night.

This, then, is the last round of the ladder of contemplation in this our pilgrimage before we stand face to face with God's own essence. But here let him whom Scripture calls *a beast*—let the unclean man take heed lest he touch this mountain or draw nigh to it; for if a beast shall touch the mount it shall be stoned. And this third degree of contemplating the life of Christ belongs to such as are already well trained and near perfection.

CHAPTER L.

On the types and prophecies of Scripture that concern the incarnation of Christ.

THE subject-matter of Holy Writ is all concerning the work of our redemption, and all it contains tends thereto. The old law foretold His coming; the new points to the work as clearly fulfilled. Reflect, therefore, within thyself how many signs in types, events, actions, prophecies, and apparitions by means of kings, prophets, and priests went before the work itself; and from these things understand aright its greatness, which will rouse thee to thankfulness. Remember the burning longings of the fathers that lived before it, and wonder at thy own lukewarmness and unthankfulness, and that of so many others.

CHAPTER LI.

On the annunciation of our Lord's coming.

THE fulness of time for the fulfilment of the aforesaid signs being now at hand, and God vouchsafing to grant the desire of the holy fathers, the Archangel Gabriel was sent to the Virgin to make known to her our Lord's incarnation. Behold her, and rejoice that the desire of the fathers and God's own words have been fulfilled. Dwell in thy soul upon the reverence shown by the angel to that peerless Virgin, and see with wonder how God stoops from on high; think on Mary's exaltation; reflect on her humility and her other virtues; dwell in thy heart on her joy and gladness and loving devotion; and forget not her kindness in visiting her kinswoman Elizabeth.

CHAPTER LII.

An abridgment of the life of Christ for the use of beginners in the school of contemplation.

IN order that thou mayst be able easily to carry about with thee the whole life of our Lord, meditate how God, having become a little child, lies wailing and weeping in a crib; see how poor He is; look upon His lowliness, and then see the angels coming down, and the shepherds keeping watch; note them as they talk among themselves, and note the wonder of Joseph and Mary; behold our Blessed Lady on her knees, adoring her child with overflowing gladness, and rejoicing in her heart. Look closely on the face and loveliness of this most beautiful babe, think on His inner greatness and wisdom, and reverently adore Him and kiss the crib.

Then call to mind how He was circumcised on the eighth day, and was called Jesus, and see how He, who was free from all sin, did not scorn to take on Himself the cure for the venom of sin, that so thou mayst cut off from thyself thy vain and disordered desires. They call Him Jesus that thou mayst understand that He is indeed a Saviour, not a Saviour of strangers, but of His own people. Weep with the tender child, now wounded and beginning to shed His blood for thee, and from His outward tears see how He inwardly grieves for wretched man.

Next see that brilliant star that leads the wise men to the infant Jesus, and their faith and devotedness, and follow them in, and offer to the Eternal Babe whatever thou hast—to-wit, thy soul and body.

Consider in what lowliness and want the wise men found Him, since, lover of poverty as He was, He would not have them ushered in with worldly pomp. And how the infant King led them out from the east under the guidance of a star, and how they worshipped Him as the true God. See here three witnesses to the birth of Christ—the star, the wise men, and the Jews, who bear witness concerning Christ and concerning the place of His birth.

How, forty days after His birth, His Mother offers Him up to God the Father in the Temple, and redeems Him as her firstborn with the ransom appointed for the poor. And gaze likewise on that procession, wherein such great and heavenly persons meet — the Virgin Mary with her child, our God and Saviour, Anne the prophetess, Simeon, and Joseph; and try, with all devotion, to go forth to meet them, and note what they say to each other, and their great devotion.

Reflect on the humility of Christ and of His Mother, who chose to keep the law, though not subject to its sway.

How Christ, while yet a babe, flying before the face of Herod, goes into exile. See His patience, and learn to suffer. Follow these pilgrims, listen to their converse, and learn from them to be poor and humble.

How from the twelfth to the thirtieth year of His age the King of Glory is hidden among the common people; for He neither preached nor wrought miracles, but, keeping a long silence, taught without speaking, and, though inactive, did many works, and by His silence taught thee that thou be in no hurry to speak, but that thou first learn to hold thy peace and be humble.

How in His thirtieth year He is baptised by John. See with what reverence John stands before Him, not daring to touch Him; and admire and imitate the wondrous humility of our God, who allows Himself, like one of the common people, to be baptised by John, and how He therein fulfilled all righteousness—to-wit, most perfect obedience. See how in visible form the whole most Blessed Trinity was here made manifest—the Father in the voice, the Son in the flesh, the Holy Ghost under the dove-like form; and how the Father sent His Son to preach, saying, Hear ye Him.

How after these changes He went forth into the desert, and fasted there for forty days and nights, and was tempted by the Evil One. Think on Christ's manner of living in the wilderness, what He did there, and on His devout prayer and contemplation. Ponder His humility, and how, according to St. Mark, he lived with wild beasts; with what wisdom He withstood Satan, and showed thee how to fight against him. Admire His dignity, seeing that angels ministered to Him. Consider how, coming down from the Mount, He chose for His followers a few fishermen and other poor men, and began through them to subdue the whole world with the sword of His word. Behold how He lives in common with His Apostles, and see His sweet converse with them. Consider His secret talk with them, at home and on their journeys, and how He is in the midst of them as if He were their servant, eating with them at the same table and out of the same dish, in nowise privileged among them.

How from thenceforth He was seen on the earth, and lived among men, walking among men, and everywhere sowing the word of God; how He wrought many wonders which God alone could work — gave sight to the blind, hearing to the deaf, cast out devils, cleansed lepers—in a word, healed all, and worked so many miracles as could scarce be written down. He forgave them that sought forgiveness for their sins. Wherever He preached He spoke in mystic parables, and in one of these He called Himself the Shepherd that had come to bring back the strayed sheep.

How a throng of people, at times four or five thousand or more, would follow Christ even into the desert. Follow thou likewise, and keep close to Jesus, that thou mayst hear His voice, and see the face of Christ and His Apostles, and witness their miracles.

How, when He chose to offer Himself in sacrifice, for which end He came, that He might show Himself the true Paschal Lamb, five days before the Passover, the Lord of heaven and earth, riding on the ass His disciples had brought, in great triumph, and amidst the joyful shouts of the Jewish children, crying out, Hosanna in the highest! entered the holy city of Jerusalem.

Mark well the marvellous humbleness of Christ our King, since He sitteth upon an ass covered with the garments of His disciples. Where are His following and His royal array? Behold Jesus, as He draweth nigh to Jerusalem, weeping over it, and grieving yet more from His gentle heart over thy sinful soul.

Thus have we briefly and in few words gone through the life of our Lord, that thou mayst the more easily bear it in mind, for with nothing else canst thou more healthfully and profitably feed thy soul; and for this motive thou oughtst every day, at some stated time, employ thy mind with the life and passion of Christ.

CHAPTER LIII.
An abridgment of the life of our Lord.

O Cross, life-giving tree,
Watered from the living Fountain,
Bedecked with the refulgent Flower,
Bringing forth sweetest Fruit,
Jesus our King, Son of the King of Heaven;
Jesus, born of God;
Jesus, foretold to the fathers;
Jesus, foreshadowed of old;
Jesus, begotten by the overshadowing of the Spirit;
Jesus, enriched with gifts;
Jesus, brought forth into this our light;
Jesus, the Sun that dawnest on the world;
Jesus, lowly Babe;
Jesus, fed with Mary's milk;
Jesus, tender Child;
Jesus, wounded with the knife;
Jesus, made subject to the law;

Jesus, borne in arms;
Jesus, shown to the kings;
Jesus, flying from Thy kingdom;
Jesus, filled with virtues;
Jesus, baptised;
Jesus, dwelling among wild beasts;
Jesus, tempted by the enemy;
Jesus, true in all Thy words;
Jesus, enkindled with zeal;
Jesus, wondrous in Thy signs;
Jesus, transfigured;
Jesus, merciful of heart;
Jesus, that sheddest tears;
Jesus, known as King of the world;
Jesus, riding on an ass;
Jesus, Servant of Thy servants;
Jesus, hallowed Bread;
Jesus, betrayed to the Jews;
Jesus, praying on the ground;
Jesus, surrounded by a crowd;
Jesus, in chains;
Jesus, led before the judges;
Jesus, denied three times;
Jesus, given up to Pilate;
Jesus, scourged;
Jesus, scoffed at;
Jesus, given up to death;
Jesus, bearing Thy Cross;
Jesus, consoling the weeping daughters of Sion;
Jesus, led along before the people;

Jesus, stripped of Thy garments;
Jesus, fastened with nails;
Jesus, lifted up on high;
Jesus, mocked by all;
Jesus, crying out with a loud voice;
Jesus, honoured with wondrous signs;
Jesus, condemned to death;
Jesus, cruelly pierced;
Jesus, reckoned with the vilest;
Jesus, coupled with thieves;
Jesus, who art given gall to drink;
Jesus, crying out in Thy agony;
Jesus, giving up the ghost;
Jesus, laid in the tomb;
Jesus, rising in glory;
Jesus, striking terror into the soldiery;
Jesus, ascending up to heaven;
Jesus, Prince most high;
Jesus, placed above the world;
Jesus, Giver of the Holy Ghost;
Jesus, given us for our Judge;
Jesus, Prince of Peace;
Jesus, beauteous Spouse;
Jesus, most just Judge;
Jesus, our wished-for King;
Jesus, Lord of all things;
Jesus, our Beginning;
Jesus, our desired End;
Jesus, cleanse us from our stains;
Jesus, cleanse our thoughts;
Jesus, perfect us in virtues;

Jesus, breathe upon us;
Jesus, defend us from our foes;
Jesus, be Thou our Guide;
Jesus, grant eternal life to men.
O Cross, most saving tree;
Watered from the living spring;
Bedecked with the most refulgent Flower,
And crowned with happiest fruit.
Mary, assumed into the highest heaven;
Mary, adorned with all kinds of loveliness;
Mary, refulgent in heaven;
Mary, dreadful to the enemy as a camp in battle array;
Mary, out of thy care for us, that art our advocate;
Mary, most pious Mother, have a care of thy children.

Remember us, we beseech thee, as thou standest before the sight of God, and crave all good things for us, who ever sing to thee, Hail Mary.

CHAPTER LIV.

On the Supper of the Lord, and how we ought prepare ourselves to receive the adorable Sacrament of the Eucharist.

AMONG all the memorials of our blessed Redeemer, the noblest is of a certainty the closing feast of that Last Supper wherein He gave Himself as food and drink to His disciples. Wherefore thou shouldst, from time to time, give thyself up to spiritual and devout meditation on this wondrous Sacrament.

Reflect, then, on His marvellous humility, and how the God of Majesty, with those His poor followers, and even with His betrayer Judas, ate at the same table and of the same dish. Think on the washing of feet; for as He wished to imprint yet more deeply on their hearts the example of His lowliness, prostrate before them, He humbly washed their feet; and learn His love and compassion from His gentle speech and the encouraging words wherewith He cheers them. But above all things thou shouldst, at all times, and most of all when thou dost approach Holy Communion, recall to mind the deep mystery that was herein instituted. For when He had eaten the typical Paschal Lamb with His disciples, after the Jewish custom, He consecrated His own most sacred Body, and gave them Himself, the true Lamb; giving them, moreover, the power of consecrating and distributing Himself to others.

O most bountiful magnificence! unheard-of goodness! love beyond compare! what can He refuse us, who hath given us Himself? What more could He have done? He hath done all He could for us; He hath given us all He had; He hath given His own kingdom; He hath given us Himself. Wherefore He said at this supper, As often as ye do these things, do them in memory of Me; that is, in memory of the things which I have done for you, while yet I bore your mortal flesh; for in your behalf have I been mocked, dishonoured, crucified. Concerning this commemoration blessed Jerome saith, He left us this last memorial of Himself as one would do who were going to a far-off land, and wished to leave a token to his beloved; so that, as often as he sees it, he may recall to mind his loving-kindness and friendship; and, if his love is true, he cannot look at it without tears and without longing after him who is afar; and thus our Saviour gave us this Sacrament to make us always mindful that He died for us. When, therefore, we partake of it at the hands of His priests, let us be mindful that it is the Body and Blood of Christ, and not be thankless for such great gifts. This Sacrament, of all sacraments the best, is healing medicine for the sick, support for the wayfarer, strength for the weak, the delight of the strong, wholesome food for the languishing, preserver of health, and it makes man gentle under chastisement, patient in toil, fervent in love, wise in counsel, quick at obedience, and devout in thanksgiving.

This most heavenly Sacrament acts as a guard on our senses, and saves us altogether from falling into mortal sin. If then, after receiving this great Sacrament, thou dost feel thyself less often harassed by the deadly movements of anger, envy, lust, and other vices, give thanks to the Body and Blood of the Lord, because the might of the Sacrament worketh in thee, and rejoice that thy festering wounds are beginning to heal.

Yet mark well that the fruit of the Sacrament is wont to be according to the dispositions and preparation of such as receive it. And Judas, though he received the Body of the Lord, yet had no share in the aforesaid gifts. And therefore, before partaking of this adorable Sacrament, we must carefully attend to prepare ourselves, that we may receive so great a Sacrament worthily; for he that receiveth unworthily the Body and Blood of the Lord eateth and drinketh judgment to himself. Now the things necessary for worthily partaking of this Sacrament are these three:

Bodily cleanliness,
Purity of spirit,
Actual devotion.

Bodily cleanliness is at all times beseeming, and sometimes absolutely required. But cleanness of spirit, to-wit, of conscience, above all from mortal sin, is necessary; and, therefore, see that thou hast contrition before approaching this Sacrament; and if thou canst, pour forth thy tears before the sight of the Lord, whereby thou mayest wash thyself from the sins thou hast committed in thought, word, and deed, and grieve for the good works thou hast neglected. To which purpose St. Gregory says, It is worth our while when we deal with these mysteries to offer ourselves up in God's sight in the sorrow of our hearts, that is to say, that we immolate not our bodies but our sins; for we who celebrate the mysteries of our Lord's passion must imitate what we perform.

After this, confess all the sins whereof thy con-. science doth accuse thee, and chiefly thy more notable faults, all which thou shouldst confess, and acknowledge thyself before the priest guilty of such also as thou canst not call to mind. And by these two means, to-wit, by contrition and confession, shalt thou wash away the uncleanness of thy conscience. Fear and love will beget in thee the third condition, namely, actual devotion : fear causes reverence, and love will inflame thy desire and affection. Approach, then, with fear and reverence : take heed how terrible is this table; and see that thou draw nigh to it with due care and great watchfulness; for in this priestly banquet Christ is Himself present, and He who celebrated the Last Supper with His Apostles doth hallow it. Nor is it man alone who changes bread and wine into the Body and Blood of Christ, but Christ Himself, who was crucified for us; the words, indeed, are uttered by the mouth of the priest, but the matter is consecrated by God's grace and His might.

How canst thou, then, fearlessly approach that table where Christ is present, and touch without dread the Son of God, on whom John the Baptist feared to lay his hand; whom Peter, Prince of the Apostles, out of fear, begged to depart from himself, saying : Go forth from me, O Lord, for I am a sinful man; whom the Dominations adore, and before whom the Powers tremble?

Consider next, that He whom thou receivest

is one day to be thy Judge. With fear, therefore, come to Him; for, shouldst thou receive Him unworthily and lightly, thou shalt feel His wrath after death, when thou must stand before His judgment-seat. And know, moreover, that wert thou for a million years to prepare thyself by constant prayer and earnest meditation, it would be naught towards worthily partaking of this Sacrament, even if thou hadst the merits of all the Saints; how much more so, seeing that thou goest to it so void of devotion, so lukewarm and unready.

Reflect, besides, after the fashion we have described, on thy own vileness, and thou wilt hold thyself unworthy, and by this means wilt gain the reverence thou needest. For this, of all things, availeth most for worthily partaking of this awful Sacrament, that thou shouldst hold thyself in thine own conceit as most unworthy of it.

Again, thou must ardently long to receive the Sacrament; for, as Augustine says, this bread requires the hunger of the inner man. And some in one way, others in another, are wont to form their desire of receiving the Blessed Sacrament: some are drawn by their longing to be one with Christ, so that they may embrace Him whom their soul loves; others are drawn to Him by the desire of being healed from their passions and vices, that they may bring Christ to themselves as a physician, by whom they may be cured from all the ills of the soul; others are brought hither by the consciousness of their own guilt, since this ineffable Sacrament has been instituted for the remission of sin; others, again, out of love and compassion towards their neighbour, that by means of this most acceptable sacrifice they may help the living and the dead.

And that the edge of thy desire may be sharpened and thou mayst burn with greater love, thou shouldst think over attentively the life of Christ.

Reflect, therefore, how He bore the sorrows of all who came to Him, and took on Himself all our woes; and how even the unclean woman that followed Him was healed; the sinner that kissed His feet was cleansed; and how the Cananean's prayer was granted, even when she followed Him with untimely cries. The lepers that came to Him were cured; those possessed by the devil, smitten with paralysis, and other outcasts of nature, by drawing nigh to Him and believing, received their cure; for a power went forth from Him and healed them all. Publicans and sinners were pardoned as they approached Him; nor did He disdain to sit at table with them. When, therefore, thou hast done what lies in thee, draw near with faith and firm hope, trusting in God's infinite goodness and pity. Moreover, before the communion of this most sweet Sacrament, thou must meditate most devoutly on the passion of our Lord, since we read that it was principally instituted in memory of His passion.

And thou wilt ask, perchance, in which of these

two affections thou oughtest to employ thyself most—in fear and reverence, or in love and desire; namely, whether it is best, as many do, to go to this delightful Sacrament with eager and burning desire, or rather, with others, to keep aloof from the frequent partaking of it by reason of the prickings of thy conscience, and out of fear bred in thee by the excellence of the Sacrament and thy own weakness.

Holy men answer by praising both these feelings, and leaving to each one's conscience to do what seems best for himself. For Zacheus hastened joyfully to welcome the Lord to his house; and yet the centurion, looking on his own lowliness, said, I am not worthy, Lord, that Thou shouldst enter under my roof; and both alike were pleasing to Christ.

However, one thing seems safe for everybody; namely, that neither should our reverence and awe shut out our desire and hope, nor should we out of hope and desire lose fear and respect; but, abiding between these two affections, trusting on the one hand and fearing on the other, we should go to receive it; for, as St. Gregory says, there is nothing safer for us than at all times to live in mingled hope and fear. However, absolutely speaking, love is a better sentiment than fear; but what is better in itself becomes in some cases and for many people worse and more dangerous.

CHAPTER LV.

That the devout contemplative man ought not by reason of harassing scruples keep aloof from partaking of this most health-giving Sacrament.

It sometimes happens that when a man wishes to approach this unspeakable mystery, at that very hour thoughts come to him concerning his own unworthiness; and, above all, it seems to him as if he had not duly confessed his sins. This, as Gerson writes, may well come from the devil's prompting, to hinder him from partaking of so great a good. Wherefore such a man ought to be aware that he can never be made worthy by his own effort, were he even to strive for a hundred years, unless God chooses to make him so out of His own good gift; and this gift He can as easily grant now as He could in the space of a hundred years.

He should, moreover, reflect that no man can tell, while in this life, with infallible and absolute certainty, whether he is in grace or not, unless it were specially revealed to him. And, indeed, whosoever should refuse to receive the Eucharist without this absolute certainty would be deceiving himself, and would seem to be possessed by a kind of pride.

There is another kind of human or moral certainty which we need and is enough for our purpose, and is when a man, upon recollecting himself and looking into his own conscience, has done all that his own prudence and other men's wholesome and wise counsel lead him to think he ought to do, and has given time enough to it, such as is usually set apart for that end; and if after this he is not aware of being in mortal sin, he may then securely and without danger go to holy communion; and even though, as is often the case, paltry doubts should occur to him, he must overcome them by slighting them, doing contrariwise to their promptings, and forcing himself to act after this fashion. I call it a frivolous doubt whenever a man deems such or such a thing to be no sin, but right and just, although he may have at the same time some trifling reasons and thoughts to the contrary, which breed a certain hesitation within him, but are not of such weight but that his former opinion—namely, that the thing is right and good—doth still remain by far the more certain of the two; so that, if he had to decide in another man's case, he would settle the question without wavering. But if he has no greater certainty for one side of the question than for the other, he ought to refrain from acting until, either by his own or somebody else's counsel, or by God's inspiration granted to him after humble prayer, he finds himself leaning to one side or the other. And if a man does not put himself on a sure footing after this manner, he will always think he has made a bad confession, and will never be at rest nor gain peace of conscience; and such a state cannot be called a good one.

All these things we have taken from the aforesaid doctor in his treatise on the several temptations of the devil.

CHAPTER LVI.
That our Lord's passion contains in itself all the perfection that man can reach in this life.

WE must know that our Redeemer fulfilled most perfectly in His passion all the works of perfection which He taught us in the Gospel; and thus we have in the cross the fulness of the Law and of all Holy Writ, and in His passion the summing up of all perfection, and in His death the fulfilment of His every word. For this reason the Apostle Paul says : I judged not myself to know anything among you but Christ Jesus, and Him crucified. And in very truth, brother, to know this is to know all that is wanted for salvation. For if we talk of voluntary poverty, who was ever poorer than Christ, who hung naked on the cross, whereon He had not where to rest His head? If we would fain speak of obedience and humility, who was ever more obedient or more lowly than the Son of God, who for us became obedient unto death, even unto the death of the cross? If of virginal purity, who was ever purer than He whose Mother is a virgin, whose Father knoweth not woman? If we speak of charity, who ever had a love like that of Christ, when He gave His life for His friends? Again, as for patience, His whole passion shows us this in its highest degree. And if we think of trampling on the world and flying from worldly things, who is farther from things of this world than Christ on the cross, lifted up on high above all earthly things? If of fasting, abstinence, and hunger, Christ in His passion tasted naught but vinegar and gall. If of chastening the body, whose body was ever more chastened than the body of Christ as He hung on the cross? If of fervent prayer, who ever prayed more fervently than Christ, who sweated drops of blood for the intensity of His fervour? If of almsgiving and works of mercy, who ever gave more generous alms than our Lord, who gave His Body for our food, and His Blood for our drink, an everlasting alms to us poor wretches? He visited the sick, He strengthened the failing hearts of His disciples, and healed so many ailments, and freed them that were in the bondage of limbo. He raised up the dead from their graves. And if we speak of loving our enemies, who ever more willingly forgave his débtors than He who not only forgave the thief his sins, but even promised him paradise.

And in like manner we may go on concerning other good works, all which, if we seek them, we shall find fulfilled in overflowing measure in Christ's passion; and which we also, if we choose to follow Christ perfectly, must fulfil, either in deed or at least in desire, and dwell in thought on them, and shape our works according to them, that what the Lord spoke in Exodus may be done: Behold, and do all things according to the pattern which was shown thee on the mount. And since our Redeemer is in many places of Scripture called the Mount, by reason of the loftiness of His exalted perfection, yet has He been so called, above all, when lifted up on the cross, on account of the exceeding merit of His most sacred passion. On this Mount, therefore, which is Christ, an example hath been set us that we may study it earnestly and diligently, and copy it in our own works. With inmost compassion, then, look on the example of our Lord's passion; receive it within thyself, and carry it out in thy life. And here it must be noted that, if we wished to describe all that Christ underwent for us in this world, His sufferings would be numberless; nor would the whole world contain the books that should be written thereon, as St. John says at the end of his Gospel. Since, then, we cannot put in writing all that our Saviour hath wrought for our welfare, let us at least endeavour with all our might to meditate leisurely and devoutly on His most glorious passion.

CHAPTER LVII.

Concerning six different ways of meditating on the passion of our Lord.

CONCERNING the passion of our Lord the devout man may exercise himself as follows. Firstly, he may meditate on it in order to imitate it; secondly, to move himself to compassion; thirdly, to stir himself up to admire it; fourthly, to rejoice over it; fifthly, to make good resolutions; sixthly, to seek his repose in it.

In the first place, I say that we ought to study the passion of Christ that we may imitate it; because the loftiest and most perfect model for Christian imitation, and the highest and most perfect way of life, is the following of Christ; and the best and holiest religion and religious perfection, the rule and model of all holiness and virtue, is to follow Christ in His death and passion. Let, therefore, our rule of life be the sufferings of Christ; and then the more like we are to Him, the more shall we be consoled; and the farther we go from this model and rule, the sadder shall we be. As far as lies in us, we must always seek to be trodden under foot by all, to undergo persecution, contempt, mockery, afflictions, and scourges, and to be despised of all men for God's service. Let us, with Christ, be stripped of all, and seek for nothing at all; rather let it be for us a most irksome suffering and pain to possess anything, and let us seek for pleasure in nothing; let us shun sweetness and delicacies in our food, and choose rather what is coarse and tasteless, desiring that all food should taste for us rather of gall than of honey, since Christ was given gall and vinegar to drink; and, in a word, let us think over all He underwent for us, and how He bore

Himself under His sufferings; and, as far as we can, let us strive to become like to Him.

Secondly, we may contemplate Christ's passion in order to awaken our sorrow and compassion for Him. Think on His words and sufferings, on the sadness of His heart, on our ingratitude, and the grief of His Mother. We should consider His scourging, the derision and insults He met with; and dwell on them in our hearts, and recall how great His shame and contempt were, His sorrow, and His affliction in mind and body, both by reason of His own sufferings and of His compassion for our sins. Let us next reflect with what bitterness our Lord, the sweetness of angels, was filled. O, how much was He tortured, not only by the pain inflicted on Him, but by our own thanklessness and the sorrow of His Mother, as she stood by, of her whom He loved so dearly, and yet had to behold overwhelmed with anguish and grief for His sufferings. The Son and Mother were crucified together, by reason of their mutual love; and their affliction was intense on account of their mutual compassion, and because each felt that the other partook in His or her agony. The Mother knew that her Son suffered for her as well as for all those whom He was to redeem; the Son knew too well that the sword of sorrow was piercing through and through His Mother's soul. Turn these things over in thy soul, filling it with these wrongs and sufferings, seeing that thy Lord, the Spouse of thy soul, suffers such pains for thee. For if thou wert indeed united with Him by love, thou wouldst grieve with Him. If thou feelest not the sorrow of Christ, who is thy Head, how art thou one with Him? And as we must have greater compassion on the head than on the other members, so should we have incomparably more pity on Christ than on any friend how beloved soever, and even than on thyself, if thou hadst to undergo all that we have described.

Therefore, most beloved brother, let us drink our fill of the myrrh and vinegar which they gave Him to drink; and let us smart under His wounds alone ; and let His shame, His wounds, and scourges pierce our hearts; and let there be nothing in us that is not filled with sorrow and compassion and touched to the quick.

In the third place, we should contemplate the passion of our Lord for the purpose of admiring it. For if we remember who suffers, from whom and for whom and what things He suffers, we cannot but be filled with wonder.

Who is He that suffers? The true Son of God, almighty, wise, and good; in a word, whatever excellence thou canst give Him is as nothing to what He is. All things that are, be they ever so good and great, compared with thy Beloved One, are but a little spark of fire.

What sufferings did He not undergo? Wanderings, banishment, hunger and thirst, heat and cold, persecutions and snares. He was defiled with spittle, and mocked, bound, scourged, scoffed at, tortured, and pierced with wounds. They spat upon the Lord of Glory, they condemned the Righteous One; the Judge was judged; He who had done no wrong was wrongfully accused, the Innocent One defamed, God blasphemed, the Anointed One trampled under foot; our Life dies, the sun is darkened, the moon blackened, the stars of heaven scattered. These things He bears as patiently as a lamb—He that with a nod could hurl the whole world into the pit of hell.

For whom did He suffer? For wicked slaves and guilty foes, for hellish men, for sons and followers of Satan, for scoffers at His majesty, and wretches thankless to God's goodness. See how One so good and great suffers all this for men so vile.

At whose hands does He suffer? At the hands of His beloved and chosen ones, towards whom He had shown every kindness; the Most High at the hands of the very lowest; the Most Wise from fools; the Holiest from the most guilty; the Brightness of God from the foulest and most hideous. On all these points let us raise our minds to wonder at the divine goodness and loving-kindness.

Fourthly, we should contemplate the passion of our Lord in order to rejoice in it. The causes of our joy should be

    1. The redemption of mankind;
    2. The filling up of the angels' ranks;
    3. The clemency of God.

Assuredly we have great reason to rejoice over the redemption of mankind wrought through Christ's passion. Who will not rejoice and be glad, seeing that by this blessed passion he is freed from everlasting damnation, from the shame of his guilt, and the power of the devil? And who would not leap for joy, seeing himself so beloved of God, that for his sake He took upon Himself such lowliness and suffering? Nor do I say that we should be glad that Christ was humbled, and that He suffered, but in the fruit thereof, and in the manifestation of God's love.

What royal prince would not exult if, while living in a foreign kingdom, he saw that the king or emperor loved him so dearly as to be ready to die for his sake? And how much more ought we, unhappy men, guilty and useless slaves, to be glad and cheerful when we see the King of kings and Lord of rulers, our own Maker, love us so unboundedly that He offered Himself up as a victim to God the Father by a shameful and hateful death for our sakes? We should rejoice with boundless joy, since He loves us more than we do ourselves.

Moreover, it beseems us to rejoice and be glad over the passion of Christ, because the ruin that was caused among the angels' host has thereby been built up. Our gladness should be intense whilst we see that by Christ's death that noble army has filled up its ranks from among ourselves, that it has become one fold and one Shepherd, and that we are one with them.

And herein both the court of heaven and the Church militant have reason for rejoicing. O passion of our Lord, worthy of all love and reverence, that bringest together what was severed, and bindest fast what had been split asunder, and with the chain of perfect love and endless gladness encirclest them for ever!

Above all, we ought to rejoice and exult at beholding in all these things the depths of the clemency of our Lord and Saviour. This, in my opinion, is the highest glory of the just, both men and angels, namely, that they can gaze upon the inmost depths of God's mercy and lovingkindness, and view the immensity of His goodness. And this is the chiefest delight of every kind of contemplation. And where doth the outpouring of the God-like goodness and merciful kindness of our most sweet and loving Father and Lord Jesus Christ shine more brightly than in His passion, in which He chose to bear such and so many pains, such shameful and grievous things, to set free and glorify His own enemy, whose folly had made him guilty of everlasting death? Let man enter into this joy, and revel in the boundlessness of God's goodness. Let man draw nigh to this exalted Heart, and exalt within his own heart the exceeding and unspeakable mercy of Jesus Christ our crucified Redeemer.

Fifthly, we should dwell on the passion of

Christ in order to soften our own hearts and transform them perfectly after His model, which happens when a man doth not only imitate, compassionate, admire, and rejoice in Jesus Christ our Redeemer, but is wholly turned to Him, so that thenceforth Christ crucified doth everywhere and at all times appear to stand before him. After this a man finds himself, as it were, softened and melted down, and he goes out of himself, and is lifted up above all things, and even above himself, and sundered from all things else, and cleaves fast to his crucified Lord; so that he sees and hears naught within himself but Christ crucified, despised, dishonoured, and suffering.

In the sixth place, we must contemplate the passion of Christ for the sake of that quiet and internal sweetness which takes place when a man, being, as we have said, softened and melted, never ceases to revolve in his heart the passion of the Lord, and, entering as best he can into his treasure, faints away within himself by reason of the fire of his devotion, and rests on Christ crucified; and the more closely he cleaves to Him, the more does he faint and pine away within himself for love and devotion; and the more he ceases to lean on himself, the faster he cleaves to his Beloved who died for him, and the more peacefully he reposes in Him. And thus this devotion and this union of love help one another until the Spouse is wholly drawn into the fiery furnace of love for the sufferings of her Beloved, and falls asleep in the love of her Spouse, who saith, I adjure you, daughters of Jerusalem, that you stir not up nor awake my beloved till she please.

Thus, therefore, shalt thou dwell upon the Lord's passion, and these fruits shalt thou gather from it: the fruit of imitation, to cleanse and enkindle thy soul; compassion, to unite thyself with Him in love; admiration, towards the lifting up of thy soul; joy and exultation, for the enlargement of thy heart; resolution, unto a perfect strengthening of the same; and repose, as needed for the safe-keeping of thy devotion. But to the end that thou mayest more easily meditate on the passion, we shall here divide it in several parts, according as it is told in the Gospel.

CHAPTER LVIII.

On the passion of our Lord, divided into six portions; and, in the first place, on a brief system of meditating it.

Thou must know that, in order to meditate more profitably and with greater ease the passion of Christ, thou shouldst attend to three things; to-wit, the fact, the manner, the cause. And these three should always be held in view in this meditation.

By the fact I mean, for example, His being seized upon, bound, buffeted, struck, scourged, &c., all which things thou must devoutly contemplate.

The manner is, for example, His behaviour; the lowliness He showed, above all, when He was brought before His judges, when He stood with bowed head and downcast eyes; how likewise He spoke to them humbly, mildly, and with sweet and gentle voice. And couldst thou hear any man speak so sweetly, it would gladden thee with delight, for His voice was as sweet as His face was beautiful.

Thou must likewise contemplate the demeanour of His inner man; for, indeed, He practised the most heartfelt humility, neither envying nor hating Pilate and the Jews, but pitying them from His inmost soul.

As for the cause, thou must remember that thou hast thyself been the cause of His passion; for He suffered in order to

Redeem thee,
Enlighten thee,
Justify thee,
Glorify thee.

And take His goodness so to heart as if Christ had suffered for thee alone. And thus, whilst thou readest and thinkest, listen to Christ saying to thee, I did this for thee, that thou mightst follow in my footsteps, and become humble and patient, and take up thy cross, and follow me.

Therefore, as to the fact, meditate on His sufferings; as to the manner, behold His humility; as to the cause, the fire of His love. And not only must thou admire these virtues in Christ, but follow them in thy works, for this it is that thy Beloved above all things desireth.

And be careful, in contemplating the passion of Christ, never to look on Him as God alone, nor as Man alone, but as one person who is true God and true Man.

First Part of our Lord's Passion.

After the solemn and regal supper was over, Christ, God and Man, arose, and, with His disciples, went forth to die. Listen to the sweet words in which He speaks to them concerning His passion, teaching and warning them in those words: When the Shepherd hath been smitten the sheep of the flock shall be scattered. And how He said to Peter, Before cock-crowing thrice shalt thou deny me.

Taking these things in their natural sense, look upon the person of Christ, God and Man, with reverence and sweetness of devotion; and give a listening and reverent ear to His words, and see what He does, with feelings of wonder and love. Next, for thine own benefit and profit, and to instruct thee in thy duty, think how sweetly He uttered those words, and with what a kind manner and speech He taught His disciples; and yet, at the same time, how full He was of sadness and grief, seeing His death so near at hand.

Then, again, reflect how He is now beginning to go forth to redeem thee, and be sacrificed for thee, and move thyself to tears and devotion.

These and other such like things must thou turn over in thy heart, attending to the three points we have already laid down—namely, the fact, the manner, the cause—for we cannot mention them over again at each part of the passion.

After this He took with Him His three chief disciples, and left the rest to themselves, and said to the former, My soul is sorrowful even unto death. And leaving them, He went higher up the mountain, to pray by Himself; and after praying there three times, so great was His dread at His fast-approaching passion, that the sweat became as drops of blood, trickling down upon the earth; and this we have never read of any other, however greatly afflicted. Consider how the angel appeared to Him and consoled Him. And forthwith rising from prayer, although still full of dread of His sufferings, yet He went out to meet His enemies, who fell to the ground like dead men at the first word He spoke. Then Judas kissed Him, and He bore the kiss in all patience. Behold how cruelly the Jews seized, bound, and dragged Him along; and all His disciples forsook Him and fled. See how they led Him first to the house of Annas, where by a most vile servant He was struck in His beautiful face. And now reflect, as we said above, who He is that is thus shamefully and scornfully treated; and bowing down, and subjecting thy reason to Him, believe that He is truly the Son of God, the Saviour of men, the just Judge of all

Second Part of Christ's Passion.

In this second part consider how Christ is savagely and cruelly dragged from the house of Annas to that of Caiphas; where the scribes, priests, and Pharisees, swelling with envy, were awaiting Him. And how Caiphas adjured Him, and when He spoke but the truth, He was cruelly beaten, as if He had falsely taken on Himself the name of God. How they covered His face, and struck, and spat upon, and mocked Him, seeking false witnesses against Him because true ones could nowhere be found. How He was denied by Peter, who had deemed himself stronger than the rest, yet when the Lord looked upon him, mindful of his guilt, he wept bitterly. Think how, at daybreak, he was led through the streets to the judge, that He might undergo the doom of death. And Judas, seeing Him led to death, grieved so bitterly that he had betrayed his most sweet Master, that he hanged himself for the very bitterness of sorrow; but first brought back the thirty pieces of silver, with which a field was bought, as it had been foretold by Jeremias. And after this, with many shouts and false accusations, the whole people being gathered together, He was accused before them. Sent away, and led through the streets, He is laughed at as a fool. Here diligently consider what manner of man He is who suffers, and become like to Him, that thou mayst feel for this most innocent, mild, noble, and loving One.

Third Part of our Lord's Passion.

In this third part see how Jesus stands most humbly before the President Pilate, and how a great tumult and shouting is raised, the Jews crying out, Crucify, crucify Him. We have a law, and by our law He must die. Then Pilate had Christ most cruelly scourged, and as if He had falsely styled Himself king, He is held up to scorn in mock royal robes, and a cloak is put about Him, and His head crowned with thorns, and beaten with a reed, and as before a king, so do they kneel before Him in mock adoration.

Now, brother, see closely how Christ bore Himself. How Pilate, seated on his judgment-seat as if he were the Lord and judge of Christ our Lord, said to Him, Knowest thou not that I have power to set Thee free, and power to crucify Thee? Look on and see the demeanour of the Jews; think on the cause wherefore Christ bore all these things, forsooth, that He might pay thy debt.

Over and over again the Jews renew their shouts. If thou settest this man free thou art no friend to Cæsar. Crucify Him, &c. Then at last Pilate, overcome with fear of Cæsar, gave Christ into their hands to be crucified. And as He went out to be crucified, He bore with Him His own gibbet, in company with thieves. With great sorrow Hé said to the women that followed Him, Weep not for me, but for yourselves and your children. And yet think what a great and glorious King of heaven and earth and Lord of hosts is He who is thus laughed to scorn and reviled under the figure of a king; and go forth to meet Him, and see how great He is, in might, in beauty, in blessedness, and eternity. Behold then with wonder how that majesty is brought to nothing, that loveliness is obscured, that blessedness is afflicted, and He who is the Everlasting One dies.

Fourth Part.

In this fourth part contemplate how, when our Lord had been led to Mount Calvary, the executioners begin to dispose themselves in order to crucify Him, stripping Him of His clothes, and so forth. Reflect most diligently on the manner of His crucifixion. First, they rear the cross, and nail His hands and feet to it, most cruelly sundering His joints. Behold, moreover, His unspeakable patience and demeanour.

Again, thou mayst meditate on this crucifixion after another fashion, seeing how they lay the cross on the ground, and whilst our Lord Himself cheerfully stretches forth His hands and feet, how they nail them to the cross, and then raise it aloft.

See Him next shedding tears on the cross, and praying for His crucifiers, and how He is blasphemed by the Pharisees as they passed by, and by the wicked thief. And how there was written above the cross a true inscription: Jesus of Nazareth, King of the Jews. Look upon the Blessed

Virgin, His glorious Mother, standing sorrowfully beneath the cross, the depth of whose sorrow equalled the fervour of her love.

Consider how He commends His Mother to John; and how after this darkness overspread the whole world. And how He then cried out with a loud voice, saying, My God, my God, why hast Thou forsaken me? By which words He showed how great His sufferings were, and that His manhood was in a certain manner forsaken by His Godhead. And this happened because the superior powers of His soul did not come to the help of the inferior powers wherein He was afflicted. And, again, behold attentively how in His thirst they gave Him vinegar mixed with gall to drink. And how at last, when all had been fulfilled, crying out with a loud voice, He gave up the ghost; showing in this that as long as He willed it He retained His strength, and that none could have taken away His life had He not chosen to lay it down of Himself. Whence the centurion in particular, moved by hearing this voice, said, Indeed this man was the Son of God.

Now here consider in what manner He suffered. As a true Lamb; most generously towards His brethren; most cruelly towards Himself; in all obedience to His Father; most wisely with regard to the enemy.

Strive, then, to gain a habit of imitating Christ, so that from the very habit of suffering for Him thou mayst acquire the practice of holiness, of kindliness and austerity, of humility and patience, and of all other virtues. And let this suffice for the fourth part.

Fifth Part.

Consider in this stage how, after Christ had died on the cross, Longinus came with other soldiers, and they broke the legs of the thieves; and when they came to Christ, and found Him already dead, they did not break His legs, that so the prophecy might be fulfilled which says: You shall not break a bone of Him. But Longinus with his spear opened His side, whence blood and water came forth, in which He consecrated the Sacraments of the Church. The veil of the temple was rent in twain, from the top even to the bottom; the sun was darkened, and darkness settled upon the whole earth; the ground trembled, the rocks were split, the graves opened, so that on the day of Resurrection the bodies of the saints that rested there might rise with the Lord. Think deeply how much the Lord hath suffered for thee, and cling fast to the cross out of a desire for suffering; so that, as thy Lord underwent scorn and derision and torments, thou mayst, in imitation of His passion, embrace all sufferings, wrongs, insults, mockeries, and tortures. And I think this will be enough for the fifth part.

Sixth Part.

We ought to remember that Christ's passion doth not only feed the memory by devout meditation, nor doth it only enkindle the will with devotion; but it doth likewise enlighten the understanding to a knowledge of truth. For before the passion of Christ seven things were hidden from the knowledge of mankind, which were then laid open: as in the Apocalypse we read of the seven seals. These seven hidden things are,

The wonders of God.
The hidden things of the rational spirit.
The world of sense.
The joys of heaven.
The terrors of hell.
The excellence of virtue.
The shamefulness of sin.

The first seal, the wonders of God, was opened in Christ's passion, because in His passion He showed Himself the Most Wise, since He kept His counsel hidden from the devil, using His wisdom and overwhelming the evil one by His might. Again, He showed Himself the Holy One, seeking therein the price of our ransom ; and displayed His mercy when He gave up His own Son for our sakes.

The second seal concerned rational spirits, and this seal was likewise broken at Christ's passion; since it was then made known how full of love of men the angels are, who suffered Christ their God to be crucified; and of what honour men are worthy, who forced Christ to suffer for their love; and how cruel are the devils, who caused their God to die such a death.

The third seal relates to the visible world, and

when it was opened at Christ's passion it was shown to be a place of darkness, where blindness reigns, since it knew not the true Light. Barrenness likewise ruleth over it, since it hath not the fruit of Christ. And iniquity reigns in it, for it doomed the Innocent One to death.

The fourth seal is paradise, which was proved by the cross to be a place filled with glory, gladness, and plenty; since Christ, that we might regain it, became lowly, poor, and wretched.

The fifth seal—to-wit, hell—was shown by the death of Christ to be a place filled with all kinds of pain and wretchedness and want; for if Christ suffered these three by destroying sin, much more must the damned undergo them, as a just punishment for their crimes.

The sixth seal is the beauty and worth of holiness, of which the cross of Christ showed the great price, the loveliness, and the fruitfulness. Of great price indeed, since Christ chose rather to lose His life than depart from it. Its beauty shines forth in the insults He suffered. Its fruitfulness is seen in this, that one perfect act of virtue robbed hell, opened heaven, and built up anew what had fallen.

The seventh seal was also opened; inasmuch as the hatefulness and guilt of sin was made known, for the forgiveness of which we needed so dear a price, so great a remedy, so sharp a cure.

Enough concerning the sixth part of Christ's passion.

CHAPTER LIX.

That the contemplative man ought in all his meditations to bear in mind the sufferings of Christ, lest the fire of his devotion be quenched.

SINCE the fervour of devotion is begotten and kept alive within us by the constant memory of our Lord's passion, as the seraphic Doctor St. Bonaventure says in his book on the Perfection of Life, so the contemplative man ought ever to strive to keep before the eyes of his heart Christ dying on the cross, to keep his devotion enkindled and not let its fire go out. For this reason the Lord said, in the Book of Exodus, The fire upon my altar shall never be quenched, and the priest shall daily feed it with wood. The altar of God is thy heart, on which the fire of ardent devotion must always be burning; and to feed and increase it thou must use the wood of the cross and the never-ceasing remembrance of our Lord's passion. And this it is that the Prophet Isaiah saith, Ye shall draw waters in joy out of the Saviour's fountains; that is to say, whosoever thirsts after the waters of grace, the waters of devotion, the waters of tears, let him drink at the Saviour's fountains, at the wounds of Christ. Draw nigh, therefore, with the feet of thine affections to Christ pierced with wounds, to Christ crowned with thorns, to Christ nailed to the wood; and do not only, with Thomas the Apostle, put thy hand into His side, but enter wholly therein, even to His heart; and when thou hast been there transformed into thy crucified love, and fastened with the nails of divine love, transfixed with the lance of heartfelt love, and wounded with inmost compassion, seek after nothing, and desire naught else, and look for consolation in nothing but in dying with Christ on the cross; so that thou mayst cry out with blessed St. Paul, I am nailed to the cross with Christ; I live now, not I, but Christ liveth in me. Thus, then, shouldst thou dwell on Christ's passion, and reflect how it was shameful, bitter, universal, and protracted.

First of all, consider the shamefulness of the passion of Christ, the Spouse of thy soul, seeing that He was crucified as if He had been a thief or robber; for no criminals used by law to be punished with this kind of death except the very worst and guiltiest, as robbers and murderers. Consider the second and yet greater ignominy of Christ; that He was crucified in a most shameful and loathsome place, to-wit, on the hill of Calvary, whereon were heaped the carcases and bones of many criminals, for whose execution that hill had been appointed, and there they used to be hanged and beheaded. And then remember, what was no less shameful, that He was placed as a thief among thieves; indeed was crucified between thieves as their prince. Hence Isaiah said, And He was reputed with the wicked. Besides, see how, to increase His shame, He was lifted up on high and hanged between heaven and earth, as if He were unworthy either to live or to die on earth.

O most unworthy and wrongful shame! that the whole world should deny the Lord of the world, and that naught should be held in greater scorn by the world than its Lord.

So that the death of the Son of God was a most shameful one, by reason of its kind, since He died on a cross; of the fellowship of the guilty men who died with Him; and for the vileness of the loathsome hill of Calvary whereon He died. O good Jesus and most kindly Saviour, Thou art put to shame, not once only, but oftentimes; and the oftener a man is put to shame, the more wretched is he held by the world. O my Lord, Thou art seized and bound in the garden. In the house of Annas Thou art struck in the face. In the house of Caiphas they spit upon Thee. In the court of Herod Thou art derided. Bearing Thy cross on Thy blessed shoulders, Thou art crucified on Calvary. Alas! the Redeemer of bondsmen, the glory of angels, the life of men is slain. O most unhappy Jews, how well have ye fulfilled your promise, Let us doom Him to a most shameful death. St. Bernard said, He annihilated Himself, taking the form of a slave that He might be subject; He who was the Son becomes the slave. Nor did He only take upon Himself the form of a slave that He might obey, but of a wicked slave that He might be chastised and pay the penalty of which He was innocent. Not only did He become the servant of the servants of God, but even the servant of the servants of the devil. Nor was this enough for Him; but He chose a death of all deaths the most shameful. For He humbled Himself, and became obedient even unto a death filled with all kinds of contempt.

In the second place, reflect devoutly how cruel our Lord's passion was; for He would not allow His body while on the cross any of those things which are wont to be a relief in suffering. Nor had His sacred and venerable head whereon to rest when He gave up the ghost on the cross.

Again, consider the bitterness of Christ's passion, since the more delicate a man is the sharper his pain. As there never was a body so delicate as the body of Christ—for His virginal flesh was formed by the Holy Ghost and born of the Virgin Mary—so His suffering was more bitter than any other suffering. For if Christ, at the mere thought of death, was so tortured in His soul by reason of the delicacy of His body that the sweat poured down in a blood-stained stream from His most sacred body upon the earth, how much more cruelly must His anguish have weighed Him down when He tasted the bitterness of His painful death! Whereupon St. Bernard says, O Lord Jesus, Thy bloody sweat showed us plainly the anguish of Thy body, seeing that while Thou didst pray it trickled down upon the earth from Thy most sacred flesh. O most holy Son of God, what hadst Thou done to be thus ill-used? O most loving youth, what crime hast Thou wrought to be thus condemned? Behold, I am the cause of Thy suffering; I am the wound that slew Thee.

Again, and more carefully, brother, examine how bitter Christ's death was. The more a man is guiltless, the harder it is to bear punishment; and if Christ had suffered for His own sins it would have been easier to bear; but He never sinned, nor was guile found in His mouth. Pilate bore witness to this, saying, I find no cause of death in Him. He is the brightness of everlasting Light, the spotless mirror, the image of God's majesty and goodness, as it is written in the Book of Wisdom. And here still more fully consider how painful was the death of thy Spouse Jesus Christ; the more universal is our suffering, the more grievous it is; now thy Spouse Christ suffered in all the members of His body, so that none of His members was free from pain, and no place on Him, however small, was not full of bitterness, so that from the sole of His foot to the crown of His head there was no place whole in Him. Hence He cried out in the excess of His agony, O all you that pass by the way, look on and behold my sorrow. Truly, O Lord Jesus Christ, never hath there been sorrow like to Thy sorrow; so great was the flood of Thy agony that Thy whole body was sprinkled over with Thy blood. O good Jesus, O most sweet Lord, not in drops but in floods did Thy blood so gush forth from the five parts of Thy body—from Thy hands at the crucifixion, from Thy head at the crowning with thorns, from Thy whole body at the scourging, from Thy heart when Thy side was pierced—that it was no wonder that not a drop of blood was left in Thee. Tell me, I beseech Thee, my most beloved Lord, since one drop of Thy blood was enough for the ransom of the whole world, why didst Thou allow so much blood to be poured out from Thy body? I know, Lord, I know well, that for this alone Thou hast willed it that Thou mightst show how deeply Thou lovest me. What, then, shall I give to the Lord for all that He hath given to me? Assuredly, O Lord, as long as I live I shall be mindful of the toil which Thou hast undergone in preaching, of Thy weary journeys, of Thy watching in prayer, of Thy merciful tears, of Thy pains and insults, how Thou wert defiled with spittle and beaten, of Thy mockeries, of Thy nails and wounds; otherwise the blood that has been poured out upon the earth will be sought for at my hands. Who will give water to my head, and a fountain of tears to my eyes, that I may bewail day and night the death of my Lord Jesus Christ, which He met, not for His own, but for my sins? For He was wounded for our iniquities and bruised for our crimes, as the Prophet Isaiah says.

Again, consider and reflect carefully how long the sufferings of Christ were drawn out; for from the day of His birth to that of His death He was always in suffering and sorrow, as He Himself says by the prophet's mouth: I am poor, and in labour from my youth. And elsewhere He says: I was scourged all day long; that is to say, throughout the whole of my life. And, moreover, the passion of Christ itself was long, nor were His pains soon over; but His death was deferred, and thus His agony was prolonged, and His affliction made more cruel.

From all we have said thou mayst infer how shameful, painful, vile, and prolonged were the death and passion of thy beloved Jesus. And all this He bore, that He might inflame thee with His love; that for all these reasons thou mightst love Him with all thy heart, with all thy soul, with all thy mind. For what is there more loving than that the Lord should take on Himself the form of a slave in order to redeem the slave? What could better lead man on to salvation than 'this example of enduring death for justice' sake and in obedience to God? What could better stir man up to love God than this loving-kindness, in that the Son of God Most High, for our sakes, and without any good desert and with many evil deserts on our side, laid down His life for us? This is a work of such love that nothing more merciful, nothing more loving could be imagined. The more grievous and lowly the things He underwent for us, the greater His love appears. For God, who did not spare His own Son, but delivered Him up for us all, has He not likewise given us all things with Him? Whence we are called upon to love Him, and from loving to imitate Him. Woe, then, to such as are ungrateful to so many loving-kindnesses, in whose souls the death of Christ hath no effect. Whence St. Bernard says: See the head of Christ bowed down to salute thee, His hands pierced to bestow favours on thee, His side opened for thy love, His whole body stretched out that He might give Himself all to thee.

Woe again to those who, crucifying Christ a second time by their sins, add to the pain of His wounds. And woe for the third time to those whose hearts cannot be softened to tears, nor provoked to love, and whom the sprinkling of so much blood, the effusion of so rich a price, the greatness of such mercy, cannot stir up to a life of holiness. These enemies of the cross of Christ do indeed crucify the Son of God, as He now sitteth at the right hand of the Father, more than they did who hanged Him on the cross. Speaking to these and concerning these, our Lord complains by the mouth of St. Bernard, saying: O man, see what I suffer for thee; see if there is any pain like mine; to thee I cry out, I who am dying for thee, Behold the sorrows that surround me, the nails that pierce me, and how I am so tormented within and without, yet my most bitter complaint is that I find thee ungrateful. Yet beware that thou remain no longer ungrateful for so great a benefit, nor careless for so great a ransom paid for thee, but set Christ crucified as a seal upon thy heart; and as a seal stamps its figure in soft wax, so stamp thou His upon thy heart, and say with the prophet: My heart hath become as melted wax. Place Him likewise as a seal upon thy arm, so that thou mayst never cease from working and toiling for the name of Jesus; but when thou hast done all, begin afresh as if thou hadst done nothing. And should ever sadness or sorrow or weariness or bitterness befall thee, or should any good work seem hard to thee, run at once to Jesus hanging on the cross; look on His thorny crown, His iron nails, the lance of His side. There contemplate the wounds of Christ—the wounds of His feet and hands, the wounds of His heart, the wound of His side—and call to mind who He is that suffers thus, that hath borne such things for thee, that hath thus loved thee. Hence the holy and seraphic Doctor Bonaventure says, writing to his sister: Believe me that at that sight forthwith thou wilt find sadness changed into joy, what was heavy will become light, what was irksome pleasant, what was harsh sweet and easy; so that thou wilt begin to cry out with holy Job, and say: What my soul once loathed has now become my food on account of the bitter passion of Christ, and has become sweet and delightful to me. Concerning which, we read that a certain man who had entered religion had grown so weary, by reason of the coarse food and other burdens of the order, that he could hardly put up with the weight thereof; and whilst he was thus in sadness, he threw himself at the feet of a crucifix, and there began, with many tears, to bewail his insufferable toils, the harshness of the order, the coarseness of the food, the poor bread and drink; and of a sudden blood began to issue from the side of the image, and as he kept on, with bitter tears, rehearsing his miseries, the said image answered him thus: Whenever thou findest an ungrateful taste in thy food or drink, steep it in the blood of my side. And ever after he bore patiently with the hardships of religion, and had a great devotion to Christ's passion, and ended his days in holiness.

CHAPTER LX.

On the resurrection and glorious ascension of our Lord, and on the sending of the Holy Ghost.

WE have spoken of the life and passion of our Lord, and shall now briefly treat of the resurrection and ascension, and of the sending of the Holy Ghost.

Firstly, think within thyself how, after our Lord had been taken down from the cross and buried, His most blessed soul went down to hell, that is to say, to the place where the holy fathers dwelt, which is usually called Limbo of the holy fathers.

Consider next what He did there; the joy of the holy fathers when they found themselves in such glory by reason of the presence of their

Lord; the wrath of the demons when they saw themselves thus overcome and despoiled, and that those holy souls were set free from their grasp. See how He rose on the third day, triumphant over death, showing us thereby that we likewise have to rise in the flesh. If, then, thou didst pity Christ in His passion, rejoice with Him in His resurrection. Consider how, when the Lord arose, the guards fell like dead men to the ground with fear. Behold, moreover, the angels seated on the sepulchre, and thou mayst well believe that a vast crowd of angels encircled the grave. Think on the visit of the women—to-wit, of Mary Magdalen and the other two—and how, when they could not find Him in the sepulchre, the greatness of their love forced them to come back to it over and over again.

Meditate on the several appearances of Christ. First He appeared to His most sweet Mother; then to Mary Magdalen, to the other two Marys, and to His disciples, and how they were gladdened at seeing Him, and how sweetly they conversed together. Again, reflect why Christ chose to appear in Galilee, that thou mightst learn to pass from sin to holiness, since Galilee signifies transmigration. And if thus we pass from a sinful to a holy life, our souls and bodies will pass to the heavenly kingdom, where we shall see Christ after the resurrection of all.

Again, contemplate how, after the lapse of forty

from Bethany to the Mount of Olives, the Lord appeared to them begirt with a countless host of angels and saints of the old law, and with words of comfort to our Lady and the others, began to be borne upwards by His own might, slowly ascending amid that mighty assemblage of holy souls, and surrounded by legions of angels. Reflect on that great and wondrous procession, wherein the angels led the way, and the holy fathers surrounded our Lord, and all with unutterable hymns of triumph and gladness entered the heavenly Jerusalem, and so great a festival was then held that the like shall never be held again till the end of the world. Think on the Apostles' sadness, and on the angels that came down to console them. Learn thou likewise to mount with Christ by those ways and exercises we have described, since, as St. Augustine says, no evil habit can ascend with Him. Moreover, consider in what manner, after the ascension, our Lady and the disciples stayed in the supper-chamber on Mount Sion, where our Lord had eaten His supper with His Apostles, and there they fasted and prayed and gave themselves to other ghostly exercises, awaiting the coming of the Holy Ghost, as the Lord had promised them. And when ten days had gone by from our Lord's ascension, and while the Blessed Virgin and the Apostles, at the third hour of the Sunday, were saying that verse of the prophet; Send forth Thy Spirit, and they shall be created, and Thou shalt renew the face of the earth; the Holy Ghost came upon them on a sudden, through whom they were at once enlightened, strengthened, and rooted in perfect unchangeable love. Behold, therefore, how He fell on them with rushing noise, in tongues of fire. Consider the gifts and fruits of the Spirit; for as the doors of the house where they were gathered together had been closed for fear of the Jews, they forthwith went out fearlessly and began to preach to the great crowd of people who had run thither in haste on hearing the noise; and how St. Peter converted about three thousand to the faith. Concerning this great mystery thou mayst ponder many things which we think it best to leave out, lest we go to too great length. We think, therefore, that this, with what we said above on our Lord's life and passion, will give thee matter enough for thy contemplation.

CHAPTER LXI.

That such as wish to gain the height of contemplation stand in need of unwavering perseverance.

WHOSOEVER thinks himself able to reach the height of contemplation, or the perfect fire of divine love, without a resolute steadfastness of purpose is like a man climbing a high mountain, and turning back at the first hard push or hindrance he meets. Such a one may likewise be compared to a man trying to light a fire with green wood or rotten sticks, and when he sees it does not catch at once, waxing wroth and scattering about what he had heaped up.

So may he be likened to one that cannot wait in patience till the wheat he has sown is ripe, or till the tree he planted has had time to take root; and all this on account of the time and risk and difficulty he finds.

He may also be compared to a monkey trying to eat a green nut, and throwing it away as soon as it tastes the bitterness of the rind, and so never getting at the sweet kernel. Or to a slothful warrior, who goes away, tired of the length and labour of the siege, before the beleaguered city has surrendered.

Thou seest, then, brother, that such a man can never reach the height of contemplation; for as he that persevereth not will never either kindle a fire, or reap his wheat, or rear a plant, or taste the kernel of the nut, or subdue the fortress, as in the examples given above, so none will ever climb the highest summit of contemplation without firm steadfastness of purpose.

CHAPTER LXII.

Concerning divers hindrances that keep the contemplative man from reaching the summit of contemplation.

LET us tarry awhile on one of the aforesaid examples; to-wit, that of him who strives to reach top of a mountain. Such a man goes a little way up the hillside, and if he chances to halt does not go down again, but resumes his climbing from his halting-place.

In like manner, he that desires to perfect himself in contemplation, should he have halted on his march, must never turn back, and must even avoid stoppages; since not to go forward is as bad as going back. For want of this perseverance so few are found who reach a perfect state of contemplation. Some, as soon as they have gone a little way, stop and go back again at the first small hardship or fatigue that crosses them.

Others there are who use neither order nor discretion in their ascents; they wish to find themselves at one stride on the mountain's top, without beginning at its foot and going on, step by step, to the highest point. The foot of the mount of contemplation is the knowledge of one's own sins and shortcomings.

Others, again, who bear heavy weights on their backs, fancy they can climb with their load; and these weights are their worldly cares and their anxieties about them, which clog the soul exceedingly and force it down to things of earth; and if it ever happens to rise, it is at once dragged down again.

Others, again, are to be found so harassed by certain flies that beset them that they give over the ascent after beginning it, and will go no farther. These buzzing flies are foolish thoughts; and the soul should never give up its task on their account, but should drive them away with holy disdain, as if by a wave of the hand. Some indeed there are who run after these flies as children do after butterflies.

Besides these, there are some who dread the howling of helldogs; that is to say, as soon as they feel any shameful temptation, at once, terror-stricken, turn back on their way, or else begin to fight against and struggle to drive it off; a useless attempt, as these temptations are more easily overcome by taking no notice of them and going our way, as the wayfarer does, who does not stop whenever he hears a dog bark, but lets it alone and speeds onward on his journey, and then the dog stops its barking; but if he stood still to fight or compel it to silence, it would bark all the more and hinder him from getting on.

Others never stretch out their hand to Him who can help them upwards, but rather withdraw it, leaning upon and trusting to the abundance of their own means and strength; and therefore it is no wonder if they keep slipping back again. For which reason the contemplative man ought always to stretch out his hand to the help of divine grace, in nowise trusting to his own strength, nor rashly hoping by his own endeavours to reach the goal of his wishes.

Some people think themselves on the summit when they are in reality at the foot of the mountain, and on that account do not care to advance, and so go backward.

Others reach the top, and at once become greedy

of vain-glory, and think they have done their journey well and manfully worked out their task, and grow careless about keeping their footing; whence they soon fall back, instead of speeding upwards as they would wish. And perhaps God will never again help them to regain the point whence they fell; and this is rightly owing to their pride and thanklessness and the ill use of the light they had received; a dreadful evil, and one that should always keep us from presuming of ourselves, when we see a man who had been so near to God and so intimate in His friendship, and had, like a bird, built his nest in heaven, afterwards cast down without recall to hell.

Then come others who, seeing themselves a little higher on the mountain than their neighbours, look down upon other men, and laugh at such as stand lower than themselves; and these are righteously permitted by God to fall, that by their own downfall they may learn how little they are worth of themselves. Some there are who strive to climb this mountain only out of curiosity, and that they may say they have been there, or to learn hidden things, or for their own recreation and pleasure, or to view its beauty, but not to please God and serve Him better and more worthily; and these soon lose God's help and His grace, or at least find themselves painfully, shamefully, and miserably deceived, and when they think themselves on the mountain of God find themselves on that of the devil.

Lastly, we see some hastening on more than is reasonable, and trying to outrun their guide, or hurrying onwards with greater speed than he advises, which is mere folly; for that guide is, as we have said, the grace of God. He, therefore, who cannot, or will not, bide the time appointed by the movement of this grace justly forfeits it, and will not find it so easily another time.

On the other hand, some are never ready to receive this grace of God, even when it calls and spurs them on, but rather shun it or turn aside to other occupations, and seem by word or deed to tell it to wait for them a little longer; and being thus driven away, it takes its leave of them. We must therefore at all times keep watch over our hearts to welcome the coming of divine grace, and let ourselves be swayed by its behests, going neither quicker nor slower than it leads the way, and ever with deep humility acknowledging ourselves unworthy even to lie down at the side of this mountain, how much more then to climb to its top? And the more deeply a man humbles himself in his own heart, the higher will he be lifted up. As a powerful king, wishing to honour his faithful knight, raises him to a higher place, and makes him sit among princes, when he sees him bashful and reluctant to be honoured; and the more he humbles himself as one unworthy thereof, the more earnestly the king forces dignities upon him. For nothing displeases God so much as presumption, nor is He pleased with such as wish to approach

Him in an unbridled and bold manner, as if he were a companion and one of themselves; but a holy and praiseworthy modesty, fear, trembling, and humility should always be our guide, joined with firm trust in His loving-kindness, since without this trust our fear would deserve blame, and would hinder us from climbing the mount of contemplation, because it lacks moderation.

CHAPTER LXIII.

On a few other hindrances to contemplation.

LET us treat of a few more hindrances and stumbling-blocks in the way of contemplation. There are some who beat their ass—that is, their body—too cruelly, so that the spirit can make no use of it. Others are too full and heavy; too weak, sleepy, and slothful, having stopped too long in the infirmary of the flesh, by excess in eating, drinking, or talking. Men like these are crippled, palsied, or drowsy, and stand in need of medicine; that is to say, they must by humble penance begin from the lowest stage.

Some at times conceive a keen spiritual hunger for the word of God, and thereupon wish to hear or read it. Whence it happens that they stay too long at their reading, and take a larger meal than reason allows to be wholesome, and, forgetful of the speed with which they had begun their ascent, they no longer walk at the same pace as before. Such a refreshment is indeed at times profitable and needful, and especially in the beginning, and when partaken of soberly. A man, therefore, while he reads, should never forget the mountain he has before him to climb, and seek rather devotion than instruction. Others kick and rear under the spur that urges them on, and these are they who fly too much from sufferings.

There are others, besides, who are not too sure of their way, and yet are not careful to ask advice from those who know it, or help from above; but abound in their own sense, and trust in themselves, and while they wish to teach themselves, often go astray and are lost.

Others, again, try to find the way by diligent inquiry and hard study, that they may know how to talk about it and teach it to others, without ever going over it themselves, and they discourse according to what they have heard from others, but never try to go themselves on the path they teach; and no wonder, if they are always at the foot of the hill; for we cannot climb by mere talk, but must use our feet. And such as these are like men in war, who encourage and teach others how to fight with bravery, but will never touch a weapon themselves; or like those who point out a path which their own silliness or cowardice keeps them from following.

There are others who no sooner have entered on one road than they turn aside into another; and this comes of their fickleness, and because they hope to find an easier and more pleasant one, which makes them profit little or nothing; just as hounds will never bring a stag to bay if they run first after one and then after another, but must run down the first they find, and leave the rest alone, as well-trained dogs will always do.

Others, heedless of themselves and of the dangers of this life, walk carelessly and rashly, and thus often roll from the top to the bottom of the mount.

Others, while climbing, look behind or below them, and if any one calls on them to come down, at once forsake all; and these become the more disabled the longer they abide below, and find it all the harder and more painful to regain the height they had lost, because worldly talk and worldly business are no small let and hindrance; and he that fixes his heart on such things, and is not quick in withdrawing himself and turning away from them to continue his ascent, creates a great stumbling-block for himself. Wherefore we must not make these our goal, and only use them as far as we are obliged to do, and while our body is here below; let our hearts, at least, be on high, which is hard for the inexperienced, because the anchor of their hearts is not yet firmly cast on the mountain, since they have not the cable of good habits with which to fasten it.

There are others who, when they have once reached the top, think they will never leave it, but will abide there as if they had it for their birthright. But they find out their frailty by falling, and learn in tribulation that it was God's grace that established them there, and kept them as long as He willed; so that, whenever they find themselves in high places, they fear to fall; and when they find themselves cast down, they bear it cheerfully, hoping through divine grace to rise again. For a man must abide firm and steadfast, not only in corporal, but likewise, and much more, in spiritual mishap; to-wit, in temptation and mental suffering, when he is bereft of those consolations which he longs for, and was wont to have.

Lastly, there are some who wear themselves out too much in their ascent, by tears and bodily afflictions, so as not to be able to fulfil those things which they are bound to do; and with these our merciful Lord dealeth mercifully, allowing them at times to fall to a lower level, so that they find themselves unable to do even what is needful.

These are the things that hinder us from climbing the mount of contemplation. There are other numberless hindrances; but all may be reduced to these, to overcome which we need a gift of steadfast perseverance with the aforesaid means—namely, humble patience, quiet retirement, and silence.

CHAPTER LXIV.

How some are wanting in steady perseverance, and on that account make little way in contemplation.

THERE are many not well forewarned concerning steadiness in persevering and the fruit of contemplation, and who cannot for that reason reach its highest point; for they never trouble themselves about prayer or meditation, unless they find themselves drawn to it by a feeling of devotion, and taste some spiritual sweetness therein; and without this feeling they think prayer and meditation useless. But this is like a man perishing with cold, and unwilling to come near a fire, unless he first feels himself warm, or dying of hunger, and resolved not to eat till hunger ceases. For what reason does a man pray or meditate, if not to warm himself at the fire of God's love, and to be filled with God's gifts and grace? These people do wrong, and fail in this—that they think it time lost if, when they go to prayer, they are not forthwith watered by the rills of devotion. To whom Gerson replies, that if they work and strive hard to be devout, and wage a constant war against their evil thoughts, being sorry that these disturb the quiet of their soul, they will often gain more than if the grace of devotion were at once granted to them without any effort. The reason of this is that they serve in God's service at their own expense, and with greater suffering and hardship. It is true, however, that whoever wishes to exercise himself in contemplation should spend a great deal of time in it, freeing himself from the burden of other occupations, whether they concern himself or others, and should constrain himself to remain even for three or four hours in the same place, whether the grace of consolation follows or not, still using all his endeavours to obtain it; and when he feels himself worn out by too much weariness he should say to himself that he can wait yet for half an hour or an hour by way of doing penance; and when the hour is gone by he can again encourage himself to wait for another hour. And it often comes to pass that in the last half-hour he makes greater profit than another would do in ten days or a month. And should he, perchance, have to go away with a repulse and without an alms—that is to say, without feeling any devotion—he should humbly turn to our Lord and acknowledge himself unworthy of this grace, and deserving rather to be scourged and afflicted than to enjoy such consolation, and say:

O Lord God of all consolation, be Thou for ever praised and glorified; and let my portion be shame and confusion, as is meet and just, unless Thy mercy dispose otherwise.

Thus he will overcome God Himself, offering Him in sacrifice the hardness of his heart. Nor will God forget to be merciful to him, and deal kindly with him, when He sees best according to His good pleasure. Nor should a man seek eagerly for the consolation of tears and devotion for his own pleasure, but that he may thereby cleave faster to God. If therefore He is better pleased that we should serve Him for the present without these consolations, it must please us likewise, and we must say:

O Lord God Almighty, well hast Thou dealt with me, that Thou dost reserve my reward for the next world; but this one thing I beseech Thee, that I may never fall under Thy anger nor lose Thy grace, and for the rest Thy will be done.

But if any one gains the devotion he sought after, let him be careful to give thanks to Almighty God, and pray yet more fervently; that the tree now planted may grow up and wax strong, so that he may not have already received his reward here below, but may await its fulness in future.

CHAPTER LXV.

Of what kind is that knowledge of God which the contemplative man enjoys in this world.

THE contemplative man must be content to hope to see God clearly in His heavenly country; but while in this exile must be satisfied with believing in Him as his Creator, Redeemer, Lord, and Rewarder, and so forth, according to what faith makes us certain of, and must not seek to have at present a clear vision of the Divine nature.

Wherefore he should take note that, according to St. Denys, how lofty soever be his contemplation of God, and though he thinks he has gained a sight of things hitherto unknown, yet, if what he sees is at all similar to anything of this world, he may rest assured he has had no clear vision of God; and this is also true concerning visions of angels. For God hath no bodily magnitude, nor is He of any colour, for example, white, red, &c.; and so likewise of angels. It is nevertheless true that God can be known in this life after a manner which no words can utter nor symbols express; but those who know God after this fashion, understand themselves what they see, and feel in their souls as it were a certain sweetness and fulness and taste and melody, which feeling must remain untold in words. For as at times we feel well within ourselves the love or joy that affects us, yet we cannot conceive of these things as being black or white, or round or square, because they are not bodily objects; so no man can make another man understand these spiritual feelings unless he has already tasted them.

However, I am not saying that no idea can be formed of the human nature that God took upon Himself; for we can well figure Him to ourselves in this His assumed nature. But what I have just said concerning God is to be understood of His Godhead.

And if a soul were well accustomed to this contemplation by means of vigorous and constant meditation, it would easily rise above itself and find numberless beautiful things to contemplate, and would thus have a safe harbour of refuge against all the troubled and bitter waves of the wide sea of the world.

CHAPTER LXVI.

That God dwells in the soul in a threefold manner.

We have hitherto only spoken of the matter of our contemplation, and have left to better skilled and more learned men other more subtle ways of contemplating; and relieving ourselves of that task, we shall now set forth the three ways in which God by His grace takes up His abode in our soul.

Firstly, by working our justification, without the soul having any sensible knowledge of it. And although she feels it not, yet it makes her dear to God.

Secondly, by means of some spiritual consolation or sentiment, as is the case with such as receive and enjoy in their contemplation divers kinds of spiritual joys and consolations. For at times they find themselves absorbed in a kind of spiritual sweetness, so that all they see and think seems full of unspeakable delight. Sometimes they feel a peaceful humility, wherein they see their own nothingness, and find relish in the things of God alone, and in what pleases Him. For whenever a man is pleased with himself, and finds satisfaction in himself, he may indeed know that he has no true humility; and whatever consolation he feels is not from God. True humility is always coupled with good and godly consolation, and makes a man know his own worthlessness and shortcomings, whence he becomes hateful to himself and seems abominable in his own eyes, knowing himself better than the whole world can know him, and he sees that God is so good and great that all else seems to be almost nothing, except as far as God is mirrored in it. Sometimes the soul tastes a kind of spiritual inebriation, which moves her to praise God and to utter sighs of devotion, so that she cannot withhold herself from letting it be seen without. Sometimes all things seem lit up with God's brightness, and seem to sing hymns of gladness to Him.

Thirdly, God is wont to dwell in the soul by a certain union like that which the most blessed Apostle Paul and other sublime men of contemplation had, concerning which I am unworthy to speak; so leaving these things to great doctors, let what I have said be enough for our dull understanding.

CHAPTER LXVII.

That all men, and above all religious, are bound to strive after perfection, under pain of present and future loss.

MANY are wont to say: An ordinary way of living is enough for me; I am content to be saved with the lowest; I do not wish for the merit of an Apostle; I have no wish to soar on high, and am quite willing to follow the common track. But let such as these remember, that not to wish to be perfect is itself an imperfection; and as Gerson says, in his *Mystic Theology*: Not to go forward in the way of God is the same as going backward. Moreover, the slothful servant who did not put out his talents at interest was condemned. Let us make this plain by a homely example: A noble and wealthy father of a family has several children, all well able to further the interests of the house. One of them, while his brethren are doing their best, sits at home idle, slothful, and careless; living in a sordid manner; never giving a thought to anything noble, great, worthy of his own talents, or his father's rank; and saying he is quite content with his fortune, and to live any kind of life. Meanwhile his father exhorts and trys to rouse him to noble and generous deeds. If the son will neither hear nor obey, he will certainly fall under his father's displeasure. In the same way must they fare with their heavenly Father, whom He calls to higher graces and a holier life, and who yet grovel sluggishly on the earth, and never strive after perfection. This must, however, be applied to those who are not fettered by some lowly state or office which forbids them to raise themselves without breach of a commandment. And for such as these it should be reckoned as the highest perfection that, out of obedience to God's bidding they restrict themselves to that state, although it hinders them from aiming at perfect contemplation.

Lastly, we must remember that, although Mary would justly have been able with Martha to serve Christ as their guest, yet Christ praised her because she chose the better part, and attended to one thing alone. Cursed then is he who, if he can do otherwise, spoileth his own portion.

From what we have said it is clear that since contemplative life, as divines teach, is more perfect than active life, whoever is apt for contemplation, and is not bound by obedience to an active life, can lay all else aside, and give himself up to contemplation. Whence Augustine says: Charity seeks after holy leisure, but necessity maketh it take up the burden of business, which burden if no man puts upon thee, thou shouldst attend to contemplation; as if he had said: Unless the Superior's behest or evident necessity bids otherwise, we should busy ourselves in contemplation. And let no one urge against this that he has talent for action, and will be condemned should he hide it, whilst he might be trafficking with it either in preaching or serving the poor; because the contemplative man is of the greatest use to the Church, if with heart and mind he gives homage to God, while others serve Him with hands, feet, and lips. On which account there are many deserving of great blame for their neglect in striving after contemplation, as, for example, those who are placed in the school of religion, which is a school of devotion, prayer, and weeping. So, likewise, ecclesiastics ought to be, who rest at their leisure, and live on the labour of the people, to keep the Lord's justifications and seek out His law; and many others in the world, men and women, who have time, knowledge, and sufficiency enough to give themselves up wholly to God. At least, let them hold fast faith, hope, and charity, since this is learning enough to be able to tend towards God with all their affections.

CHAPTER LXVIII.

That in certain cases the contemplative man must descend from the height of contemplation, and break off for a time his spiritual exercises.

IN two ways must the contemplative man interrupt his exercises and come down from the mount—to-wit, by descending to himself, or by attending to his neighbour. In three ways he may have to descend to himself.

Firstly, when a man who is in a higher grade

descends at times to exercise himself more perfectly in some lower degree, lest through negligence while climbing upwards he might lose what he had gained below. For in the aforesaid exercises no one ought so to stretch himself forward to what is before him as never to think it needful to look behind, but he should, while going onwards, and advancing from virtue to virtue, not forget the steps he has already made, and that on which he stands, but should use every care to ground himself in them; for example, thou didst through fear first conceive a sorrow for sin, and through fear and the thought of death, judgment, and the pains of hell, and other good works, thou wentest through the Way of Purity. Thou camest next to hope, while dwelling on the works of God's love, in the Way of Enlightenment. Finally, thou didst unite thyself to God by burning and seraphic love in the Way of Union. But tell me, brother, since thou hast reached this union, oughtest thou to forsake altogether thy fear and the thoughts of death and judgment? By no means. Rather shouldst thou from time to time descend to an attentive consideration of the emptiness of this world, the fewness of thy days, the bitter pains of hell, fearing to go down there, that by this very fear thou mayst be drawn to heavenly things, and mayst, as by a spur, be driven on thy upward career; and thus in all thine exercises by hope and love thou should ascend, and yet descend by fear, until charity be so perfected in thee that fear be driven out; and so thou wilt not fall into presumption and carelessness and grow torpid. And after this manner holy men are wont to ascend to heaven by hope, love, and desire, and then descend again into the depths by careful meditation on the pains of hell.

Secondly, thou must descend to thy own level, to attend to the due composure and ordering of thy outer man, so that thy inward devotion and holiness may appear without; for we must in such a manner control our demeanour and watch over ourselves as to make ourselves exemplary and amiable to all men. And this we shall best fulfil if we are careful to observe three things in our outward behaviour. The first is gravity; the second, humility; the third, kindness. Gravity gives others good example, humility defends us, kindness makes us beloved by all.

Thirdly, we must come down to ourselves when we have to undertake some bodily toil or work with our hands. For we must so arrange our exercises that we may every day, at allotted times, work with our hands; and at other times again attend to spiritual exercises; though even while working we can still pray, meditate, and rouse ourselves up to ghostly and holy thoughts. Our holy fathers held this as a rule; and the more they busied themselves at working with their hands, the higher the degree of purity and love they hoped to arrive at. Thus, as we are but weak men, let us not imagine ourselves angels, who always feed on spiritual food which we cannot eat; and let us not wish to be at all hours employed in spiritual things, but rather at certain times in working with our hands, and this for several reasons.

The first is, lest we grow so tired of spiritual things as to give them up altogether. Nor ought we think ourselves holier and more spiritual men than the great Anthony, who, if he had not been taught by an angel to use prayer and work by turns, would have been overcome by the irksomeness of his life, and have gone back to the world. For this, Cassian says, that whoever does not choose to work with his hands for some time daily, cannot long abide in his cell.

The second is, that although these manual employments do for a moment withdraw us from contemplation, yet they make us afterwards stronger and more willing; for we cannot ascend together with the lusts of the flesh, and we must therefore subdue them, and this is done by work, whereas the sluggard is always forming desires. Thus, then, manual labour is often of use for ghostly exercises, inasmuch as it does away with the hindrance to our ascent of the mount of contemplation.

The third is, that our heart is very unsteady; and, like a ship at sea, is tossed hither and thither by many thoughts and wishes. Make thy heart, then, fast by some anchor, as Cassian says, and steady it by the weight and occupation of some manual labour.

The fourth reason is, that the enemy finds fewer gates open to temptation when we are busy than when we are idle: for a man who is employed has only one devil to tempt him, and the idler is beset with numberless devils. For these and many other reasons, which I have advisedly left out to avoid being lengthy, the holy fathers, and especially those of Egypt, were so fond of manual labour, and on this account are so highly praised by the Saints. But in order not to be carried too far from our contemplation, we must, as far as it lies in us, make choice of those kinds of work which appear best fitted for spiritual things; as, for example, the writing of spiritual books, which withdraws our mind less from things of the spirit, and is in itself of greater profit to our souls.

We should, therefore, go faithfully to work with our hands, not like worldlings, who only get their earthly reward, while we shall not only be requited here, but shall earn an undying crown in heaven.

See how the holy angels bore a special message of Christ's birth to the shepherds at their work. Yet let us not be excessive nor over-anxious about our work, but moderate and wise, being careful to keep silence while at work, because silence is our strength, as the prophet says; and though it is well to keep it at all times and places, yet is it more needed when we are at work, according to the Apostle's saying: We beseech you in the Lord Jesus to eat your bread in silence.

It is likewise often necessary to leave our contemplation awhile for our neighbour's sake; and this may be either for the sake of our superiors, our equals, or our inferiors. First, on account of our superiors: because although we may for our own part wish to be always engaged in spiritual things, weeping over our sins with Lazarus, and exciting feelings of compunction by the memory of our sins and of the last judgment, or sitting down with Mary at the Lord's feet, that is to say, refreshing our mind with the thought of Christ's life and passion, and with any other good spiritual exercise; yet if the Superior comes and tells us to leave off our contemplation, we must forthwith lay everything aside and obey, and place ourselves at the feet of God's Vicar, namely, of our Superior, and say: My heart is ready, O God, my heart is ready. Ready to give myself to contemplation at Thy bidding, and ready when Thou dost command to employ myself in outward things. This we are bound to do, not only at the Superior's command, but even sometimes out of charity at a brother's request; since our holy fathers were most willing to forego all their exercises in order to keep unswervingly to obedience, and reckoned it above all else if they did another man's will and not their own. And though the bond of obedience is stricter in case of precept, yet thou must never question whether thou art bound or not, for obedience fulfilled out of love is often the more meritorious, and when devoutly fulfilled increaseth charity.

Secondly, on account of our equals we may lawfully at times forego our spiritual works, to help them out of pity and compassion, with deed or counsel, lending ourselves to such as are in bodily need, and much more to the spiritually afflicted; and we must assist them as far as we can with advice, warning, and encouragement, and by counselling and cheering them up in times of sorrow and trial. For if Paul had not come down from the third heaven, and had not stooped to his weak brethren from the height of his rapture, he had never brought any to Christ, but by descending thence he became all things to all men. And to carnal men he preached Jesus and Him crucified, and to spiritual men he gave spiritual food. After the same manner we must become all things to all, helping every one as far as he needs it; and, above all, drawing towards us, admonishing and correcting those whom we see going astray from the yoke of Christ by mortal sin. Say not in thy heart: My own salvation is enough for me; I wish to take care of myself, not of others. Say not: Am I appointed his superior or his guardian? It is not the zeal of God that breeds these thoughts. Thou must help thy neighbour, when he is in bodily need, with alms; and when in spiritual want, strive to afford him some ghostly help, praying for him, advising, teaching, and guiding him, chiefly in his temptation and spiritual exercises. But do not take upon thee to teach others the things thou knowest not thyself; rather acknowledge thyself ignorant than dare to teach rashly. And let thy counsel be ever in agreement with Holy Writ. Whatever thou hearest in counsel or should come to thy knowledge, if secret, be careful lest thou make it known, especially if it concerneth other men's temptation, for hence dangers often arise. In giving counsel take heed lest thou follow thy passion or the bent of nature, for this would twist thy judgment, and zeal knows not how to be wise. Again, before giving advice, above all in troublesome matters, think a long time, and do not say what comes first into thy head, but take counsel with thyself, yielding thy own views to other men's opinions so as to shun stubbornness; and desire rather to agree with the lowliest ones than that they should agree with thee, for which reason thou must make light of no man's counsel, seeing that God often reveals to the little ones what He hides from the wise; but hear every man's thoughts, without however embracing them, as the Apostle says : Try all things, and hold fast what is good.

Thirdly, we must descend from the height of our contemplation to those below us; as, for example, prelates and others having to govern those under them are often obliged to cease from contemplation to watch over the safe-keeping and discipline of their subjects. I say the *safe-keeping*, with respect to those who stand as it were upright, that they be worthily upheld in their firmness; and *discipline* with respect to erring and disorderly subjects who need correction, otherwise God will require their blood at the hands of their Superiors; and unless the least of the brethren be brought safe, as far as they are able, they shall not see the face of Joseph, that is of Christ, the true Saviour. See now how dangerous the condition of Superiors is, since a man must needs so often forsake himself, and, often by forgetting himself, is in danger of being lost; for when a man has much outward work, and is at a standstill in the concerns of his soul, he grows dull and hard of heart, perceiving only outward things, and losing the taste of spiritual ones, as St. Bernard well shows in his book on *Consideration.* Therefore following the advice of holy men, as far as in thee lies, always keep far from the dignity of Superior and from too much external occupation, saving always humble and speedy obedience. But when a man is forced to yield himself to these employments, he must, whenever he can, find time to return eagerly to himself and give himself to spiritual exercises, lest, as we have said, he should become hard of heart. Whence St. Gregory says: Holy men, when they are obliged by the duties of their state to engage in exterior business, are always careful to retreat into the hiding-place of their heart; and there they station themselves in the highest summit of perfection, and receive the law of God, as it were on a mountain, laying aside the bustle of temporal pursuits and entering into the decrees of the Divine Will; for as they serve God in external duties without transgressing, they are ever striving to return to the secret places of their own hearts.

CHAPTER LXIX.

Concerning sundry doctrines which the devout man must carefully observe in the matters that have been treated of; and the conclusion of this work.

SINCE we have now, with God's help, described in what manner a man ought to unite his soul to God by the practice of prayer, meditation, and contemplation, according to the three ways of Purity, Enlightenment, and Union, as a conclusion to this work we have resolved to add a few points about the aforesaid, although they may have been, at least in part, treated of above. And that they may be more easily remembered, we shall arrange them in paragraphs, and shall put at the beginning of each paragraph its title.

ABDICATION, or cutting off from oneself. He that wishes to give himself up in real earnest to meditation must cut off all concupiscence or thirst of honour, riches, pleasures, and worldly pursuits, because the thoughts of these things distract the mind greatly.

HOLINESS OF LIFE. He must live holily, because the spirit of wisdom and the spirit of meditation will not enter the soul that wishes evil.

UNSHAKEN TRUST in his Beloved. He must not be easily drawn away from the love of his

Beloved One by reason of the temptations that come upon him. For the devil loves to fight the devout man with many temptations, and to hinder him in the exercise of meditation. Say, therefore: I trust in Him who hath said, Son, give Me thy heart, who willeth not the death but the salvation of sinners. Think nothing harsh or cruel of thy Beloved, but say with Job: Should He even kill me, I will hope in Him.

OUTWARD DEMEANOUR. If alone, thou mayst use gestures and ceremonies, as raising thy hands like Aaron; bending thy knees like Solomon; at times falling on thy face, and then again rising and kneeling as Christ did on the Mount of Olives; sitting down like Mary at the feet of our Lord; stretching out thy arms in the manner of a cross, as Christ our Lord did on His cross; at times casting down thine eyes to the ground like the publican; sometimes lifting them up to heaven with the Apostles at our Lord's ascension. This outward variety of ceremonies helps to beget different feelings in the soul. Beginners should pray on bended knees and with downcast eyes, or with arms stretched out in the form of a cross, or with frequent prostrations. Those more advanced should pray on bended knees, but with uplifted hands and eyes; the perfect standing upright and with eyes raised to heaven, with inward desires and sighs. The contemplative may raise their hearts, sitting down at the feet of our Lord.

But whenever thou art with others shun whatever is unusual; bow thy head when the rest do so, showing thereby filial reverence to God as to thy most loving Father; kneel when others kneel, doing homage to God as a servant to his lord; if others fall on their faces on the ground, do thou the same, acknowledging God for thy judge, and thyself a guilty man, and that thou hast to become dust.

VARIETY IN THY EXERCISES. Thou shouldst vary thy practices as it has been said: Now read, now pray, then go to work with fervour, and thy time will be short and thy labour light. If thou strivest to keep always at one thing, thou wilt profit little, and wear thyself out.

OBJECT OF MEDITATION. Let not the scope of thy meditation, prayer, and contemplation be thy own pleasure, nor to escape punishment, nor any gain or heavenly reward or sweetness of spirit, but that thou mayst have in readiness an abode for God in thy heart, and mayst make room for His grace in thee, and mayst do the will of Him whose delight is to be with the sons of men, and who rejoices greatly in our salvation. For to this end was man's heart made, that lovingly and in its inmost being it might be united to its most sweet Maker in this life by prayer, meditation, and contemplation; and in the next by enjoying Him for ever. In a word, thou must in all thy exercises seek God's glory, the honour of His saints, the good of the Church, and thy own well-being; referring all to the glory of God, according to the word of the Apostle: Whether you eat or drink, or whatever else you do, do all for the glory of God.

THANKFULNESS FOR GRACE. If thou seest any good in thyself, give glory to God, and thank Him for it, and be not proud; for it is not of him that striveth, nor of him that runneth, but of God that showeth mercy. Neither be thou puffed up, for the grace of meditation is given not only to the good, but sometimes to bad men also.

ABUNDANCE OF POINTS FOR MEDITATION. Gerson says that thou shouldst have in the beginning of thy prayer abundance of points for meditation, wherewith thou mayst excite thyself, and of this we have spoken above.

KEEPING CLOSE TO CHRIST. Whithersoever thou goest, thou shouldst always have thy Beloved, as it were, before thy eyes, in His cradle, in Egypt, on the cross, &c., praising Him with inward gladness of thy heart, speaking to Him lovingly and as to a friend, laying before Him thy wants, and asking His help.

BROTHERLY LOVE. As thou wishest God to show Himself towards thee—to-wit, kind and merciful—so do thou show thyself towards thy neighbour. Despise none, and thus shalt thou make a friend of God, who turneth away from none, and despiseth none. And friends have the same will, and the same dislikings. Again, we easily grow cold, and hence we need to seek the fire of love by the sighs of prayer, by meditating on our Lord's passion, by the sorrow of compassion, by a desire for union with Him, saying, as above in the Way of Union: O Lord, when shall I love Thee? &c.

LABOUR. Thou must work hard, and not without good reason; because in all undertakings beginnings are toilsome, and later on the load is lightened by habit. See what toil husbandmen undergo to reap the fruits of the earth, and merchants in crossing seas, and the wounds and risks of soldiers in time of war. Yet they do all those for a passing gain; much harder, then, shouldst thou work for thy everlasting good.

MODERATION or DISCRETION. In all things keep due measure; be neither too hot nor lukewarm, neither too careless nor again too restless, according to that saying, Use moderation in all things, for in this lies the greatest beauty of virtue.

NATURAL DISPOSITION. Look carefully to what is most in keeping with the bent of thy nature; for some can best abide at length in prayer, others in meditation; some are best swayed by reasons, others by thinking on God's works of love; some are fitter for the active, others for the contemplative, life. Likewise, in eating and drinking have a care of thy health, and use both with moderation, since what is not enough for one man is too much for another; and so let not thy heart be weighed down with feasting and drunkenness.

ORDER. Begin from the Way of Purity, washing and *cleansing* thyself, in order to be next *enlightened*, before thou canst cling to thy Beloved in the

Way of *Union*; for he that is foul and soiled ought not to approach to the royal kiss before he has cleansed himself, nor shouldst thou attempt to climb the roof before thou canst walk on the ground.

READINESS. Make such use of food and sleep as to be at all times ready to lift up thy heart, so that in thee may come to pass what is written: Lift up your hearts; we have lifted them up unto the Lord; and thou mayst say: O God, my God, to Thee do I watch at break of day. Be thou, then, ever on the watch, willing and prudent.

QUIET OF MIND. Fly from all things that distract thy mind, and rest in the peace of thy Lord, unless out of duty or obedience thou art tied down to some outward employment, thus likewise never judging and suspecting ill of others, because this makes our heart very restless. And if thoughts of suspicion arise within thee, cast them from thee without deciding anything, and saying: He that hath to judge us is the Lord. Always put the best meaning on what is doubtful. And when a man is fallen, compare thyself with him, and say: Had I been thus tempted, I should perhaps have fallen yet lower.

RECOLLECTION. Often strive to recall thy thoughts from things below to those above, from time to eternity, from things without to things within, from fleeting things to such as are everlasting. Never wish to listen to useless talk, and say: I have seen all things under the sun, and behold all are vanity, and my Beloved alone is good, lovely, beautiful, and all-sufficient for me.

DEVOTION TO THE SAINTS. Thou shouldst be devout to some saints in particular, to whom thou shouldst offer some homage every day, that they may vouchsafe ever to intercede for thee in the sight of God; above all to our Lady, thy Angel Guardian, and to some one of the Apostles, Martyrs, Virgins, or Confessors, or to several of them, that they may pray for thee.

FULL RESIGNATION. Bow thyself wholly down to the will of God, saying: O my most merciful Lord Jesus Christ, as Thou willest and seest best, so do Thou with me. And if He grants thee the gift of prayer, meditation, or contemplation, receive it with fear; if not, bear up in patience, and be content without grumbling with whatever He sends thee, and thus become one spirit with Him, so as to think no more of aught else than Christ crucified.

SEEKING FOR A HIGHER RESTING-PLACE IN CONTEMPLATIVE REPOSE. If thou art in religion, thou art bound, as Gerson says, to aim at that quiet which is the end of contemplation, even though in the whole course of thy life thou canst hardly reach it, since such is the religious state. Soldiers have to defend the oppressed, husbandmen to till the earth, and religious to aim at contemplation. As St. Bonaventure says, begin to-day where thou didst leave off yesterday, and do like one that is climbing a high mountain: when he wishes to halt he never goes back to his starting-place, but sits him down to rest wherever he happens to be, and, gathering strength, goes on his way. And for this reason we make little or no way in contemplation, because if with God's grace we have been able to master something one day, we lose it the next by eagerly running after trifles, idle talk, and amusements. And then we give up the ascent of the mount, and go down again into the valley, by not abiding in frequent contemplation.

CHRIST. Have nothing dearer to thee than Christ, and beseech Him to vouchsafe to be thy Help, Safeguard, and Leader, and the End of thy journey.

The end of the treatise called *The Book of Exercises of the Spiritual Life*, in which, if any one doth carefully exercise himself by reading, praying, meditating, and contemplating, he will, with ease and in a short time, be borne along on the arms of God's grace, cleave fast to the Lord as if with a seraphic love, and it will at last be given him, as the reward of his toil, to hope firmly for life everlasting.

This treatise was written in the Monastery of St. Mary of Monserrat, and ended in the year of the Lord one thousand five hundred, on the thirteenth of November.

THE END.

PAX.

A

Directory for the Canonical Hours.

WRITTEN BY

GARCIAS CISNEROS,

ABBOT OF THE ORDER OF ST. BENEDICT.

LONDON: BURNS AND OATES,
Portman Street and Paternoster Row.
1876.

PREFACE.

THE following short but beautiful treatise, though written for the benefit of Benedictine monks, is so full of spiritual wisdom, and of gentle and loving piety, that no one can read it without feeling himself moved to devotion. In language of inexpressible sweetness and power, it sets before us the threefold office of divine worship—praise, thanksgiving, and prayer; and with maxims culled from the writings of Saints and Fathers of the Church, develops this threefold office throughout the several hours of the Divine Office. Should a beginner find the number of subjects laid down for meditation too great a strain on his intellect, nothing can be easier than to single out the chief ones and dwell on them, not for the space of one psalm only, as the author directs, but during two or three. A like easy arrangement will at once remove any difficulty that may be met with by ecclesiastics not using our monastic Breviary, which Abbot Cisneros had in view in allotting the subjects for meditation to the several canonical hours.

CONTENTS.

CHAP.		PAGE
I.	That a religious should make the divine office his most earnest care	9
II.	How necessary it is for a religious to be well prepared before going to the night office, in order to fulfil it as he ought.	10
III.	Three several ways of preparation for the Divine office; and in particular, how a religious should prepare himself for the night office	11
IV.	In what manner a devout religious will be best able to be attentive during the psalmody, so as to keep his mind lifted up to God	17
V.	What a monk should do at Prime and Tierce throughout the whole week, taking the benefits received from God for his object according to the days of the week	26
VI.	How a religious should employ his thoughts at Sext and None	37
VII.	Concerning Vespers	41
VIII.	Concerning Compline	42
IX.	How to end the canonical hours, and on what a good monk ought to reflect during the pause we make on our knees in choir after each canonical hour	44
X.	What we should think upon while *Gloria Patri* is being sung at the end of the psalms	47

A

DIRECTORY FOR THE CANONICAL HOURS,

WHEREIN A RELIGIOUS IS TAUGHT HOW HE MAY JOIN IN THE DIVINE OFFICE BY DAY AND NIGHT WITH DUE ATTENTION AND REVERENCE.

CHAPTER I.

That a religious should make the Divine Office his most earnest care.

IN the second book of Paralipomenon, chapter the twenty-ninth, it is written: My sons, be not negligent; the Lord hath chosen you to stand before Him, and to minister to Him, and to worship Him. Since, then, God has chosen the religious man as His minister, to worship and serve Him, he ought to know how God is to be served. For, as Gerson says, nothing so beseems a religious as the worthy and careful performance of divine worship—to-wit, of the canonical hours, which our father and captain, St. Benedict, calls in his Rule the work of God; more especially because it is the first duty of a religious, as St. Jerome says, to employ himself in praising God, offering Him hymns, psalms, prayers, and sacrifice; and by these means to appease the anger of God against His people, and bewail the sins of his brethren. Wherefore a monk must be watchful and diligent in worthily discharging the debt of his service to God, lest the fearful curse of Jeremias the prophet fall upon him: Cursed be the man that doth the work of God with negligence.

CHAPTER II.

How necessary it is for a religious to be well prepared before going to the office of the night, in order to fulfil it as he ought.

WE read in the eighteenth chapter of Ecclesiasticus: Before prayer prepare thy soul, and be not as a man that tempteth God. We read also in the conference of Abbot Isaac, that as we would fain find ourselves at prayer so should we strive to make ourselves before going to it. It is likewise written in the book called the *Mirror for Monks:* Strive to rouse thy heart, forestalling by some devout practice the canonical hour thou art about to recite. Learn from the example of a poor man who, when he wishes to beg an alms of a rich man, does his best to dispose him beforehand, and studies his words that he may prevail on him to give the desired alms. Think, moreover, on a man condemned to death before his doom is pronounced; how eagerly he tries to think, while waiting to go before the judge, how to plead his cause so as to move him to mercy. In like manner the servant of God, before appearing in the sight of the Divine Majesty, ought to weigh well how and by what prayers he may be able to bend Him to mercy.

It is therefore, brethren, the greatest rashness to go before so great a Majesty utterly unprepared. For the whole fruit of both day and night office depends on our foregoing preparation, according as the Prophet says: Thy ear hath heard the preparation of my heart. And there can be no perfect prayer unless forestalled by meditation, as Hugh of St. Victor says in his *Treatise on Prayer*. Gerson also, in his book on *Mystic Theology*, tells us that a religious should lay everything else aside to dispose his spirit for saying the canonical hours.

Therefore, most beloved brethren, let us not grudge rising from our beds a little before the night-watches. And let us barter this little time with God, and we shall see how plentifully He will requite it. And in order that we may have some fixed arrangement in this preparation, and it be not in vain for us to rise before daylight, we will here briefly describe three ways of preparing ourselves.

CHAPTER III.

On three several ways of preparation for the Divine Office; and in particular, how a religious should prepare himself for the night office.

DEAREST brethren, holy men teach us three ways of preparing ourselves, to-wit:

The remote preparation of a holy life;
The special one of deep meditation;
The immediate preparation of fervent prayer.

The first is a general one, and we observe it by living well and holily, shunning all vanity in word and deed, using every endeavour to keep watch over our hearts and spend our time profitably, directing the last end of our works to God, lest our heart at prayer-time be entangled in foolish fancies. And if we find ourselves before going to prayer beset with these thoughts, we should read a while, and try to think of what we read, and the subject of this reading should be such as may help us to pray with purity.

The second preparation is a nearer and more special one, and must be made during the quarter of an hour before the night office begins, after this manner. When we have risen from our beds and are dressed, staying a while in our cells, and standing up where we are wont to pray, we should gather our thoughts together as best we can, and think thus within ourselves: what we are going to do, and why we have risen from our beds; for whosoever does not think before acting must needs be careless in his work.

And what are we about to do, brethren, at the time of the Divine Office, unless it be to appear before the sight of God and His holy angels, in the company of our just and holy brethren? Wherefore we must diligently bear in mind that we are going to

  Adore God,
  Give thanks to God, and
  Pray to Him.

First, we have to adore God—Three in Persons, One in Essence—with adoration of highest worship, for the judgments of His justice. By these judgments or decrees, brethren, we must understand the Incarnation of His only-begotten Son our Saviour, His birth and circumcision, His manifestation to the kings, His presentation in the temple; and lastly, His most holy passion, resurrection, and all the other works which our glorious Lord vouchsafed to work while on earth for our redemption. These are styled the judgments of the Divine justification, because through these we were ransomed and justified. This, then, is the first thing we must call to mind with earnestness and devotion as soon as we have risen from our beds. And for these judgments the saints tell us we should adore, bless, praise, and glorify the Lord, and take them as the object of our worship at the nightly office, as we shall say hereafter, treating of that portion of the office.

The second thing to be remembered when we are going to the Divine Office is that we are about to give thanks to God, and to praise Him for His goodness; and this should be our object at the day hours, as we shall explain below for Prime and Tierce.

The third point to be noticed is that we have to beseech God's boundless mercy for ourselves, for all ranks of men in the Church, taking on ourselves the person of each class, as we shall set forth concerning Sext and None.

It will encourage us to do all this if we bear in mind that nothing is

More worthy of adoration,
More deserving of our praise,
More useful and needful to us
than Almighty God.

When we have devoutly turned these things over in our mind, we must forthwith look back upon ourselves, and see whether we are duly prepared to appear in God's presence, with whom we are about to hold converse; since in the psalms we speak to God, and He in turn speaks to us. For this we need three things, namely:
That our heart be cleansed;
That our thoughts be collected;
That our affections be inflamed.

We must first have our soul cleansed from all deadly sin, that we may worthily appear before the sight of God. Secondly, our thoughts must be recalled from every distraction, to be able to say the Divine Office attentively. Thirdly, our mind must be enkindled with some devout feeling, that we may bestir ourselves from our sloth, and sing to God with reverence, as will be better seen in the preparation that follows.

The third preparation, which is called immediate, consists in prayer; for human effort availeth naught unless helped by divine grace. Therefore, after dwelling on the aforesaid points, let us on our knees humbly beseech the Lord to grant us worthily to adore Him in the judgments of His justice, and devoutly to pay Him the duty of our homage. When, therefore, the sound of the bell hath struck upon our ears, rising from prayer, we should say: This is the sign of the great King; let us go and seek His face, and offer Him gold, incense, and myrrh: the gold of devotion, the incense of devout attention, the myrrh of respectful and manly demeanour.

We next go to the place of prayer, singing in our hearts gladsome hymns of joy, and saying over again: Behold thy Lord and Ruler hath come to His holy temple; rejoice and be glad, O Sion, going forth to meet thy God. See here, O my soul, the Lord of the whole world; and sing with wisdom in the sight of His boundless majesty. With such seraphic words as these a monk should awaken his soul, and lift up his whole self to God. Going into choir and sprinkling ourselves with holy water, we must say, *Asperges me*, &c., and make a general act of sorrow for our venial sins, and on entering say likewise: I will enter into Thy house. And while we are saying this, we should fix our eyes on the Blessed Sacrament of the Eucharist, and bowing down with deep reverence and adoring our God, go on and say: We adore Thee, O Christ, and bless Thee, &c. Then let us say: Thou art my God, and I will confess to Thee; Thou art my God, and I will praise Thee; to Thee be praise, glory, thanksgiving; rightly do all Thy creatures praise, adore, and glorify Thee. This is called the adoration of supreme worship, which kind of honour is owed to God alone. And thus each one standing in his place, with eyes closed and thoughts recollected, may form his intention, saying in his heart: In the sight of the angels I will sing praise to Thee, &c.; in praise, glory, and thanksgiving to the Highest and Undivided Trinity, the Manhood of Jesus Christ, and in union with all the most burning aspirations and prayers of my Lord Jesus Christ while on earth, and who now intercedeth for us at the right hand of God the Father; in union with the inspiration of the Holy Ghost; and in honour of the Blessed Virgin Mary, of the saint whose memory we honour to-day, and of all the saints; for the welfare also of the whole Church, I desire to fulfil this office of praise; would that I could do so worthily. Know, brethren, that this forming of our intention after a careful consideration of the aforesaid points is of great value, and gives to the whole office of Matins a degree of merit, as St. Ambrose and other saints bear witness. And, moreover, if in the course of the office our mind should out of weakness wander through other thoughts, we are hereby excused from the guilt of wilful distraction, because the whole is referred to our first intention, formed as above; and thus our prayer is always meritorious, unless we give way knowingly to distractions, and do not use our best efforts to recall our wandering thoughts.

And this is what we had to say concerning the preparation for Matins, which a monk ought to make during the aforesaid quarter of an hour if he wishes to go onward in the ways of the Spirit, and that his homage be pleasing to God; and after this he will all day long be devout and cheerful, and in a proper mood for the Divine Office.

After he has accustomed himself to this, he had best, at the day hours, briefly reflect that he is going to place himself in the sight of the Lord, to adore Him, thank Him, and ask favours of Him, as we have already said. And whenever he enters the oratory he should sprinkle himself with holy water, saying, as above: We adore Thee, O Christ, &c.; adding, Thou art my God, &c. And standing in his place, during the brief space we are used to wait on our knees let him form his intention; and gathering his thoughts together, let him mentally go through the above prayer, to-wit: In the sight of the angels, &c.

CHAPTER IV.

In what manner a devout religious will be best able to be attentive during the psalmody, so as to keep his mind lifted up to God.

DEAREST brethren, holy men tell us of divers kinds of attention during the Divine Office. But because men in these days are dull of understanding, and but little skilled in things divine, few are able to catch the spiritual meaning of what these holy men tell us; I have therefore thought best to choose one easy method out of the many taught by holy doctors, and to arrange the whole office according to this one as far as our own psalmody is concerned,* so that any one, however simple, can at once understand and make use of it.

The Triple Prayer.†

First, then, during the triple prayer that begins the office and in our mental preparation we must firmly believe that we are in the presence of God, and strive to be there with reverence, attention, and devotion, and as if we were angels in heaven before the throne of the Divine Majesty, so should we take our place among them. And when he that presides gives the sign, we should think ourselves called by God, and make ourselves ready to hold converse with Him. And seeing that we are unworthy, we must beg Him to make us worthy, saying as we begin Matins: O God, incline unto my aid; O Lord, make haste to help me. Thou, O Lord, shalt open my lips, and my tongue shall tell Thy praise. O Lord, why are they multiplied that afflict me? In which words we humbly beg that all the stumbling-blocks of our foes may be taken away from our path, to the end that we may worthily and reverently adore, praise, and magnify our Lord for the judgments of His justice, as we have said above. Next follows the psalm,

Come, let us adore.

* Namely, that of the Benedictine Order.
† A prayer in honour of the Three Divine Persons, formerly in use in our monasteries, described in the ms. *Consuetudines*

During which we must look upon the angels as standing beside us, and speaking to and calling on us, that we may together with them adore and praise our Lord. And we must devoutly reflect on the meaning of each verse of this psalm. Then follows the

Hymn,

which is a certain manner of praising God, and we may offer it to Him in honour of His presence, and, as it were, greeting Him. Next follow the psalms of the first Nocturn, wherein a monk must keep his mind in some fixed place, and set down a number of these resting-places, lest it should wander hither and thither. As far as he can, he should adapt the meaning of the psalms to the scenes he has in his mind; and he can thus go through the whole of the office, reckoning, for example, all the psalms of Matins on the joints of the four fingers of his left hand after this fashion: let him place the tip of his thumb on the first joint of his forefinger, and first meditate on the

I. ANNUNCIATION.

At the first psalm he should meditate on the coming of the angel to Nazareth, as if he saw the angel going into our Lady's poor dwelling, and saying: Hail, full of grace, &c.; and with him a host of angels singing praises, in whose company he may sing the first psalm, adapting it as much as he can to what is being done in that mystery, to-wit, to the Incarnation of the Son of God.

II. BIRTH OF CHRIST.

The first psalm being ended (placing his thumb at the second joint of his forefinger), let him now see in his mind's eye the city of Bethlehem, and behold the new-born Child laid in the crib, listen to the angels' and shepherds' hymns of praise, and with them let him recite the second psalm, adapting, where he can, its meaning to the things that pass before his mind; and should his thoughts wander, he may easily recall them by pressing his finger with his thumb-nail.

III. THE CIRCUMCISION.

The third psalm is to be sung in honour of our Lord's circumcision, doing as above directed concerning this bodily circumcision, by which that of our own souls is signified; and concerning the imposition of the name Jesus, which means Saviour, and the outpouring of His precious blood, and His sufferings and tears, &c.

IV. THE ADORATION OF THE KINGS.

Sing the fourth psalm with the kings, who came to adore the King of kings, adapting its meaning as above.

V. THE PRESENTATION.

Sing the fifth psalm with Simeon and Anna, whilst the Child is presented in the temple.

VI. THE FLIGHT INTO EGYPT.

The sixth, with our Lady and St. Joseph in

Egypt, and at the loss of Christ in the temple, and be present at His baptism, temptation in the wilderness, and at His transfiguration.

Thus the first Nocturn is ended. Sitting down, attend to the meaning of the lessons and responsories, and be transfigured with our Lord on the mount.

Next we come to the second Nocturn, in which we must make six more stations. Let the first be at the

VII. ENTRY OF OUR LORD INTO JERUSALEM.

Reflect minutely on what took place when He entered the city—how He rode upon an ass, and wept; and with the pious Jewish crowds say the first psalm of the second Nocturn, which is the seventh in the whole tale, adapting it as already explained.

VIII. THE LAST SUPPER.

The next psalm should be said with the Apostles at the last supper; and note well what takes place there.

IX. THE PRAYER OF OUR LORD.

The ninth should be said with our Lord praying in the garden, with Michael the Archangel and the other angels there present.

X. FROM HIS CAPTURE TO THE HOUSE OF ANNAS.

At the tenth psalm, follow Him from the garden to the house of Annas with St. John, and see Him dragged along in bonds.

XI. IN THE HOUSE OF ANNAS.

Say the eleventh in the house of Annas, where He was struck in the face and buffeted.

XII. IN THE HOUSE OF CAIPHAS.

The twelfth station is in the house of Caiphas, where He was blindfolded, and where they spat in His face.

And here endeth the second Nocturn.

While the lessons are read, visit our Lord in prison, without, however, failing to listen to the lessons and responsories.

The third Nocturn follows, with its three canticles.

The First Canticle

is to be said with our Lord as He is led from the house of Caiphas to that of Pilate.

The Second Canticle,

from the house of Pilate to Herod.

The Third Canticle,

whilst He is led back from Herod to Pilate. At the

Homily,

behold our Lord scourged and crowned with thorns. After the last responsory, contemplate our Lord led forth crowned with thorns, and how they show Him to the people, and the words, Behold the man; and, to atone for their blasphemies, say the

Te Deum laudamus.

Then see how our Lord is led before Pilate to hear His doom, which is signified by the Gospel, and do thou give attentive ear to it.

But if it be a ferial office, make the stations allotted to the canticles and *Te Deum* at the *Pater noster* and *Ave Maria*, which are said at the beginning of Lauds, and at the psalms *Deus misereatur* and *Miserere*, so that the psalm *Miserere* be ended outside the city, where our Lord laid down His cross. And in the psalms that follow make the stations told off for Lauds on festivals.

The psalms of Lauds are to be said with the following stations :

1. *Deus misereatur*. When after His sentence He was bidden go back to the place of His scourging, to put on His own garments.

2. *Dominus regnavit*. When He was léd forth from Pilate's house, bearing His cross as far as the gate of the city.

3. *Jubilate*. From the gate of the city to Mount Calvary.

4. *Deus, Deus meus*. When He was stripped, laid on the cross, and nailed to it.

5. *Benedicite*. When He was raised up on the cross.

6. *Laudate*. The taking down from the cross, on His Mother's knees, and burial.

Chapter, &c. His going down to the prison of the fathers.

Hymn. The joy of the fathers at seeing Him.

Benedictus. With the holy fathers thanking Him for their deliverance.

Pater noster and Prayer. The reunion of the body and soul of Christ in His tomb.

Antiphon of our Lady. The first apparition of our Lord to His Mother, our Blessed Lady.

Thus Lauds are ended. And in this manner our mind will have been throughout employed in thoughts of our Lord, adoring, blessing, praising, and glorifying Him and praying for our wants. For these are the three things we do at each canonical hour: we adore God for the judgments of His justice, we thank Him for His benefits, and beseech Him for ourselves and for the whole of His people; although at the night office we make it our especial end to praise Him for His judgments, and at the day office we do the like in praying for the welfare of the Church and acknowledging His goodness. We must therefore be attentive at all the hours of the work of God, and at every canonical hour; so that, whenever the meaning of psalm or verse calls on us to adore, to give thanks, or to pray, we may do as it inviteth us. And because some do not know any form for adoring, giving thanks, or praying while at the office, we here give one.

A Form of Adoration.

We may adore as follows, rather with our heart than in words:

O Most High God, I adore Thee for Thy most

righteous decrees fulfilled in Thy most beloved Son.

With these or suchlike words we must adore our Lord in the divine psalmody.

A Form of Thanksgiving.

We may give thanks after this manner:

O Lord Most High, my soul offers thanks and praises to Thee for Thy most burning love, out of which before the world was made Thou hast loved me, predestined me, created me, redeemed me, made me a Christian, drawn me to Thee, led me forth from the world.

And in this wise the aforesaid words may be used to give thanks for any benefit whatever.

A Form of Prayer at the Divine Office.

We may pray in the form here set down, during the psalmody, either for ourselves or for holy Church, or for sinners, or for our kindred, for our benefactors, living or dead, or for any other state of men. At the first psalm, therefore, of Matins, as we are ending it, we may quickly say over in our mind as follows:

O Lord, by Thy holy Incarnation, be merciful to me, a sinner; free me from such and such a temptation; make me humble, chaste, and patient. Or, Grant me Thy grace and glory.

Or we may say:

O Lord, have mercy on Thy Church; or, on sinners; or, on the souls in Purgatory, &c.

At the second psalm we may pray as follows:

O Lord, by Thy blessed nativity, have mercy on me, a sinner, &c., as above. Thus likewise:

By Thy blessed circumcision, by Thy appearing to the kings, by Thy presentation in the temple, by Thy flight into Egypt, and Thy sacred tears which Thou sheddest on entering Jerusalem, grant me contrition and tears of sorrow; by Thy last Supper, &c.

In this manner a monk may throughout the whole psalmody pray, as well for himself as for all states of men in the Church, uttering divers affections according to the different wants of those he prays for.

CHAPTER V.

What a monk should do at Prime and Tierce throughout the whole week, taking the benefits of God for his object according to the days of the week.

On Monday he may consider the goodness of God in creating him.

On Tuesday, in giving him His grace.

On Wednesday, in his vocation.

On Thursday, in his justification.

On Friday, in enriching him with gifts.

On Saturday, in guiding him safely.

On Sunday, in the future gifts of glory.

Each of these benefits is divided into six

heads, three of which are allotted to Prime and three to Tierce.

Hence at each of these six articles we say one psalm, giving thanks to God after this manner:

I thank Thee, O Lord God Most High, for such or such a benefit.

At the hymns of Prime, Tierce, and Sext throughout the whole week, rejoice in the divine presence.

On Monday.

On Monday, meditate on God's goodness in thy creation, thanking Him that He

At Prime: 1. Predestined thee; 2. Created thee; 3. Gave thee a body.

At Tierce: 4. Gave thee a soul; 5. Appointed thee a guardian angel; 6. Gave thee Christian parents.

At Prime on Monday.

From all eternity He predestined thee, loved thee with everlasting love, and had a care of thee.

When it pleased Him He created thee, and gave thee thy place among men, His noblest creatures, and did not make thee a stone or any other such senseless creature.

He gave thee a body, integrity of limbs, and health, freeing thee from many miseries, and fitting thee to serve Him.

At Tierce on Monday.

He gave thee a soul made to His image and

likeness, capable of enjoying Him and living for ever, adorned with many faculties and powers.

He gave thee an angel for thy guardian from the moment thou wast formed, to watch over thee and do thee many loving-kindnesses.

He gave thee Christian parents, so that thou hast not been born an infidel or a Jew; and He caused thee to be born in Christian times.

On Tuesday.

At Prime and Tierce, on Tuesday, consider the gifts of God's grace, in the manner set down for Monday.

Give Him thanks, therefore, that He

At Prime: 1. Hath given thee His grace; 2. His Holy Spirit; 3. His sacraments.

At Tierce: 4. Hath washed thee in the water of Baptism; 5. Hath strengthened thee in Confirmation; Hath made thee a Christian.

At Prime on Tuesday.

He made thee pleasing to Himself in the grace of His beloved Son, not sparing Him, but giving Him to thee as thy reward, example, and companion.

He gave thee the Holy Ghost as an earnest of thy adoption, as a gift of His love, and as the wedding-ring of thy soul, sharing with thee His gifts, fruits, and holy inspirations. He opened the sacraments for thy welfare, and, above all, hath given thee His Church as thy refuge, where thou mayest be safe from the flood of guilt, as Noah was in the ark from the deluge of waters.

At Tierce on Tuesday.

He cleansed thee in Baptism, wherein He forgave thee original sin, gave thee back thy innocence, clothed thee with His justice. He strengthened thee with the sacrament of Confirmation, of which many are bereft, wherein He loaded thee with divers good gifts, and set thee free from many evils.

He made thee a Christian, calling thee by His own name, to show thee that thou art in His grace and favour; and gave thee this name as a memorial of Himself, making thee a child of God and heir to the kingdom of heaven.

On Wednesday.

At Prime and Tierce on Wednesday consider the goodness of God in thy vocation, after the manner set down for Monday.

Give thanks to God, who

At Prime: 1. Bore with thee; 2. Called thee back to Himself; 3. Gave thee a good will.

At Tierce: 4. Welcomed thee; 5. Led thee forth from the world; 6. Placed thee in a well-ordered community.

At Prime on Wednesday.

He hath borne with thee patiently; though thou didst turn back on Him after receiving so many good things, and didst by thy crimes throw thyself away on creatures, yet He waited long for thee, and would not that thou shouldst die in such a state and be lost.

He often called thee back in many ways when thou hadst strayed from the path; at times by His inward whisperings, and again by warnings from others; sometimes by the words of Holy Scripture; sometimes by lavishing His gifts on thee, by putting before thee everlasting joys and sufferings, and in many other ways.

He enriched thee with the will to do good, the first of His gifts; opening the deafness of thy heart, making His voice a voice of might, and clearing from thy path the hindrances to thy conversion.

At Tierce on Wednesday.

As often as thou wert willing to return to Him, with fatherly welcome He kissed and embraced thee, and gave thee back thy robe and ring, as did the father of the prodigal son.

Moreover, He received thee to repentance, led thee out of the world, like Lot out of Sodom and Abraham from the Chaldees and Noah from the flood.

He set thee in a well-ordered house, amid holy brethren living according to rule, and preserved thee from the assembly of evil-doers. He gave thee time to do penance, a time of priceless worth, and granted thee forgiveness of all thy past sins through thy profession, as in a second baptism.

On Thursday.

On Thursday consider, as above, God's goodness in the work of thy justification, thanking thy Lord because He

At Prime: 1. Changed thy will; 2. Gave thee perseverance; 3. Gave thee hope.

At Tierce: 4. Fed thee with the Eucharist; 5. Opened the Scriptures before thee; 6. Bequeathed to thee the adornments of virtue.

At Prime on Thursday.

He wrought a change in thy will, so that the once bitter works of penance became sweet, and what had been sweet to thee turned to bitterness; and He gave thee the noble gift of keeping thyself pure from sin.

He gave thee perseverance and steadfastness, without which no man can be saved, since many have begun without abiding to the end.

He bestowed on thee the gift of hope and the grace of not giving up what thou hadst undertaken; the hope of having forgiveness, grace, and glory from Him; strengthening thee in this by many inward consolations, and giving thee grace to go forward by the hatred of thy past evils, and by yearning after the blessedness to come.

At Tierce on Thursday.

He hath given thee the Sacrament of the Altar, spreading a table before thee, at which thou mayst eat and be strengthened, lest thou shouldst faint on the way; He hath given thee the Sacrament of His Body and Blood, and the bread of thy pilgrimage as a sacrament of union and a victim for thy ransom.

He hath unfolded the books of Scripture before thee, where, as in a mirror, thou mayst view thy failings, enkindle thy desires, and cleanse and justify thyself ever more and more.

He hath robed thee in the ornaments and exercises of virtue, covering with these the foulness of thy sins.

And lest thou shouldst grow faint and cold in the works of righteousness, He hath given thee the example of His saints with which to instruct and encourage thyself.

On Friday.

At Prime and Tierce on Friday reflect how God has bestowed His gifts on thee, and thank Him that He has

At Prime: 1. Clothed thee from the first with many gifts; 2. Added many more; 3. Given thee the grace of meditation.

At Tierce: 4. Enkindled His love in thee; 5. Kept thee from sin; 6. Raised thee when thou hadst fallen.

At Prime on Friday.

He made thee adorned with noble gifts of nature, giving thee understanding and memory, strength, and the beauty of the human form; and gave thee those of grace, the true faith, and the wish to follow Him.

He has added many other good things, leading thee back from thy wayward paths, teaching the darkness of thy mind, raising thee when fallen.

He gave thee grace for inward meditation and outward employments, enlightening thy understanding, kindling His love in thy heart, guiding thy affections.

At Tierce on Friday.

He enkindled His love in thee; for He did not only make His light shine on thy understanding, but, which is yet more, gave thee sweetness and devotion, and cheered thee with His inward consolations, giving thee an earnest of everlasting life.

He hath guarded thee from sin, warding off occasions, strengthening thee to fight against them, and healing thy affections lest thou shouldst fall back. He hath raised thee up after thy falls. And if ever He let thee be overcome with temptation, He gave thee to rise again with greater strength; He enabled thee to renew the fight more vigorously, and placed His hand on thee to save thee from being overthrown.

On Saturday.

At Prime and Tierce on Saturday consider His goodness in guiding thee, and thank Him that He has

At Prime: 1. Preserved thy being; 2. Saved thee from many harms; 3. Given thee support for all thy wants.

At Tierce: 4. Supplied thee with many other good things; 5. Preserved other creatures for thy well-being; 6. Watched over and governed thee.

At Prime on Saturday.

He hath preserved thy being, nourished thee daily, and given thee health and gladness; whilst of thyself thou art nothing.

From thy cradle to this day He hath kept thee safe from many dangers, illnesses, enemies, and many other evils.

He hath sustained thee in all thy wants, giving thee as thou hadst need thy daily food and clothing.

At Tierce on Saturday.

All other needful things He hath lavished on thee—a dwelling, and a bed to sleep in; and not only things needful, but many other things for thy use and comfort.

He hath kept other creatures in being for thy sake, governing the change of seasons, and bringing forth divers kinds of fruit to afford thee pleasure.

He hath governed and guided thee, being thy leader in adversity as well as in prosperity; and in adversity itself hath bestowed many good gifts on thee, cleansing thee from sin, and heaping up thy merits. And what is more, He has always such care and guard over thee as if He had a care of none besides. And He is always with thee, and beholdeth all thy works.

On Sunday.

At Prime and Tierce on Sunday meditate on the gift of thy future blessedness in glory, and thank God for His gifts of glory, which are to be

At Prime: 1. Above thee; 2. Beside thee; 3. Within thee.

At Tierce: 4. Without thee; 5. Beneath thee; 6. Around thee.

At Prime on Sunday.

He hath promised thee the joys of heaven. Above thee are the enjoyment of the Godhead, the sight of our Saviour and of His glorious Mother. Reflect, then, what a great joy it will be to see the King of heaven in His glory, and our Blessed Lady, His Virgin Mother, illumined and glorified by God.

Beside thee thou wilt have for thy delight the company of the saints, who are most beautiful and noble, full of love, and countless in numbers.

Within thee thou wilt enjoy the glorification of soul and body, which latter will be adorned with the four gifts of glory, and clothed with immortality, and will shine more brightly than the sun.

At Tierce on Sunday.

Without thee He will give a most lovely and

delicious abode, filled with all delights, with sweetest fragrance, with music and all kinds of harmony, boundless in extent, and resplendent with light.

Below thee He will grant thee other joys. For thou shalt reap delight not only from things above, but likewise from such as are below thee; seeing thou hast in the might of God overthrown thy fierce and dreaded foes, and that out of His mercy thou hast washed away thy sins with tears, and hast escaped such fearful pains.

Around thee He will set forth for thee many other good things, beyond all reckoning, measureless and peerless in value; in a word, thou shalt be freed from all harm, and all thy wishes shall be fulfilled, having all thou wishest, and having naught thou wouldst not.

ON THE USEFULNESS OF THANKSGIVING FOR BENEFITS.

Thus far, dearest brethren, we have at Prime and Tierce on every day in the week called to mind the benefits received from God; that none may be able to plead excuse, saying that he does not know how to give thanks, while this should be the foremost of a religious man's duties, to become worthy of benefits by being thankful for those he has received. It is because we are ungrateful that we get such scanty measure of virtues and gifts from above, and chiefly so little of the love of God. For we can never be apt to have a perfect love of God unless we meditate often on His goodness; for these are the bonds by which we are drawn, and are made fit for and cleave fast to God, as He bears witness in the Prophet Osea, saying: I will draw them with the cords of Adam. What are these bonds of Adam, brethren, if not the constant thoughts of God's benefits, as Hugh of Lincoln and St. Bonaventure tell us? With every effort, therefore, must we strive to accustom ourselves to gain skill in these exercises; and we shall assuredly find our souls enlightened and set on fire by God; because, as St. Augustine says, nothing kindles in us the love of God so much as often to remember His gifts.

CHAPTER VI.

How a religious should employ his thoughts at Sext and None.

As we have said above, we ought to pray to our Lord, not for ourselves alone, but for the whole world, and with the utmost fervour of our heart, that He would vouchsafe to show His mercy to all His creatures, for whom the Prince of glory, Christ our Redeemer, deigned to suffer, that all may be brought to the knowledge of the Catholic faith, whether they be Christians, Jews, or infidels; and may not be bereft of that most delightful fellow-

ship of the blessed, and lose the beatific vision of
the Godhead, for the contemplation and enjoyment
of which all rational beings were made; for whom,
likewise, the precious treasure of Christ's blood
was poured out on the cross. Above all, we are
bound to pray to the Divine Majesty for the people
of Christ as it befits us. Jeremias the prophet,
when he saw his people oppressed and led captive
into Babylon by the wicked king Nabuchodonosor,
said with grief: Who will give water to my head
and a fountain of tears to my eyes, and I shall
weep day and night over the slain of my people?
Who is this wicked king, brethren, if not the
devil, who leads the souls of Christians captive to
Babylon, that is to say, to hell? And who is the
prophet, if he be not the devout religious, who
cleaves fast to God by love, and, standing before
God, filled with the spirit of compassion, ceases
not to pour forth heartfelt prayers and to weep day
and night for the slain of his people? We ought
therefore, brethren, at Sext and None to take upon
us in our prayers, with earnest affection, the person of each particular state of men in the Church,
whilst we recall to mind those seven words which
our Saviour uttered in His agony on the cross,
asking of the Divine Majesty, for the sake of each
of these words, whatever is needed for the seven
different classes of men for whom we pray.

The first word: *Father, forgive them, for they
know not what they do.* For our enemies, whether
Christians, Mahometans, Jews, or other infidels.

The second: *Woman, behold thy son; son, behold thy Mother.* For our relations.

The third: *To-day thou shalt be with Me in Paradise.* For our benefactors.

The fourth: *My God, My God, why hast Thou forsaken Me?* For all in temptation, sorrow, and captivity.

The fifth: *I thirst.* For all in mortal sin.

The sixth: *It is finished.* For the just.

The seventh: *Father, into Thy hands I commend My spirit.* For the sick and those in their agony.

At Sext throughout the Week.

While reciting the first psalm bear in mind the first word, Father, forgive them, for they know not what they do. Pray for thy enemies, whether Christians, Mahometans, Jews, or other infidels; wishing from thy heart that they may come to the knowledge of the truth, lest they be shut out from everlasting blessedness. And make thy prayer with heartfelt devotion, saying: Most merciful Lord, by that first word Thou didst speak on the cross, have mercy on all these souls.

Say the second psalm in the name of all thy kindred, having before thy mind the second word our Lord spoke on the cross: Woman, behold thy son. And to the disciple: Behold thy Mother. And form thy prayer thus: O Lord, by this Thy word, have pity on our relations.

Say the third psalm for thy benefactors, remembering the third word our Lord spoke on the cross when He said to the thief: To-day thou shalt be with Me in Paradise. And form thy petition thus: O Lord, by the power of this Thy sacred word so full of pity, have pity on our benefactors.

At None throughout the Week.

Thou mayest recite the hymn in the name of all in temptation, trouble, and bondage, having present to thy mind the fourth word of Christ: My God, My God, why hast Thou forsaken Me? Thy prayer should be as follows: O Lord, by the might of this Thy word, vouchsafe to help all that are in woe, in temptation, and in prison.

Recite the first psalm in the person of such as are in mortal sin, recalling the fifth word of Christ on the cross: I thirst; that is, for the salvation of souls. And let this be thy prayer: O my God, by the power of this most sacred word, have pity on all in mortal sin, and bring them to true penance.

The second psalm should be said in the name of all the just, in memory of the sixth word of Christ: It is finished; to-wit, all that hath been foretold of the decrees of the justice of My Father. And pray thus: O Lord, by this most sacred word, keep all just men in works of righteousness.

The third psalm is to be sung in behalf all the sick and dying; and it represents the seventh word spoken by Christ on the cross, namely—

Father, into Thy hands I commend My spirit. And the prayer should be in this form: O Lord, by this sacred word of Thine, have mercy on all in sickness, and receive the souls of such as are in their agony.

CHAPTER VII.

Concerning Vespers.

A RELIGIOUS should prepare himself carefully for the office of Evensong, to offer up to the Lord his Vesper sacrifice; and after going over again his preparation as at the night office, he should at his place in the choir collect his thoughts, and mount up to heaven in spirit, and place himself before the throne of God's Majesty, and of the multitude of the angels, and of all the saints who sing around the throne of God, and with deepest awe should praise God, as it were, among them, singing the first psalm with the angels, the second with the patriarchs, the third with the prophets, the fourth with the apostles, the chapter and responses with the martyrs, the hymn with the confessors, the first half of the *Magnificat* with our Blessed Lady, and the latter half with the virgins; the *Pater noster* and collect with the whole Church militant.

CHAPTER VIII.
Concerning Compline.

THE last of the canonical hours is Compline, and as it ends the day and the works of our active life, so a devout religious should pass from these works to contemplation, and from outward to inward employments. For this reason we say *Converte nos*, &c. at the beginning of Compline, asking of God to turn us from active works to contemplation.

Say the first psalm with all the holy fathers in behalf of the souls in Purgatory, thinking on our Lord's descent into hell. And thus shouldst thou pray: O Lord, by Thy most holy going down into Limbo, having pity on all the souls that are in Purgatory.

The second psalm should be said in the person of holy Church, calling to mind our Lord on Mount Olivet, the day of His ascension, with our Lady and the college of Apostles bearing the figure of the Church. And pray thus: O Lord, by Thy holy ascension, have mercy on Thy Church, and on all orders and classes of the faithful.

Say the third psalm in the name of all our congregation, with our Lady, the Apostles, and the holy women in the supper-chamber, in memory of the coming of the Holy Ghost. And pray thus: O Lord, by the coming of the Holy Ghost, have pity on our congregation; vouchsafe to shed the grace and gifts of the same Holy Ghost upon it, that He may ever guide and rule us.

CONCLUSION OF THIS WORK.

We have thus far spoken of divers holy thoughts and subjects which a religious may bear in mind at each psalm of the Divine Office. For as we have said, it helpeth much to keep us devout and attentive, if we have our mind steady in one fixed place. Holy men have used these objects in divers ways; some have adapted them to the several hours of Christ's passion; others to the life of our Lord, according to the days of the week, as St. Bonaventure teaches in his book on the contemplation of the life of Christ. Others on the letter of the Gospel, as Gerson writes in his *Monotesseron*. Others on the benefits received from God. And because all things do not suit all men, we have suited ourselves to the capacity of men in our days, by culling from each of the above what could be practised with most profit and least trouble. Wherefore he that wishes worthily to offer up God's praise, let him carefully think over the method we have laid down. And if he doth so, he will be able with tranquil conscience to plead before God's clemency in behalf of his distractions in time of office, doing what he can, since it belongeth to angels, and not to men, to sing to God without any distraction. And that the unlettered may understand what we mean when we talk of an *object*, we call by that name any pious thought concerning, for example, the life of Christ, the goodness of God, the wants of men, &c., as above.

CHAPTER IX.

How to end the canonical hours, and on what subject a good monk ought to think during the pause we make on our knees in choir after each hour.

We have, then, dealt with the beginning and progress of the canonical hours, and shall now explain how to end them. For we read in Ecclesiastes, that the end of a speech is better than its beginning. And this is said rightly, because praise is given at the end. And every work must be held as well done when it ends well. Therefore, brethren, it ill beseems us to hurry out of choir as soon as the hour of prayer is over. And holy men find great fault with this; and say that rather, when our duty is discharged, we should inwardly beseech our Lord from the bottom of our hearts to vouchsafe to be pleased with our service, and should humbly ask His forgiveness, return thanks, and offer Him sacrifice.

First, let a monk reflect whether he has been duly attentive, devout, and reverent, and for whatsoever he finds he has done amiss let him ask pardon of God; let the lowliness of his prayer make up for his lack of devotion, and let him say with contrite heart the words of the publican: Lord, be merciful to me, a sinner; words of great virtue and marvellous devotion. If they had efficacy enough to reconcile the publican with God, we may well trust that they will atone for the shortcomings we fall into against our will in the Divine Office. And while saying this, let us strike our breasts, as the publican did.

Secondly, let him be mindful to thank God, who hath vouchsafed to admit us to praise Him, and to pour out His grace and consolation on us, and give us a firm hope that He has heard us.

Thirdly, let him be careful about offering up the sacrifice of the night office, as well as that of Lauds, and of the other canonical hours, which is in the highest degree needful, lest the birds of the air, to-wit, the devil and our bad thoughts, come and carry off the seed of God's word that had been sown in the field of our heart during the time of holy psalmody, and which godly seed must be forthwith hidden by prayer. Know, therefore, brethren, that each good work ye do should at once be offered up to God by prayer, that the seed of God may always take root in the heart, and that the ghostly fruit of good works may grow and ripen in you, so that your life be pleasing to God, and fruitful to His Church. And this offering should never be left out at the end of the work of God, that our Lord may deign to let us hold fast what He hath vouchsafed to grant us.

And this offering should be made through the prayers of the saints whose feasts we keep and of the Blessed Virgin, after this manner :

O Lord my God, receive the homage of my service through the prayers and merits of the most glorious Virgin Mary, and of all thy saints, and especially of the angels and apostles, and of the saint whose festival we keep to-day. And if I have done aught worthily in this homage of praise look on it with clemency, and what I have done amiss, do thou mercifully forgive. Through Christ our Lord.

Or thus :

My morning (or evening) sacrifice is now fulfilled. Accept it, O Lord, by the intercession of the most Blessed Virgin Mary, and of the saint whose memory we celebrate this day, and of all Thy saints, to the praise and glory of Thy name, and for the salvation of our souls and of all Christians, and the repose of the departed. Through Christ our Lord.

At the end of the other hours, the offering may be made thus :

The sacrifice of praise is ended. Receive it, &c.

And thus we ought to keep ourselves always in the same devout mood and gravity of demeanour after prayer, as if we had just risen up from it, turning our mind to our wonted exercises, and to such as we have described above, and meditating leisurely upon them.

CHAPTER X.

What we should reflect upon while Gloria Patri is being sung at the end of the psalms.

ST. BONAVENTURE writes that all God's benefits are gifts either of nature, of grace, or of reparation, which answer to the gifts of creation, justification, and redemption. And these three priceless gifts are attributed to the three Divine Persons.

The work of our creation is wont to be attributed in a special manner to the Father; our redemption, to the Son; our justification, to the Holy Ghost. Therefore, whenever we say the *Gloria Patri,* we should call to mind these three gifts, saying: Glory be to the Father, who created me out of nothing; to the Son, who redeemed me when I was lost; to the Holy Ghost, who justified me when I was a child of wrath.

Otherwise: Glory to the Father, who made all things; to the Son, who redeemed the world; to the Holy Ghost, who justified all the saints.

And be He glorified thus for all and each of these works, as He was glorified in the beginning, when the morning stars praised Him, and with the glory He hath now, and will have from the whole Church in this world, and from all the citizens of heaven for ever and ever in our true country, who hath given me all these good things. Amen.

Here endeth the Directory of the Canonical Hours, to the honour and glory of God, and of His most glorious Mother, our Blessed Lady the Virgin Mary. Amen.

SUMMARY OF THIS TREATISE.

This treatise has four principal parts:
1. Preparation for the Divine Office.
2. Acts of adoration for Matins, Lauds, and Vespers.
3. Acts of thanksgiving at Prime and Tierce.
4. Petitions at Sext, None, and Compline.

The ways of preparing for the Divine Office are three:
1. Remote, or the preparation of a holy life; 2. Special, or devout meditation; 3. Immediate, or fervent prayer.

That of living holily consists:
    In keeping watch over our heart;
    Spending our time usefully;
    Giving a right direction to our works.

Secondly, we must devoutly meditate that we are going to
    Adore God;
    Give thanks to Him;
    Ask favours of Him.

Because He is most worthy of adoration, He is our fittest object of praise, and our most needful and useful end.

In order to pray fervently, we must have our mind pure, recollected, and filled with holy affections.

Our tribute of adoration is thus set forth:

At Matins we must adore Christ's life on earth, His passion and glorification.

At Vespers we must adore God in company with our Blessed Lady, with the Church triumphant, and with the Church militant.

At Prime and Tierce we thank God, calling to mind all His benefits in the following order:

On Monday, the work of our creation; on Tuesday, the gifts of grace; on Wednesday, our vocation; on Thursday, our justification; on Friday, the other gifts of body and soul; on Saturday, the providence of God in this our pilgrimage; on Sunday, our glorification.

Each of the aforesaid benefits is divided into six articles, so that each article answers to one of the six psalms which are recited at Sext and None throughout the week, as we have explained more at length elsewhere.

Our petitions at Sext and None are made for seven classes of men, in reverence for the seven words spoken by our Lord on the cross.

At the three psalms of Sext we pray: 1. For our enemies, whether Christians or infidels or Jews; 2. For our kindred; 3. For our benefactors.

At the hymn and three psalms of None we pray: 1. For all in suffering, trial, and bondage;

2. For such as are in mortal sin; 3. For the just; 4. For the sick, and such as are in their agony.

At Compline we pray: 1. For the suffering souls in Purgatory; 2. For the welfare of the whole Church; 3. For our own congregation.

THE END.

LONDON:
ROBSON AND SONS, PRINTERS, PANCRAS ROAD, N.W.

A Select Catalogue of Books

LATELY PUBLISHED BY

BURNS AND OATES,

17, 18 PORTMAN STREET

AND

68 PATERNOSTER ROW.

LONDON:
ROBSON AND SONS, PRINTERS, PANCRAS ROAD, N.W.

Books lately published

BY

BURNS AND OATES,

17, 18 PORTMAN STREET, W., & 63 PATERNOSTER ROW, E.C.

Sin and its Consequences. By His Eminence the CARDINAL ARCHBISHOP OF WESTMINSTER. Second edition. 6s.

    CONTENTS: I. The Nature of Sin. II. Mortal Sin. III. Venial Sin. IV. Sins of Omission. V. The Grace and Works of Penance. VI. Temptation. VII. The Dereliction on the Cross. VIII. The Joys of the Resurrection.

'We know few better books than this for spiritual reading. These lectures are prepared with great care, and are worthy to rank with the old volumes of sermons which are now standard works of the English tongue.'—*Weekly Register.*

'We have had many volumes from his Grace's pen of this kind, but perhaps none more practical or more searching than the volume before us. These discourses are the clearest and simplest exposition of the theology of the subjects they treat of that could be desired. The intellect is addressed as well as the conscience. Both are strengthened and satisfied.'—*Tablet.*

'Of the deepest value, and of great theological and literary excellence. More clear and lucid expositions of dogmatic and moral theology could not be found. No one can read these very forcible, searching, and practical sermons without being deeply stirred and greatly edified.'—*Church Herald.*

'His Grace has added to Catholic literature such a brilliant disquisition as can hardly be equalled.'—*Catholic Times.*

'As powerful, searching, and deep as any that we have ever read. It construction, as well as in theology and in rhetoric, they are more than remarkable, and are amongst the best from his Grace's pen.'—*Union Review.*

The Prophet of Carmel: a Series of Practical Considerations upon the History of Elias in the Old Testament; with a Supplementary Dissertation. By the Rev. CHARLES B. GARSIDE, M.A. Dedicated to the Very Rev. JOHN HENRY NEWMAN, D.D. 5s.

'There is not a page in these sermons but commands our respect. They are Corban in the best sense; they belong to the sanctuary, and are marked as divine property by a special cachet. They are simple without being trite, and poetical without being pretentious.'—*Westminster Gazette.*

'Full of spiritual wisdom uttered in pure and engaging language.'—*The Universe.*

'We see in these pages the learning of the divine, the elegance of the scholar, and the piety of the priest. Every point in the sacred narrative bearing upon the subject of his book is seized upon by the author with the greatest keenness of perception, and set forth with singular force and clearness.'—*Weekly Register.*

'Under his master-hand the marvellous career of the Prophet of Carmel displays its majestic proportions. His strong, nervous, incisive style has a beauty and a grace, a delicacy and a sensitiveness, that seizes hold of the heart and captivates the imagination. He has attained to the highest art of writing, which consists in selecting the words which express one's meaning with the greatest clearness in the least possible space.'—*Tablet.*

'The intellectual penetration, the rich imagination, the nervous eloquence which we meet with throughout the whole work, all combine to give it at once a very high place among the highest productions of our English Catholic literature.'—*Dublin Review.*

'Is at once powerful and engaging, and calculated to furnish ideas innumerable to the Christian preacher.'—*Church Review.*

'The thoughts are expressed in plain and vigorous English. The sermons are good specimens of the way in which Old Testament subjects should be treated for the instruction of a Christian congregation.'—*Church Times.*

Mary magnifying God: May Sermons. By the Rev. Fr. HUMPHREY, O.S.C. Cloth, 2s. 6d.

'Each sermon is a complete thesis, eminent for the strength of its logic, the soundness of its theology, and the lucidness of its expression. With equal force and beauty of language the author has provided matter for the most sublime meditations.'—*Tablet.*

'Dogmatic teaching of the utmost importance is placed before us so clearly, simply, and unaffectedly, that we find ourselves acquiring invaluable lessons of theology in every page.'—*Weekly Register.*

By the same,

The Divine Teacher. Second edition. 2s. 6d.

'The most excellent treatise we have ever read. It could not be clearer, and, while really deep, it is perfectly intelligible to any person of the most ordinary education.'—*Tablet.*

'We cannot speak in terms too high of the matter contained in this excellent and able pamphlet.'—*Westminster Gazette.*

Sermons by Fathers of the Society of Jesus.
Third edition. 7s.
CONTENTS: The Latter Days: Four Sermons by the Rev. H. J. Coleridge. The Temptations of our Lord: Four Sermons by the Rev. Father Hathaway. The Angelus Bell: Five Lectures on the Remedies against Desolation by the Very Rev. Father Gallwey, Provincial of the Society. The Mysteries of the Holy Infancy: Seven Sermons by Fathers Parkinson, Coleridge, and Harper.

Also, printed separately from above,

The Angelus Bell: Five Lectures on the Remedies against Desolation. By the Very Rev. Father GALLWEY, Provincial of the Society of Jesus. 1s. 6d.

Also Vol. II. in same series,

Discourses by the Rev. Fr. Harper, S.J. 6s.
Also, just published, Vol. III. 6s.
CONTENTS: Sermons by the Rev. George R. Kingdon: I. What the Passion of Christ teaches us; II. Our Lord's Agony in the Garden; III. The Choice between Jesus and Barabbas; IV. Easter Sunday (I.); V. Easter Sunday (II.); VI. Corpus Christi. Sermons by the Rev. Edward I. Purbrick: VII. Grandeur and Beauty of the Holy Eucharist; VIII. Our Lady of Victories; IX. The Feast of All Saints (I.); X. The Feast of All Saints (II.); XI. The Feast of the Immaculate Conception; XII. The Feast of St. Joseph. Sermons by the Rev. Henry J. Coleridge: XIII. Fruits of Holy Communion (I.); XIV. Fruits of Holy Communion (II.); XV. Fruits of Holy Communion (III.); XVI. Fruits of Holy Communion (IV.). Sermons by the Rev. Alfred Weld: XVII. On the Charity of Christ; XVIII. On the Blessed Sacrament. Sermons by the Rev. William H. Anderdon: XIX. The Corner-Stone a Rock of Offence; XX. The Word of God heard or rejected by Men.

WORKS WRITTEN AND EDITED BY LADY GEORGIANA FULLERTON.

The Straw-cutter's Daughter, and the Portrait in my Uncle's Dining-room. Two Stories. Translated from the French. 2s. 6d.

Life of Luisa de Carvajal. 6s.

Seven Stories. 3s. 6d.
 CONTENTS: I. Rosemary: a Tale of the Fire of London. II. Reparation: a Story of the Reign of Louis XIV. III. The Blacksmith of Antwerp. IV. The Beggar of the Steps of St. Roch: a True Story. V. Trouvaille, or the Soldier's Adopted Child: a True Story. VI. Earth without Heaven: a Reminiscence. VII. Ad Majorem Dei Gloriam.
 'Will well repay perusal.'—*Weekly Register.*
 'Each story in this series has its own charm.'—*Tablet.*
 'In this collection may be found stories sound in doctrine and intensely interesting as any which have come from the same pen.'—*Catholic Opinion.*
 'As admirable for their art as they are estimable for their sound teaching.'—*Cork Examiner.*

A Sketch of the Life of the late Father Henry Young, of Dublin. 2s. 6d.

Life of Mère Marie de la Providence, Foundress of the Order of the 'Helpers of the Holy Souls.'
 The materials of this Biography have been drawn from the 'Notice sur la Révérende Mère Marie de la Providence,' published in Paris in 1872; the work of the Rev. Père Blôt, 'Les Auxiliatrices des Ames du Purgatoire;' and some additional documents furnished to the authoress by the Religious of the Rue de la Barouillière. 2s.

Laurentia: a Tale of Japan. Second edition. 3s. 6d.
 'Has very considerable literary merit, and possesses an interest entirely its own. The dialogue is easy and natural, and the incidents are admirably grouped.'—*Weekly Register.*
 'Full of romantic records of the heroism of the early Christians of Japan in the sixteenth century. Looking at its literary merits alone, it must be pronounced a really beautiful story.'—*Catholic Times.*

Life of St. Frances of Rome. 2s. 6d.; cheap edition, 1s. 8d.

Rose Leblanc: a Tale of great interest. 3s.

Grantley Manor: the well-known and favourite Novel. Cloth, 3s. 6d.; cheap edition, 2s. 6d.

Germaine Cousin: a Drama. 6d.

Fire of London: a Drama. 6d.

OUR LADY'S BOOKS.
Uniformly printed in foolscap 8vo, limp cloth.

No. 1.
Memoir of the Hon. Henry E. Dormer. 2s.

No. 2.
Life of Mary Fitzgerald, a Child of the Sacred Heart. 2s.; cheap edition, 1s.

Meditations for every Day in the Year, and for the Principal Feasts. By the Ven. Fr. NICHOLAS LANCICIUS, of the Society of Jesus. With Preface by the Rev. GEORGE PORTER, S.J. 6s. 6d.

'Most valuable, not only to religious, for whom they were originally intended, but to all those who desire to consecrate their daily life by regularly express and systematic meditation; while Father Porter's excellent little Preface contains many valuable hints on the method of meditation.'—*Dublin Review.*

'Full of Scripture, short and suggestive. The editor gives a very clear explanation of the Ignatian method of meditation. The book is a very useful one.'—*Tablet.*

'Short and simple, and dwell almost entirely on the life of our Blessed Lord, as related in the Gospels. Well suited to the wants of Catholics living in the world.'—*Weekly Register.*

'A book of singular spirituality and great depth of piety. Nothing could be more beautiful or edifying than the thoughts set forth for reflection, clothed as they are in excellent and vigorous English.'—*Union Review.*

Meditations for the Use of the Clergy, for every Day in the Year, on the Gospels for the Sundays. From the Italian of Mgr. SCOTTI, Archbishop of Thessalonica. Revised and edited by the Oblates of St. Charles. With a Preface by his Grace the ARCHBISHOP OF WESTMINSTER.

Vol. I. From the First Sunday in Advent to the Sixth Saturday after the Epiphany. 4s.

Vol. II. From Septuagesima Sunday to the Fourth Sunday after Easter. 4s.

Vol. III. From the Fifth Sunday after Easter to the Eleventh Sunday after Pentecost. 4s.

Vol. IV., completing the work. 4s.

'This admirable little book will be much valued by all; but especially by the clergy, for whose use it is more immediately intended. The Archbishop states in his Preface that it is held in high esteem in Rome, and that he has himself found, by the experience of many years, its singular excellence, its practical piety, its abundance of Scripture, of the Fathers, and of ecclesiastical writers.'—*Tablet*.

'It is a sufficient recommendation to this book of meditations that our Archbishop has given them his own warm approval. . . . They are full of the language of the Scriptures, and are rich with unction of their Divine sense.'—*Weekly Register*.

'A manual of meditations for priests, to which we have seen nothing comparable.'—*Catholic World*.

'There is great beauty in the thoughts, the illustrations are striking, the learning shown in patristic quotation considerable, and the special applications to priests are very powerful. It is entirely a priest's book.'—*Church Review*.

The Question of Anglican Ordinations discussed. By the Very Rev. Canon ESTCOURT, M.A., F.A.S. With an Appendix of Original Documents and Photographic Facsimiles. One vol. 8vo, 14s.

'A valuable contribution to the theology of the Sacrament of Order. He treats a leading question, from a practical point of view, with great erudition, and with abundance of illustrations from the rites of various ages and countries.'—*Month*.

'Will henceforth be an indispensable portion of every priest's library, inasmuch as it contains all the information that has been collected in previous works, sifted and corrected, together with a well-digested mass of important matter which has never before been given to the public.'—*Tablet*.

'Marks a very important epoch in the history of that question, and virtually disposes of it.'—*Messenger*.

'Canon Estcourt has added valuable documents that have never appeared before, or never at full length. The result is a work of very great value.'—*Catholic Opinion*.

'Indicates conscientious and painstaking research, and will be indispensable to any student who would examine the question on which it treats.'—*Bookseller*.

'Superior, both in literary method, tone, and mode of reasoning, to the usual controversial books on this subject.'—*Church Herald*.

May Papers; or Thoughts on the Litanies of Loreto. By EDWARD IGNATIUS PURBRICK, Priest of the Society of Jesus. 3s. 6d.

'There is a brightness and vivacity in them which will make them interesting to all, old and young alike, and adds to their intrinsic value.'—*Dublin Review*.

'We very gladly welcome this volume as a valuable addition to the now happily numerous manuals of devout exercises for the month.'—*Month*.

'Written in the pure, simple, unaffected language which becomes the subject.'—*Tablet*.

'We cannot easily conceive a book more calculated to aid the cause of true religion amongst young persons of every class.'—*Weekly Register*.

'They are admirable, and expressed in chaste and beautiful language. Although compiled in the first place for boys at school, they are adapted for the spiritual reading of Catholics of every age and condition of life.'—*Catholic Opinion*.

WORKS OF THE REV. FATHER RAWES, O.S.C.

Homeward: a Tale of Redemption. Second edition. 3s. 6d.

'A series of beautiful word pictures.'—*Catholic Opinion.*
'A casket well worth the opening; full to the brim of gems of thought as beautiful as they are valuable.'—*Catholic Times.*
'Full of holy thoughts and exquisite poetry, and just such a book as can be taken up with advantage and relief in hours of sadness and depression.'—*Dublin Review.*
'Is really beautiful, and will be read with profit.'—*Church Times.*

God in His Works: a Course of Five Sermons. 2s. 6d.

SUBJECTS: I. God in Creation. II. God in the Incarnation. III. God in the Holy See. IV. God in the Heart. V. God in the Resurrection.

'Full of striking imagery, and the beauty of the language cannot fail to make the book valuable for spiritual reading.'—*Catholic Times.*
'He has so applied science as to bring before the reader an unbroken course of thought and argument.'—*Tablet.*

The Beloved Disciple; or St. John the Evangelist. 3s. 6d.

'Full of research, and of tender and loving devotion.'—*Tablet.*
'This is altogether a charming book for spiritual reading.'—*Catholic Times.*
'Through this book runs a vein of true, humble, fervent piety, which gives a singular charm.'—*Weekly Register.*
'St. John, in his varied character, is beautifully and attractively presented to our pious contemplation.'—*Catholic Opinion.*

Septem: Seven Ways of hearing Mass. Fifth edition. 1s. and 2s.; red edges, 2s. 6d.; calf, 4s.; French Translation, 1s. 6d.

'A great assistance to hearing Mass with devotion. Besides its devotional advantages it possesses a Preface, in clear and beautiful language, well worth reading.'—*Tablet.*

Great Truths in Little Words. Third edition. Neat cloth, 3s. 6d.

'A most valuable little work. All may learn very much about the Faith rom it.'—*Tablet.*
'At once practical in its tendency, and elegant; oftentimes poetical in its diction.'—*Weekly Register.*
'Cannot fail to be most valuable to every Catholic; and we feel certain, when known and appreciated, it will be a standard work in Catholic households.'—*Catholic Times.*

Hymns, Original, &c. Neat cloth, 1s.;
cheap edition, 6d.

**The Eucharistic Month.* From the Latin of
Father LERCARI, S.J. 6d.; cloth, 1s.

*ial*Twelve Visits to our Lady and the Heavenly
City of God.* Second edition. 8d.

**Nine Visits to the Blessed Sacrament.* Chiefly
from the Canticle of Canticles. Second edition. 6d.

**Devotions for the Souls in Purgatory.* Second edition. 8d.

* Or in one vol.,
Visits and Devotions. Neat cloth, 3s.

WORKS BY FATHER ANDERDON, S.J.

Christian Æsop. 3s. 6d. and 4s.

In the Snow: Tales of Mount St. Bernard.
Sixth edition. Cloth, 1s. 6d.

Afternoons with the Saints. Eighth edition,
enlarged. 5s.

Catholic Crusoe. Seventh edition. Cloth gilt,
3s. 6d.

Confession to a Priest. 1d.

What is the Bible ? Is yours the right Book ?
New edition. 1d.

Also, edited by Father Anderdon,
What do Catholics really believe ? 2d.

Cherubini: Memorials illustrative of his Life.
With Portrait and Catalogue of his Works. By EDWARD
BELLASIS, Barrister-at-Law. One vol., 429 pp. 10s. 6d.

Louise Lateau of Bois d'Haine: her Life,

her Ecstasies, and her Stigmata: a Medical Study. By Dr. F. LEFEBVRE, Professor of General Pathology and Therapeutics in the Catholic University of Louvain, &c. Translated from the French. Edited by Rev. J. SPENCER NORTHCOTE, D.D. Full and complete edition. 3*s.* 6*d.*

'The name of Dr. Lefebvre is sufficient guarantee of the importance of any work coming from his pen. The reader will find much valuable information.'—*Tablet.*

'The whole case thoroughly entered into and fully considered. The Appendix contains many medical notes of interest.'—*Weekly Register.*

'A full and complete answer.'—*Catholic Times.*

Twelve New Tales. By Mrs. PARSONS.

1. Bertha's Three Fingers. 2. Take Care of Yourself. 3. Don't Go In. 4. The Story of an Arm-chair. 5. Yes and No. 6. The Red Apples under the Tree. 7. Constance and the Water Lilies. 8. The Pair of Gold Spectacles. 9. Clara's New Shawl. 10. The Little Lodgers. 11. The Pride and the Fall. 12. This Once.

3*d.* each; in a Packet complete, 3*s.*; or in cloth neat, 3*s.* 6*d.*

'Sound Catholic theology and a truly religious spirit breathes from every page, and it may be safely commended to schools and convents.'—*Tablet.*

'Full of sound instruction given in a pointed and amusing manner.'—*Weekly Register.*

'Very pretty, pleasantly told, attractive to little folks, and of such a nature that from each some moral good is inculcated. The tales are cheerful, sound, and sweet, and should have a large sale.'—*Catholic Times.*

'A very good collection of simple tales. The teaching is Catholic throughout.'—*Catholic Opinion.*

Marie and Paul: a Fragment. By 'Our Little Woman.' 3*s.* 6*d.*; gilt edges, 4*s.*

'We heartily recommend this touching little tale, especially as a present for children and for schools, feeling sure that none can rise from its perusal without being touched, both at the beauty of the tale itself and by the tone of earnest piety which runs through the whole, leaving none but holy thoughts and pleasant impressions on the minds of both old and young.'—*Tablet.*

'Well adapted to the innocent minds it is intended for. The little book would be a suitable present for a little friend.'—*Catholic Opinion.*

'A charming tale for young and old.'—*Cork Examiner.*

'To all who read it the book will suggest thoughts for which they will be the better, while its graceful and affecting, because simple, pictures of home and family life will excite emotions of which none need be ashamed.'—*Month.*

'Told effectively and touchingly, with all that tenderness and pathos in which gifted women so much excel.'—*Weekly Register.*

'A very pretty and pathetic tale.'—*Catholic World.*

'A very charming story, and may be read by both young and old.'—*Brownson's Review.*

'Presents us with some deeply-touching incidents of family love and devotion.'—*Catholic Times.*

Dame Dolores, or the Wise Nun of Eastonmere; and other Stories. By the Author of 'Tyborne,' &c. 4s.

CONTENTS: I. The Wise Nun of Eastonmere. II. Known Too Late. III. True to the End. IV. Olive's Rescue.

'We have read the volume with considerable pleasure, and we trust no small profit. The tales are decidedly clever, well worked out, and written with a flowing and cheerful pen.'—*Catholic Times.*

'The author of *Tyborne* is too well known to need any fresh recommendation to the readers of Catholic fiction. We need only say that her present will be as welcome to her many friends as any of her former works.'—*Month.*

'An attractive volume; and we know of few tales that we can more safely or more thoroughly recommend to our young readers.'—*Weekly Register.*

Maggie's Rosary, and other Tales. By the Author of 'Marian Howard.' Cloth extra, 3s., cheap edition, 2s.

'We strongly recommend these stories. They are especially suited to little girls.'—*Tablet.*

'The very thing for a gift-book for a child; but at the same time so interesting and full of incident that it will not be contemned by children of a larger growth.'—*Weekly Register.*

'We have seldom seen tales better adapted for children's reading.'—*Catholic Times.*

'The writer possesses in an eminent degree the art of making stories for children.'—*Catholic Opinion.*

'A charming little book, which we can heartily recommend.'—*Rosarian.*

Scenes and Incidents at Sea. A new Selection. 1s. 4d.

CONTENTS: I. Adventure on a Rock. II. A Heroic Act of Rescue. III. Inaccessible Islands. IV. The Shipwreck of the Czar Alexander. V. Captain James's Adventures in the North Seas. VI. Destruction of Admiral Graves's Fleet. VII. The Wreck of the Forfarshire, and Grace Darling. VIII. The Loss of the Royal George. IX. The Irish Sailor Boy. X. Gallant Conduct of a French Privateer. XI. The Harpooner. XII. The Cruise of the Agamemnon. XIII. A Nova Scotia Fog. XIV. The Mate's Story. XV. The Shipwreck of the Æneas Transport. XVI. A Scene in the Shrouds. XVII. A Skirmish off Bermuda. XVIII. Charles Wager. XIX. A Man Overboard. XX. A Loss and a Rescue. XXI. A Melancholy Adventure on the American Seas. XXII. Dolphins and Flying Fish.

History of England, for Family Use and the Upper Classes of Schools. By the Author of 'Christian Schools and Scholars.' Second edition. With Preface by the Very Rev. Dr. NORTHCOTE. 6s.

Tales from the Diary of a Sister of Mercy. By C. M. BRAME. New edition. Cloth extra, 4s.

CONTENTS: The Double Marriage. The Cross and the Crown. The Novice. The Fatal Accident. The Priest's Death. The Gambler's Wife. The Apostate. The Besetting Sin.

'Written in a chaste, simple, and touching style.'—*Tablet.*
'This book is a casket, and those who open it will find the gem within.'—*Register.*
'They are well and cleverly told, and the volume is neatly got up.'—*Month.*
'Very well told: all full of religious allusions and expressions.'—*Star.*
'Very well written, and life-like; many very pathetic.'—*Catholic Opinion.*

By the same,

Angels' Visits: a Series of Tales. With Frontispiece and Vignette. 3s. 6d.

'The tone of the book is excellent, and it will certainly make itself a great favourite with the young.'—*Month.*
'Beautiful collection of Angel Stories.'—*Weekly Register.*
'One of the prettiest books for children we have seen.'—*Tablet.*
'A book which excites more than ordinary praise.'—*Northern Press.*
'Touchingly written, and evidently the emanation of a refined and pious mind.'—*Church Times.*
'A charming little book, full of beautiful stories of the family of angels.'—*Church Opinion.*

ST. JOSEPH'S THEOLOGICAL LIBRARY.
Edited by Fathers of the Society of Jesus.
Vol. I.

On some Popular Errors concerning Politics and Religion. By the Right Honourable Lord ROBERT MONTAGU, M.P. 6s.

CONTENTS: Introduction. I. The Basis of Political Science. II. Religion. III. The Church. IV. Religious Orders. V. Christian Law. VI. The Mass. VII. The Principles of 1789. VIII. Liberty. IX. Fraternity. X. Equality. XI. Nationality, Non-intervention, and the Accomplished Fact. XII. Capital Punishment. XIII. Liberal Catholics.

XIV. Civil Marriage.   XV. Secularisation of Education.
XVI. Conclusion.   Additional Notes.

This book has been taken from the 'Risposte popolari alle obiezioni piu diffuse contro la Religione; opera del P. Secondo Franco. Torino, 1868.' It is not a translation of that excellent Italian work, for much has been omitted, and even the forms of expression have not been retained; nor yet is it an abstract, for other matter has been added throughout. The aim of the editor has been merely to follow out the intention of P. Franco, and adapt his thoughts to the circumstances and mind of England.

Considerations for a Three Days' Preparation for Communion. Taken chiefly from the French of SAINT JURE, S.J. By CECILIE MARY CADDELL. 8d.

'In every respect a most excellent manual.'—*Catholic Times.*
'A simple and easy method for a devout preparation for that solemn duty.'—*Weekly Register.*
'A beautiful compilation carefully prepared.'—*Universe.*

The Spiritual Conflict and Conquest. By Dom J. CASTANIZA, O.S.B. Edited, with Preface and Notes, by Canon VAUGHAN, English Monk of the Order of St. Benedict. Second edition. Reprinted from the old English Translation of 1652. With fine Original Frontispiece reproduced in Autotype. 8s. 6d.

The Letter-Books of Sir Amias Poulet, Keeper of Mary Queen of Scots. Edited by JOHN MORRIS, Priest of the Society of Jesus. Demy 8vo, 10s. 6d.

Sir Amias Poulet had charge of the Queen of Scots from April 1585 to the time of her death, February 8, 1587. His correspondence with Lord-Treasurer Burghley and Sir Francis Walsingham enters into the details of her life in captivity at Tutbury, Chartley, and Fotheringay. Many of the letters now published are entirely unknown, being printed from a recently-discovered manuscript. The others have been taken from the originals at the Public Record Office and the British Museum. The letters are strung together by a running commentary, in the course of which several of Mr. Froude's statements are examined, and the question of Mary's complicity in the plot against Elizabeth's life is discussed.

Sœur Eugenie: the Life and Letters of a
Sister of Charity. By the Author of 'A Sketch of the Life of St. Paula.' Second edition, enlarged. On toned paper, cloth gilt, 4s. 6d.; plain paper, cloth plain, 3s.

'It is impossible to read it without bearing away in one's heart some of the "odour of sweetness" which breathes forth from almost every page.'—*Tablet.*
'The most charming piece of religious biography that has appeared since the *Récits d'une Sœur.*'—*Catholic Opinion.*
'We have seldom read a more touching tale of youthful holiness.'—*Weekly Register.*
'The picture of a life of hidden piety and grace, and of active charity, which it presents is extremely beautiful.'—*Nation.*
'We strongly recommend this devout and interesting life to the careful perusal of all our readers.'—*Westminster Gazette.*

Count de Montalembert's Letters to a School-
fellow, 1827-1830. Qualis ab incepto. Translated from the French by C. F. AUDLEY. With Portrait. 5s.

'Simple, easy, and unaffected in a degree, these letters form a really charming volume. The observations are simply wonderful, considering that when he wrote them he was only seventeen or eighteen years of age.'—*Weekly Register.*
'A new treasure is now presented for the first time in an English casket—the letters he wrote when a schoolboy. The loftiness of the aspirations they breathe is supported by the intellectual power of which they give evidence.' —*Cork Examiner.*
'Reveal in the future ecclesiastical champion and historian a depth of feeling and insight into forthcoming events hardly to be expected from a mere schoolboy.'—*Building News.*
'Display vigour of thought and real intellectual power.'—*Church Herald.*

Ecclesiastical Antiquities of London and its
Suburbs. By ALEXANDER WOOD, M.A. Oxon., of the Somerset Archæological Society. 5s.

'O, who the ruine sees, whom wonder doth not fill
With our great fathers' pompe, devotion, and their skill?'

'Will prove a most useful manual to many of our readers. Stores of Catholic memories still hang about the streets of this great metropolis. For the ancient and religious associations of such places the Catholic reader can want no better cicerone than Mr. Wood.'—*Weekly Register.*
'We have indeed to thank Mr. Wood for this excellent little book.'—*Catholic Opinion.*
'Very seldom have we read a book devoted entirely to the metropolis with such pleasure.'—*Liverpool Catholic Times.*
'A very pleasing and readable book.'—*Builder.*
'Gives a plain, sensible, but learned and interesting account of the chief church antiquities of London and its suburbs. It is written by a very able and competent author—one who thoroughly appreciates his subject, and who treats it with the discrimination of a critic and the sound common sense of a practised writer.'—*Church Herald.*

LIBRARY OF RELIGIOUS BIOGRAPHY.
Edited by EDWARD HEALY THOMPSON.

Vol. I.
The Life of St. Aloysius Gonzaga, S.J.
Second edition. 5s.

'Contains numberless traces of a thoughtful and tender devotion to the Saint. It shows a loving penetration into his spirit, and an appreciation of the secret motives of his action, which can only be the result of a deeply affectionate study of his life and character.'—*Month.*

Vol. II.
The Life of Marie Eustelle Harpain; or the Angel of the Eucharist. Second edition. 5s.

'Possesses a special value and interest apart from its extraordinay natural and supernatural beauty, from the fact that to her example and to the effect of her writings is attributed in great measure the wonderful revival of devotion to the Blessed Sacrament in France, and consequently throughout Western Christendom.'—*Dublin Review.*

'A more complete instance of that life of purity and close union with God in the world of which we have just been speaking is to be found in the history of Marie Eustelle Harpain, the sempstress of Saint-Pallais. The writer of the present volume has had the advantage of very copious materials in the French works on which his own work is founded; and Mr. Thompson has discharged his office as editor with his usual diligence and accuracy.'—*Month.*

Vol. III.
The Life of St. Stanislas Kostka. 5s.

'We strongly recommend this biography to our readers.'—*Tablet.*

'There has been no adequate biography of St. Stanislas. In rectifying this want Mr. Thompson has earned a title to the gratitude of English-speaking Catholics. The engaging Saint of Poland will now be better known among us, and we need not fear that, better known, he will not be better loved.'—*Weekly Register.*

Vol. IV.
The Life of the Baron de Renty; or Perfection in the World exemplified. 6s.

'An excellent book. The style is throughout perfectly fresh and buoyant.'—*Dublin Review.*

'This beautiful work is a compilation, not of biographical incidents, but of holy thoughts and spiritual aspirations, which we may feed on and make our own.'—*Tablet.*

'Gives full particulars of his marvellous virtue in an agreeable form.'—*Catholic Times.*

'A good book for our Catholic young men, teaching how they can sanctify the secular state.'—*Catholic Opinion.*

'Edifying and instructive, a beacon and guide to those whose walks are in the ways of the world, who toil and strive to win Christian perfection.'—*Ulster Examiner.*

Vol. V.
The Life of the Venerable Anna Maria
Taigi, the Roman Matron (1769-1837). Third edition. With Portrait. 6s.

This Biography has been written after a careful collation of previous Lives of the Servant of God with each other, and with the *Analecta Juris Pontificii*, which contain large extracts from the Processes. Various prophecies attributed to her and other holy persons have been collected in an Appendix.

'Of all the series of deeply-interesting biographies which the untiring zeal and piety of Mr. Healy Thompson has given of late years to English Catholics, none, we think, is to be compared in interest with the one before us, both from the absorbing nature of the life itself and the spiritual lessons it conveys.'—*Tablet.*

'A complete biography of the Venerable Matron in the composition of which the greatest care has been taken and the best authorities consulted. We can safely recommend the volume for the discrimination with which it has been written, and for the careful labour and completeness by which it has been distinguished.'—*Catholic Opinion.*

'We recommend this excellent and carefully-compiled biography to all our readers. The evident care exercised by the editor in collating the various lives of Anna Maria gives great value to the volume, and we hope it will meet with the support it so justly merits.'—*Westminster Gazette.*

'We thank Mr. Healy Thompson for this volume. The direct purpose of his biographies is always spiritual edification.'—*Dublin Review.*

'Contains much that is capable of nourishing pious sentiments.'—*Nation.*
'Has evidently been a labour of love.'—*Month.*

The Hidden Life of Jesus: a Lesson and
Model to Christians. Translated from the French of BOUDON, by EDWARD HEALY THOMPSON, M.A. Cloth, 3s.

'This profound and valuable work has been very carefully and ably translated by Mr. Thompson.'—*Register.*

'The more we have of such works as the *Hidden Life of Jesus* the better.'—*Westminster Gazette.*

'A book of searching power.'—*Church Review.*

'We have often regretted that this writer's works are not better known.'—*Universe.*

'We earnestly recommend its study and practice to all readers.'—*Tablet.*

'We have to thank Mr. Thompson for this translation of a valuable work which has long been popular in France.'—*Dublin Review.*

'A good translation.'—*Month.*

Also, by the same Author and Translator,

Devotion to the Nine Choirs of Holy Angels,
and especially to the Angel Guardians. 3s.

'We congratulate Mr. Thompson on the way in which he has accomplished his task, and we earnestly hope that an increased devotion to the Holy Angels may be the reward of his labour of love.'—*Tablet.*
'A beautiful translation.'—*Month.*
'The translation is extremely well done.'—*Weekly Register.*

New Meditations for each Day in the Year,
on *the Life of our Lord Jesus Christ.* By a Father of the Society of Jesus. With the imprimatur of the Cardinal Archbishop of Westminster. New and improved edition. Two vols. Cloth, 9s.; also in calf, 16s.; morocco, 17s.

'We can heartily recommend this book for its style and substance; it bears with it several strong recommendations. . . . It is solid and practical.' —*Westminster Gazette.*
'A work of great practical utility, and we give it our earnest recommendation.'—*Weekly Register.*

The Day Sanctified; being Meditations and
Spiritual Readings for Daily Use. Selected from the Works of Saints and approved Writers of the Catholic Church. Fcp. cloth, 3s. 6d.; red edges, 4s.

'Of the many volumes of meditations on sacred subjects which have appeared in the last few years, none has seemed to us so well adapted to its object as the one before us.'—*Tablet.*
'Deserves to be specially mentioned.'—*Month.*
'Admirable in every sense.'—*Church Times.*
'Many of the meditations are of great beauty. . . . They form, in fact, excellent little sermons, and we have no doubt will be largely used as such.' —*Literary Churchman.*

Reflections and Prayers for Holy Com-
munion. Translated from the French. With Preface by the CARDINAL ARCHBISHOP OF WESTMINSTER. Fcp. 8vo, cloth, 4s. 6d.; bound, red edges, 5s.; calf, 9s.; morocco, 10s.

'The Archbishop has marked his approval of the work by writing a preface for it, and describes it as "a valuable addition to our books of devotion."'—*Register.*
'A book rich with the choicest and most profound Catholic devotions.'— *Church Review.*

Lallemant's Doctrine of the Spiritual Life.
Edited by the late Father FABER. New edition. Cloth, 4s. 6d.

'This excellent work has a twofold value, being both a biography and a volume of meditations. It contains an elaborate analysis of the wants, dangers, trials, and aspirations of the inner man, and supplies to the thoughtful and devout reader the most valuable instructions for the attainment of heavenly wisdom, grace, and strength.'—*Catholic Times.*

'A treatise of the very highest value.'—*Month.*

'The treatise is preceded by a short account of the writer's life, and has had the wonderful advantage of being edited by the late Father Faber.'—*Weekly Register.*

The Rivers of Damascus and Jordan: a
Causerie. By a Tertiary of the Order of St. Dominic. 4s.

'Good solid reading.'—*Month.*

'Well done and in a truly charitable spirit.'—*Catholic Opinion.*

'It treats the subject in so novel and forcible a light that we are fascinated in spite of ourselves, and irresistibly led on to follow its arguments and rejoice at its conclusions.'—*Tablet.*

Legends of our Lady and the Saints; or
our *Children's Book of Stories in Verse.* Written for the Recitations of the Pupils of the Schools of the Holy Child Jesus, St. Leonard's-on-Sea. 2s. 6d.

'It is a beautiful religious idea that is realised in the *Legends of our Lady and the Saints.* The book forms a charming present for pious children.'—*Tablet.*

'The "Legends" are so beautiful that they ought to be read by all lovers of poetry.'—*Bookseller.*

'Graceful poems.'—*Month.*

The New Testament Narrative, in the Words
of *the Sacred Writers.* With Notes, Chronological Tables, and Maps. Cloth, 2s.

'The compilers deserve great praise for the manner in which they have performed their task. We commend this little volume as well and carefully printed, and as furnishing its readers, moreover, with a great amount of useful information in the tables inserted at the end.'—*Month.*

'It is at once clear, complete, and beautiful.'—*Catholic Opinion.*

QUARTERLY SERIES.

Conducted by the Managers of the 'Month.'

VOLUMES PUBLISHED.

The Life and Letters of St. Francis Xavier.
By the Rev. H. J. COLERIDGE. Sec. edit. Two vols. 18s.

'We cordially thank Father Coleridge for a most valuable biography.... He has spared no pains to insure our having in good classical English a translation of all the letters which are extant.... A complete priest's manual might be compiled from them, entering as they do into all the details of a missioner's public and private life.... We trust we have stimulated our readers to examine them for themselves, and we are satisfied that they will return again and again to them as to a never-exhausted source of interest and edification.'—*Tablet.*

'A noble addition to our literature.... We offer our warmest thanks to Father Coleridge for this most valuable work. The letters, we need hardly say, will be found of great spiritual use, especially for missionaries and priests.'—*Dublin Review.*

'One of the most fascinating books we have met with for a long time.'—*Catholic Opinion.*

'Would that we had many more lives of saints like this! Father Coleridge has done great service to this branch of Catholic literature, not simply by writing a charming book, but especially by setting others an example of how a saint's life should be written.'—*Westminster Gazette.*

'This valuable book is destined, we feel assured, to take a high place among what we may term our English Catholic classics.... The great charm lies in the letters, for in them we have, in a far more forcible manner than any biographer could give them, the feelings, experiences, and aspirations of St. Francis Xavier as pictured by his own pen.'—*Catholic Times.*

'Father Coleridge does his own part admirably, and we shall not be surprised to find his book soon take its place as the standard Life of the saintly and illustrious Francis.'—*Nation.*

'Not only an interesting but a scholarly sketch of a life remarkable alike in itself and in its attendant circumstances. We hope the author will continue to labour in a department of literature for which he has here shown his aptitude. To find a saint's life which is at once moderate, historical, and appreciative is not a common thing.'—*Saturday Review.*

'Should be studied by all missionaries, and is worthy of a place in every Christian library.'—*Church Herald.*

The Life of St. Jane Frances Fremyot de Chantal.

By EMILY BOWLES. With Preface by the Rev. H. J. COLERIDGE. Second edition. 5s. 6d.

'We venture to promise great pleasure and profit to the reader of this charming biography. It gives a complete and faithful portrait of one of the most attractive saints of the generation which followed the completion of the Council of Trent.'—*Month.*

'Sketched in a life-like manner, worthy of her well-earned reputation as a Catholic writer.'—*Weekly Register.*

'We have read it on and on with the fascination of a novel, and yet it is the life of a saint, described with a rare delicacy of touch and feeling such as is seldom met with.'—*Tablet.*

'A very readable and interesting compilation. . . . The author has done her work faithfully and conscientiously.'—*Athenæum.*

'Full of incident, and told in a style so graceful and felicitous that it wins upon the reader with every page.'—*Nation.*

'Miss Bowles has done her work in a manner which we cannot better commend than by expressing a desire that she may find many imitators. She has endued her materials with life, and clothed them with a language and a style of which we do not know what to admire most—the purity, the grace, the refinement, or the elegance. If our readers wish to know the value and the beauty of this book, they can do no better than get it and read it.'—*Westminster Gazette.*

'One of the most charming and delightfu volumes which has issued from the press for many years. Miss Bowles has accomplished her task faithfully and happily, with simple grace and unpretentious language, and a winning manner which, independently of her subject, irresistibly carries us along.'—*Ulster Examiner.*

The History of the Sacred Passion.

From the Spanish of Father LUIS DE LA PALMA, of the Society of Jesus. The Translation revised and edited by the Rev. H. J. COLERIDGE. Third edition. 7s. 6d.

'A work long held in great and just repute in Spain. It opens a mine of wealth to one's soul. Though there are many works on the Passion in English, probably none will be found so generally useful both for spiritual reading and meditation. We desire to see it widely circulated.'—*Tablet.*

'A sterling work of the utmost value, proceeding from the pen of a great theologian, whose piety was as simple and tender as his learning and culture were profound and exquisite. It is a rich storehouse for contemplation on the great mystery of our Redemption, and one of those books which every Catholic ought to read for himself.'—*Weekly Register.*

'The most wonderful work upon the Passion that we have ever read. To us the charm lies in this, that it is entirely theological. It is made use of largely by those who give the Exercises of St. Ignatius; it is, as it were, the flesh upon the skeleton of the Exercises. Never has the Passion been meditated upon so before. . . . If any one wishes to understand the Passion of our Lord in its fulness, let him procure this book.'—*Dublin Review.*

'We have not read a more thoughtful work on our Blessed Lord's Passion.

It is a complete storehouse of matter for meditation, and for sermons on that divine mystery.'—*Catholic Opinion.*

'The book is—speaking comparatively of human offerings—a magnificent offering to the Crucified, and to those who wish to make a real study of the Cross will be a most precious guide.'—*Church Review.*

Ierne of Armorica: a Tale of the Time of Chlovis. By J. C. BATEMAN. 6s. 6d.

'We know of few tales of the kind that can be ranked higher than the beautiful story before us. The author has hit on the golden mean between an over-display of antiquarianism and an indolent transfer of modern modes of action and thought to a distant time. The descriptions are masterly, the characters distinct, the interest unflagging. We may add that the period is one of those which may be said to be comparatively unworked.'—*Month.*

'A volume of very great interest and very great utility. As a story it is sure to give much delight, while, as a story founded on historical fact, it will benefit all by its very able reproduction of very momentous scenes. . . . The book is excellent. If we are to have a literature of fiction at all, we hope it will include many like volumes.'—*Dublin Review.*

'Although a work of fiction, it is historically correct, and the author portrays with great skill the manners and customs of the times of which he professes to give a description. In reading this charming tale we seem to be taken by the hand by the writer, and made to assist at the scenes which he describes.'—*Tablet.*

'The author of this most interesting tale has hit the happy medium between a display of antiquarian knowledge and a mere reproduction in distant ages of commonplace modern habits of thought. The descriptions are excellent, the characters well drawn, and the subject itself is very attractive, besides having the advantage of not having been written threadbare.'—*Westminster Gazette.*

'The tale is excessively interesting, the language appropriate to the time and rank of the characters, the style flowing and easy, and the narrative leads one on and on until it becomes a very difficult matter to lay the book down until it is finished. . . . It is a valuable addition to Catholic fictional literature.'—*Catholic Times.*

'A very pretty historico-ecclesiastical novel of the times of Chlovis. It is full of incident, and is very pleasant reading.'—*Literary Churchman.*

The Life of Dona Luisa de Carvajal. By Lady GEORGIANA FULLERTON. 6s. (See p. 6.)

The Life of the Blessed John Berchmans. By the Rev. FRANCIS GOLDIE, S.J. 6s.

'A complete and life-like picture, and we are glad to be able to congratulate Father Goldie on his success.'—*Tablet.*

'Drawn up with a vigour and freedom which show great power of biographical writing.'—*Dublin Review.*

'One of the most interesting of all.'—*Weekly Register.*

'Unhesitatingly we say that it is the very best Life of Blessed John

Berchmans, and as such it will take rank with religious biographies of the highest merit.'—*Catholic Times.*

'Is of great literary merit, the style being marked by elegance and a complete absence of redundancy.'—*Cork Examiner.*

'This delightful and edifying volume is of the deepest interest. The perusal will afford both pleasure and profit.'—*Church Herald.*

The Life of the Blessed Peter Favre, of the
Society of Jesus, First Companion of St. Ignatius Loyola. From the Italian of Father GIUSEPPE BOERO, of the same Society. With Preface by the Rev. H. J. COLERIDGE. 6s. 6d.

This Life has been written on the occasion of the beatification of the Ven. Peter Favre, and contains the *Memoriale* or record of his private thoughts and meditations, written by himself.

'At once a book of spiritual reading, and also an interesting historical narrative. The *Memoriale, or Spiritual Diary*, is here translated at full length, and is the most precious portion of one of the most valuable biographies we know.'—*Tablet.*

'A perfect picture drawn from the life, admirably and succinctly told. The *Memoriale* will be found one of the most admirable epitomes of sound devotional reading.'—*Weekly Register.*

'The *Memoriale* is hardly excelled in interest by anything of the kind now extant.'—*Catholic Times.*

'Full of interest, instruction, and example.'—*Cork Examiner.*

'One of the most interesting to the general reader of the entire series up to this time.'—*Nation.*

'This wonderful diary, the *Memoriale*, has never been published before, and we are much mistaken if it does not become a cherished possession to thoughtful Catholics.'—*Month.*

The Dialogues of St. Gregory the Great.
An old English version. Edited, with Preface, by the Rev. H. J. COLERIDGE. 6s.

'The Catholic world must feel grateful to Father Coleridge for this excellent and compendious edition. The subjects treated of possess at this moment a special interest. . . . The Preface by Father Coleridge is interesting and well written, and we cordially recommend the book to the perusal of all.'—*Tablet.*

'This is a most interesting book. . . . Father Coleridge gives a very useful preface summarising the contents.'—*Weekly Register.*

'We have seldom taken up a book in which we have become at once so deeply interested. It will suit any one; it will teach all; it will confirm any who require that process; and it will last and be read when other works are quite forgotten.'—*Catholic Times.*

'Edited and published with the utmost care and the most perfect literary taste, this volume adds one more gem to the treasury of English Catholic literature.'—*New York Catholic World.*

The Life of Sister Anne Catherine Emme-rich. Edited, with Preface, by the Rev. H. J. COLERIDGE. 5s.

St. Winefride; or Holywell and its Pil-grims. By the Author of 'Tyborne.' Third edition. 1s.

Summer Talks about Lourdes. By Miss CADDELL. Cloth, 1s. 6d.

Blessed Margaret Mary Alacoque: a brief and popular Account of her Life; to which are added Selections from some of her Sayings, and the Decree of her Beatification. By the Rev. CHARLES B. GARSIDE, M.A. 1s.

A Comparison between the History of the Church and the Prophecies of the Apocalypse. Translated from the German by EDWIN DE LISLE. 2s.

CATHOLIC-TRUTH TRACTS.

NEW ISSUES.

Manchester Dialogues. First Series. By the Rev. Fr. HARPER, S.J.

- No. I. The Pilgrimage.
- II. Are Miracles going on still?
- III. Popish Miracles tested by the Bible.
- IV. Popish Miracles.
- V. Liquefaction of the Blood of St. Januarius.
- VI. 'Bleeding Nuns' and 'Winking Madonnas.'
- VII. Are Miracles physically possible?
- VIII. Are Miracles morally possible?

Price of each 3s. per 100, 25 for 1s.; also 25 of the above assorted for 1s. Also the whole Series complete in neat Wrapper, 6d.

Specimen Packet of General Series, containing 100 assorted, 1s. 6d.

www.ingramcontent.com/pod-product-compliance
Lightning Source LLC
Chambersburg PA
CBHW020238240426
43672CB00006B/569